'Be prepared to feel a sense of relief. Wiggins and Hughes offer a clear exposition of the ideas informing relational change. They argue persuasively that our organizations and our interactions within those organizations are simply what we make them. They draw attention to the need to think reflexively, to take our own reactions seriously and not to succumb to the delusion of control. The rich examples help bring their arguments to life and might just help change yours.'

Professor Robert MacIntosh, Head of School, School of Management and Languages, Heriot-Watt University Edinburgh

'This book addresses an important area of fundamental importance in a new and refreshing way, reflecting the many years of experience the authors have had working with leaders "in the real world". While rooted in strong academic research, the book is accessible and understandable, and full of useful insights and conceptual frameworks that can really help the busy executive as they work to improve their organization's performance.'

Richard Lucas, Serial Entrepreneur

'Ashridge is justly famous for its pioneering work in organizational change. This wise and friendly book is a typically generous and accessible offer of help, in a field that too often daunts and bamboozles. The combination of light-touch theory and case studies makes it both robustly grounded and practical, and no-one contemplating organizational change should be without it.'

Dr Eve Poole, Partner, Leadersmithing LLP

'Engaging, clear, human, rigorous, enlivening. This is a must-read for people leading change in organizations. It is an intensely practical distillation of years of accumulated wisdom and it may change the way you go about leading. Wiggins and Hunter offer an antidote to the top-down change programmes we still see in too many organizations. Make sure you get your copy.'

George Binney, author of *Living Leadership*

'I have practiced OD using an HR perspective for 30 years. During this time I have read many books, attended a few courses and listened to keynote speakers. Whilst this has helped inform me about "change", I was usually left with a feeling that I still did not know what to actually do! If you have had this experience and would like to know what actually works, then buy (and read) this book. My journey to find "what works" has ended with this book. Let it be your destination too – just take the time to enjoy the OD journey knowing you are in very safe hands.'

Karin Rundle, Director of HR/OD, Centre for Environment Fisheries and Aquaculture Science

'This is an important book for all MSc and MBA students interested in how change actually works. Practical and pragmatic, it takes an informed and uncompromising look at change as it really is: messy, unpredictable, fundamentally about people and how they feel. The authors are practitioners first and foremost, but the theory in which the advice is grounded is solid, well-researched and sound. I particularly valued the stories, each of which thoroughly explored the application of theory to practice. An excellent addition to the genre.'

Roger Delves, *Dean of Qualifications, Hult International Business School*

'I am delighted that we now finally have a handbook which appreciates the messiness of change, makes sense of it and teaches us to work with it. In the superbly written case studies we can follow the chemistry of relational change, where, to quote Jung, "if there is any reaction, both are transformed". Sophisticated consulting methodologies seep through in those case studies. And helpful cross-referencing enables us to conceptualise how helping relationships can change an organization in the same way a parent can change a baby – not just for the better but with all the messiness taken on board and worked through.'

Erik de Haan, Professor of Organization Development at the VU University, Amsterdam

'*Relational Change* is an eminently readable book, combining practical advice, just the right amount of untangling of relevant change-management theory, and wise reflections on relevant real-life scenarios. I could take away and use many practical suggestions, not just to help with the challenges of managing change in a fast-moving world, but also in the everyday situations in the office, in board meetings and even at home! Reading the book was more like having a chat with a very wise friend over a glass of wine – enjoyable and very helpful.'

Michelle Jarrold, Development Director, Jarrold Retail Division

'This book is helpful for managers and leaders. It's incredibly accessible and engaging, with just the right balance between theory and practice for a busy manager. It's very readable, practical and relevant to a wide cross-section of leaders. You can tell the authors have "been there" and challenge you to stop and reflect your practice in a meaningful way that, unlike some more theoretical approaches, you find yourself applying.'

Chris Stirling, Site Director, Western General Hospital

'This isn't just informative, evocative and stimulating – I really enjoyed reading it. The authors share what at times are complex concepts, in a coherent and structured way. At times I found myself nodding vigorously in wholehearted agreement; whilst at others I pursed my lips and furrowed my brow as I was encouraged to consider things from a different than usual perspective. I think this book will be useful for all leaders who are interested in getting below the surface of their leadership gestures to the thoughts, feelings and beliefs that underpin them.'

David Julien, CEO, First Contact Clinical

'This book is as refreshing as it is powerful. A tour de force. Written from a relational perspective, it is full of practical guidance on the complex processes of organizational change and development. For those interested in change in organizations, and particularly for those responsible for managing or leading it, this excellent book is a must-read.'

Donald MacLean, Professor of Strategic Management, The University of Glasgow, Adam Smith Business School

'The authors have crafted a book that's practical, down-to-earth and supportive, intellectually stimulating without wallowing in theory. Everyone working with transformational change can use this book as a provocative and supporting guide and will relish the wealth of examples that make the ideas leap into life through stories from the field.'

Philippa Hardman, Co-Founding Partner, GameShift

'Change is around us all the time - we are asked to do more, do better. Leading change and improvement isn't easy and we all know that. This book provides a refreshingly different narrative on what is possible and reminds us all that organizations are all about people and relationships. It is the choices made by leaders that pave the way for really helping to unlock the potential for improvement, no matter how big or small. The tips, reflections and examples within this book provide a range of different ideas and approaches to help leaders to navigate and respond to the opportunities and challenges around us. It raises more questions than answers, but the words here enable leaders to reflect on and experiment with ways to work through the ambiguity and unknown to create new and better together.'

Bridget Turner, Director of Policy & Care Improvement, Diabetes UK

'Finally, a book that speaks frankly to us about the complexities and challenges of leading organizational change. With an engaging mixture of academic theory and practical advice, Liz and Harriet provide sound guidance, share the wealth of their experience, and offer us generative frameworks to help us see organizations differently. They enable us to focus our gaze on deeply ingrained patterns of emotions, politics and power that can so often undermine our change initiatives. The authors invite us to pay attention to what is happening in organisation, as they say, both "above and below the waterline" and to embrace change as a relational practice; happening one conversation at a time and between people.'

Michele Martin, Organizational Development Practitioner, Barclays

'The practical ideas and examples presented are strikingly readable and memorable. Familiar scenarios - which in the workplace usually sink without impact - are explored, advanced and transformed, enabling managers to relish organizational change.'

Imogen Gibbon, Chief Curator and Deputy Director, Scottish National Portrait Gallery

'Leadership is challenging and rewarding in equal measures, and whilst the power of networking can provide structural support and community for a leader, this is no replacement in really understanding human behaviours, the power of relationship and the dynamics of change. This book is a great read, it gives the leader a strong reference and theoretical base whilst signposting practical solutions to complexity, and is really accessible. Too many books in this field fail to interpret theory and move this to practicality, the "so what should I do or how should I lead in this situation?" The authors deliver this consistently. This book should furnish your desk if you as a leader want to make a difference, are committed to continuing personal development and organizational development. I hope you enjoy it and dip into regularly.'

Dr Ian Bullock, Chief Executive, Royal College of Physicians, London

'A wise, practical and thought-provoking guide to leading and/or enabling change from a relational perspective in organizations - this book really brings theory to life and makes it accessible. I wish I'd had it alongside me when I was an operational leader and then when I started my career in OD.'

Carolyn Northgate, OD consultant, Civil Service; former OD consultant in the NHS

'These insights have made me a better leader, doctor, father, husband. It's the best educational experience I have ever had'. This is the feedback given by a consultant surgeon having finished his time on the Generation Q leadership programme. Liz Wiggins and Harriet Hunter have distilled the essence of this programme in *Relational Change*. Read, reflect, and be changed.'

Dr Jennifer Dixon, CEO, The Health Foundation

'Like a professional coach in your pocket – this book offers practical advice to managers and leaders on how develop their working relationships and improve performance.'

Suzie Bailey, Director of Leadership and Quality Improvement, NHS Improvement

'Wiggins and Hunter's *Relational Change* is a breath of fresh air in the change literature. They explain why the typical top-down, change management approach usually doesn't work and offer, instead, practical tools and models for engaging the people who will have to change in *being* the change. Unlike most change books, it's not just for the most senior leaders. Anyone in the organizational trenches looking for guidance will find some here. Well written, with many true to life examples, easy to read without insulting the reader's intelligence ... managers who accept the messy, unpredictable, political world of organizational change will find value in this book.'

Gervase R. Bushe, Professor of Leadership and Organization Development, Beedie School of Business, Simon Fraser University

'"Change happens through changing conversations and relationships!" To me this is the heart of this book and it is what attracted me to reading it. The authors describe relational change as an art and leaders in organizations as artists navigating the complexity of change. Focusing on the human behaviour side of change, this book is a collection of the key theories on change leadership as well as a guide with practical exercises and tips for leaders, HR, L&D and OD consultants. I will recommend this book to everyone in my team, department and the wider organization as a "must-have" resource guide.'

Stephanie Conway, Lead Learning and Development Business Partner, Google

'A combination of unrivalled academic expertise and an intimate knowledge of how organizations work, make for a truly transformational yet helpfully practical approach. A must read for anyone in a leadership position, not least because we live in a world in which relentless change is the new normal. Every leader should have this in their back pocket.'

Amelie Roland Gosselin, Global Communications Manager, Foods, Unilever

Relational Change

Relational Change

The Art and Practice of Changing Organizations

Liz Wiggins and Harriet Hunter

Bloomsbury Business
An imprint of Bloomsbury Publishing Plc
B L O O M S B U R Y
LONDON • OXFORD • NEW YORK • NEW DELHI • SYDNEY

Bloomsbury Business
An imprint of Bloomsbury Publishing Plc

1385 Broadway
New York
NY 10018
USA

50 Bedford Square
London
WC1B 3DP
UK

www.bloomsbury.com

BLOOMSBURY and the Diana logo are trademarks of Bloomsbury Publishing Plc

First published 2016

British Library Cataloguing-in-Publication Data
A catalogue record for this book is available from the British Library.

ISBN: HB: 978-1-4729-3267-9
ePDF: 978-1-4729-3268-6
ePub: 978-1-4729-3265-5

Library of Congress Cataloging-in-Publication Data
Names: Wiggins, Liz, author. | Hunter, Harriet, 1972- author.
Title: Relational change : the art and practice of changing organizations / by Liz Wiggins and Harriet Hunter.
Description: London ; New York, NY : Bloomsbury Business, 2016. | Includes bibliographical references and index.
Identifiers: LCCN 2016035463 (print) | LCCN 2016048640 (ebook) | ISBN 9781472932679 (hardback) | ISBN 9781472932655 (ePub) | ISBN 9781472932686 (ePDF) | ISBN 9781472932662 (eXML)
Subjects: LCSH: Organizational change. | Organizational behavior.
Classification: LCC HM796 .W54 2016 (print) | LCC HM796 (ebook) | DDC 658--dc23
LC record available at https://lccn.loc.gov/2016035463

Cover image © Pete Atkinson/Getty Images

Typeset by Fakenham Prepress Solutions, Fakenham, Norfolk NR21 8NN
Printed and bound in Great Britain

Contents

Acknowledgements

Thanks from Liz

Much of the thinking in this book had its genesis in working, and learning, with a body of good colleagues and friends whom I got to know at Ashridge Consulting. The Ashridge Masters in Organisational Consulting (AMOC) and the Ashridge Masters in Executive Coaching (AMEC) were fundamental to the development of my own thinking about relational change. I am, therefore, grateful for the many conversations and interactions I enjoyed which fed into the development of our collective work in, and for, organizations.

Much of my own reflection and thinking about leading change in practice has been honed and encouraged though my role in developing the Ashridge Masters in Leadership (AML), which is marketed as GenerationQ. From 2009 to 2015, I led the development and running of this along with my dear friend and colleague, Janet Smallwood. She has helped me grow, given me the confidence to share what I know and also to accept my own strengths and limitations as a leader. We have talked often, planning leadership fora, moderating assignments, navigating politics and just generally mulling and musing together on the phone and at her kitchen table, talking about what we have always felt is important and good work. She has been unfailing supportive, giving praise and encouragement, as well as telling me when, in Baddeley and James' terms, I was about to be a 'donkey' or had got hooked by my own Personal Drivers.

Thanks, too, to the rest of the GenQ faculty - Brian Marshall, Guy Lubitsh, Pete Dudgeon, Andrew Day, Howard Atkins and Georgie Hewitt-Penfold, who all contributed to the thinking and smooth running of the programme, as well as to my own learning. Thanks, as well, to the commitment and dedication of the GenQ coaches: George Binney, Sarah Beart, David Birch, Billy Desmond, Phil Glanfield, Louisa Hardman, Susanne Parsons, Tricia Boyle and Isobel Downs. Together you have helped Janet and me develop a programme that challenges and supports the leadership practice and learning of all the Fellows who have come on it, and who hold significant and challenging roles in the NHS and the charity and policy worlds in the United Kingdom.

Thank you to the Health Foundation for commissioning Ashridge and Unipart Expert Practices to develop GenerationQ back in 2009 - and to Will Warburton, Frances Wiseman and Sophie Bulmer for their current support to the programme.

Thanks to Professor Vicki Culpin who initiated the development of the Ashridge Bloomsbury series and encouraged Harriet and me to put forward our ideas for this book, and to Andrew Day, and then Roger Delves, for giving me the time to get my ideas down on paper.

Thank you to all the leaders I have had the privilege of working with on GenerationQ and in my other work as a leader myself, as a change consultant, executive coach and leadership development consultant. I have learnt much from your stories and your questions in so many ways that are impossible to document or know.

Harriet and I talked about writing something five years before we actually managed to make the time to get going. It has been a truly collective endeavour and involved much conversation, redrafting, talking, engaging in dialogue when we disagreed about a particular point and discovering together what we really meant by a relational approach to change. Harriet's unfailing good humour and optimism has significantly added to the fun of writing.

My family have been tolerant and supportive, so a big thank you to Clive, Esther and Josh who have brought me cups of tea and done more jobs round the house than they would have chosen to, while I was finishing this manuscript.

Thanks from Harriet

Thank you to the faculty of GenerationQ and my fellow Cohort One colleagues. The experience of participating on this programme with everyone revolutionized my working life and led to my involvement in the writing of this book.

Thanks to all those people, too numerous to name, who have had, and continue to have, an influence on my thinking. If we've ever shared a coffee or a glass of wine and talked animatedly about work and what it all means, then you are one of these people. Our conversations have undoubtedly contributed to this book!

In particular, thank you to three people who have given me fantastic opportunities to grow and learn at work over the years; Annette Henderson, Chris Stirling and Nicky Richards.

To my family; Jonathan is just an all-round brilliant husband, and has helped in the writing of this book in more ways than I can name. My mum and dad, who don't believe in book acknowledgements, but who are getting one anyway, for all the conversations we've had over the years, which have undoubtedly contributed to this book even if they won't believe me.

So, last but not least, to Liz, who has taught me so much and with whom it has been a joy and a privilege to work.

From us both

Many people were kind enough to read chapters in various draft forms. Special thanks to Rachel Williams, Helen Lucas, Hilary Macpherson, Susanne Parsons, Robert Richards, Cath Guest, Geoffrey Robb, Clive Wiggins, Emma Adams, Helen Crimlisk, Niladri Ghoshal, Lauren Wiggins, Anthony Hughes, Fiona Pender and Mark Cheetham, who all fitted reading and commenting into their busy work schedules.

A particular thanks to Brian Marshall, Janet Smallwood, Frances Wiseman, Eileen Moir, Peter Wilson, Martyn Brown and Dave Julien who challenged the thinking, flow and clarity of earlier versions of Chapter 1. Their tough love in giving supportive but challenging feedback encouraged the writing of what we believe is now a much better chapter as a result of their interventions and conversations. We, of course, take responsibility for any remaining areas of confusion, misunderstanding or inaccuracies in this and other chapters of the book.

Thanks also to those who were willing to share their stories. You will remain anonymous for obvious reasons, but your openness to talk about the ups and downs of leading change relationally has been truly appreciated.

Our editors at Bloomsbury, Ian Hallsworth and Emily Bedford, have been supportive throughout and a delight to work with. We have appreciated their willingness to engage in conversations about the title and cover and their practical advice and encouragement.

Lastly our thanks to Sue Jabbar, our project manager, without whom this book would never have happened. She has lightly held us to the plan that we made, helping us flex timings and priorities as stuff emerged, while enabling us to keep track of what we had done and where we needed to go next. Having her as part of the team has been a constant source of reassurance that at least one of us knew where we were. She has also been the guardian of multiple versions of chapters, fortnightly checklists, reference lists and progress charts, as well as helpfully spotting repetitive words, clunky sentences and poor grammar. We have benefitted enormously from her good humour, calm efficiency and teamwork. Thank you Sue.

Introduction

Why did we write this book? A view from the authors

Our intention in writing this book has been to give those involved in leading change some practical, down-to-earth ideas and support that will help them lead change relationally, thus working *with* others rather than doing *to* them. We have found that many current books on change contain much theory, but rarely seem to give enough practical detail to guide those in the thick of leading change as to what to do next. At the other extreme are the 'how to' manuals that proffer a simple model of change and a recipe book of exercises and lists to tick off on completion. While their intent is often worthy, and the desire to reassure the reader admirable, the downside is that in trying to 'keep it simple', a highly sanitized and, therefore, distorted view of leading change is often presented.

Thus, we have endeavoured to offer practical ideas, rooted in academic theory and research, but which also acknowledge the messiness and complexity of organizational life. This is a book that draws strongly on our own experiences of change in the public and private sectors, and it will, therefore, be relevant in any context. The touchstone for an idea to be included is that it has practical relevance for anyone involved in leading change. We hope that this book will achieve the following:

- reflect the experience of you, the reader
- acknowledge the hopes and challenges of change without fobbing you off with some easy template or toolkit that masquerades as a 'cookie-cutter solution'
- offer encouragement and practical ideas
- remind you that you are not alone when you experience the inevitable moments of annoyance, despondency and frustration

- inspire you to experiment with breaking stuck patterns; and
- help you be more 'choiceful' around the options you have when leading change. (We know that the word 'choiceful' does not exist, grammatically speaking, but we believe it should. It conveys the need to be aware of the different options for action open to you and to then make a deliberate choice about what to do next when leading change.)

In Chapter 1, we look at organizations through different metaphors. In doing so, we hope you will begin to recognize some of your assumptions about how you think organizations *should* work, as well as how they appear to work in practice. We will show how the way in which you see organizations has practical consequences for the ways in which you both lead and approach change. In Chapter 2, we look at two different approaches to leading change – the directive and the facilitative. In Chapter 3, we explore ways of engaging people relationally through dialogue and the dynamics of push and pull, inquiry and advocacy. We also consider what is needed to foster the different kinds of conversation that enable new ways of thinking to emerge. Chapters 4, 5 and 6 look at the sources of significant unpredictability during organizational change – politics, power and emotions – and suggest how to work with them. Chapters 7 and 8 offer ways of reimagining meetings and noticing what is going on 'in the moment', so that you can respond choicefully to both your own responses and to other people, rather than just being on automatic pilot. Chapter 9 looks at your options when everything is feeling stuck and Chapter 10 examines the question of how to sustain yourself, others and the change. In all of the first ten chapters, there are short, real life but anonymous stories to illustrate the points being made.

Chapters 11 to 13 differ from the previous ones in that each is an extended account of the lived experience of a relational leader of change. The stories recount the ups and downs of leading change, illustrating the key ideas of relational change in an authentic way, warts and all. While true to events, significant details have been changed to protect the anonymity of those involved.

We hope that reading this book will be like talking to a good friend who has some experience to share and ideas that are helpful in guiding you to lead relational change.

Part I

Chapter 1

Seeing organizations differently

A few words of introduction

Relational change takes into account three features of organizational life that are played down in traditional approaches to change management. First, relational change embraces the fact that work only happens through other people and that relationships therefore matter greatly. Second, despite the rhetoric of leaders needing to be in control and have 'grip', relational change acknowledges and works with the unexpected and unpredictable, rather than pretending that the reality of the messiness of organizational change can be airbrushed out and managed through a fixed plan. Third, relational change recognizes that the way we think and the stories that we tell ourselves, and others can constrain the possibilities of acting differently.

In this first chapter, we begin by introducing three contrasting ways of looking at organizations. This is to help you challenge your own thinking and assumptions, which, in turn, may well have limited the way in which you have approached change so far. We have found that helping leaders think differently about organizations, change and leadership has significant practical consequences in that it gives them new possibilities for action going forwards. We hope the same will be true for you.

Many leaders today are trapped in very traditional and mechanistic ways of understanding organizations and change. They wonder why, despite the effort, pain and aggravation, the change didn't really deliver. They can turn their anger on others, blaming 'them' or they can turn it on themselves, believing they somehow 'failed' or 'didn't do it right'. Leaders tell us that they are always firefighting and that organization life can feel mad at times. We start by exploring how the traditional way of viewing organizations, which is rooted in the metaphor of organization as machine, can lead to this apparent madness. Looking through this metaphor or lens, suggests change should be predictable and controllable and that the leader is like a master engineer who knows how to dismantle and then reassemble the complex machine, replacing or repairing individual parts as necessary. The second metaphor we consider presents organizations as organisms. Looking through this lens encourages us to pay attention to relationships: to that between the organization and its environment, and the multiple ones that exist internally between people and the different parts of an organization. Seen through this lens, change is a natural process of growth and development, and the role of the leader is to ensure that the organization knows how to learn and adapt to context in order to survive and thrive.

Last of all, we consider regarding organizations as complex responsive processes with the focus on local, unpredictable interactions between people. When they come to understand the implications of this way of seeing organizations, leaders often say this in particular challenges their assumptions about how they have hitherto thought organizations *ought* to work. Yet, paradoxically, it is the description that often resonates most with the way they *actually* experience organizations on a day-to-day basis. This way of understanding organization – or perhaps we should say *organizing* – offers an explanation for the complexity, messiness and unpredictability, and what sometimes seems the sheer madness of organizations. It emphasizes the multiple, non-linear relationships and interactions between people that are taking place all the time and explicitly draws attention to the importance of relationships and to paying attention to what is emerging.

Relational change draws on insights from all three ways of looking at organizations, but, in particular, uses the ideas generated by seeing organizations as complex responsive processes. It is an approach that challenges the dominant orthodoxy around change management by encouraging you to pay attention to what is *really* happening, rather than what you think ought to be happening; to be facilitative and focus on working with people, rather than 'doing to' them, and sees relationships as the source of insight, creativity and energy. It recognizes that as a leader you are in charge, but cannot be in control, which many leaders tell us can ultimately liberate them from feeling they ought to know and be able to fix everything.

Frustrations with change and a practical response

Whichever level you are in an organization, being able to lead change has become an integral part of work. Nobody gets on in his or her career by making the case for keeping everything the same. Yet people tell us of their frustration at the way that their initial excitement and enthusiasm for improving things evaporates after a while, often worn down by the sheer effort and energy required to make change happen in practice. We once worked with a global insurance company and the Chief Executive drew a sketch of a large aeroplane standing on the tarmac. There was a small figure tethered to the front trying to haul it back from the stand. 'That's how I feel,' he said. 'I'm that small guy with the rope around his middle and that's how it feels trying to turn around this organization. Exhausting.'

This is a practical book that recognizes leading change can feel exhausting. With this in mind, we share ideas from academic theory, research and our own experience of using those ideas in practice. We draw on our work with leaders from many different sectors, knowing what they have found helpful for getting themselves and those around them unstuck, involved and engaged in the process of change. There are many academic articles and management books written on specific aspects of change. While having the virtue of depth, if you are busy and pressed for time it can be laborious to wade through hundreds of pages to find the practical nugget of gold. We have endeavoured to do that mining for you. This first chapter is the most theoretical and gives the logic and academic foundations for relational change, but you can always revisit this later. The other chapters are very practical. To bring the ideas to life we have included true stories in each chapter, along with three longer stories at the end of the book. These stories have not been sanitized to pretend change is easy. Instead, we use them to illustrate and bring to life the points and practical suggestions we are making. A few details have been altered and names fictionalized to protect anonymity but otherwise these are unvarnished accounts of people like you who are trying to lead change in their organizations. We share these leaders' experiences of relational change, including the highs and lows, the choices and moments of indecision. We hope reading this book will be like conversing with a trusted friend, giving you practical ideas and confidence without pretending it is all straightforward.

We concentrate on the *'how'* rather than the *'what'* of change. So, rather than covering specific topics such as organizational design, strategy, mergers and acquisitions, attracting and keeping top talent or improvement methodologies, we concentrate on the process of leading change. W. Edwards Deming[1] wrote: 'Change is required. There is a process of change just as there is a process of manufacturing or for growing wheat. How to change is the problem.'

In exploring different ways of looking at organization, we are inviting you to surface your own assumptions about organizations. In doing so, you will become more aware of what the American psychologist Chris Argyris[2] calls your 'theories in use'. Argyris undertook extensive research into the differences between people's thinking and their actions in practice, contrasting 'theories in principle' with 'theories in use'. The former inform our beliefs about how we think the world *should* work; the latter how we *actually* behave in practice. Leaders, who are able to examine their own thinking and assumptions about organizations, can become more choiceful and confident about how they personally want to lead change in practice. (We know that the word 'choiceful' doesn't exist, but we believe it should. We use it regularly in our work with leaders who seem to find it useful too as it reminds them that there are always different possibilities for action open to them!)

To help you look at your assumptions about change, we start by describing different ways of seeing organizations. To do this, we draw on different metaphors that have been used by thinkers and researchers on organizations. A metaphor is, according to the *Oxford Dictionary* online: 'a figure of speech in which a word or phrase is applied to an object or action to which it is not literally applicable'.[3] In introducing metaphors to illuminate organizations, we are not suggesting that an organization **is** a machine or **is** an organism. Metaphors are like a lens, a way of seeing something in a particular way, but at the same time this draws our attention away from other aspects of the object or phenomenon. Metaphors are, therefore, by definition, offering a partial or limited view.

So, although academic theories and ways of thinking about organizations have shifted over time, we have found that many leaders' mental models remain rooted in old ways of seeing change. As we will show, the machine metaphor so dominates, it can seduce you into believing that it is the only way of organizing and the only approach to change management. As we analyse the three different ways of looking at organizations, you might want to consider the extent to which each recognizes the nature of people as you experience them when leading change in your organization, and the messiness and unpredictability of 'stuff' happening.

The machine metaphor

The first formal research into organizations emerged in the early twentieth century. It drew, in part, on studies of the army, but was most heavily influenced by the growing use of production lines, as pioneered by the Ford Motor company in the United States. As machines became more and more widespread, so did the idea that human activity at work needed to be organized in a mechanistic way to ensure the highest productivity levels possible. This line of thinking reached its apogee in Frederick Taylor's scientific management theory.[4] He was the first to introduce time and motion studies. By watching every move a bricklayer made, he reduced the number of steps in the process from fifteen to eight, saving time and money. Just as an engineer will design a machine by defining the different interdependent parts, so organizations were then conceived as a network of parts with interdependent functional departments. Within each functional department, each job was precisely defined, all rationally organized, planned in an orderly fashion and mapped onto a hierarchical organization chart. People were, in effect, seen as cogs in the machine. Policies and procedures would specify what each part of the organization should do, when and how, very much as you would with a machine. Looking at organizations through this metaphor, it is unsurprising that standardization, replicability and efficiency are the goals.

Social attitudes, when Taylor was writing, were undoubtedly more conformist than now, and social boundaries maintained class and professional hierarchies. Whether or not people enjoyed work or got on well together was largely seen as irrelevant. If the social element of work was noticed, it was treated as a technical problem to be fixed through rational means. Engaging people in their work, let alone in change, has no place in this schema. Instead, workers are viewed as passive objects, receiving and doing what is asked of them, rather than being seen as active participants. There are echoes here too of traditional views of the army - command and control for the leaders, following orders for the foot soldiers and troops. This way of looking at organizations has also been likened to Newtonian science, as it is very rational, reduces the whole to its constituent parts in order to understand it and believes in iron laws that assure certainty and predictability.[5]

Looking at organizations through the machine metaphor has implications for how we understand leadership. The leadership required is highly directive: the task of leadership is to ensure that people do as they are told and reliably perform their function. This, in turn, makes planning, measurement and control important. There is an assumption that control of the organization as a whole is possible and lies with those at the top. Control can be through governance procedures, reporting lines and management by objectives to align individuals' efforts with the corporate endeavour. Deficiencies are identified and understood through diagnosis, problem solving and trying to identify linear cause and effect, so that the organization can be steered towards desired and predictable outcomes - again, from the top. Indeed, the more a leader knows about a situation, the more tightly she or he can manage what happens and the better the outcome achieved; hence, the value placed on technical expertise.

Whenever we use a metaphor, it focuses our attention on some aspects of a phenomenon to the exclusion of others. This limits what we see and means that we can unwittingly ignore other aspects. In envisaging the organization as a closed entity, this metaphor diverts our attention away from the organization's context and the environment, which is often the source of much unpredictability and things we can't control. People and how they respond, interact and relate to one another are a further source of unpredictability when leading change, yet the machine metaphor gives people a very limited role, perceiving them as neither sources of creative energy and innovation nor of resistance.

In early research studies undertaken when the machine view of organization was the only one in town, leaders were regarded as born and not made. Some people have it. Others don't. Known as the trait theory, it was the leadership equivalent of the worker as the cog in the wheel. It was a case of fit and fitting in – it was just that leaders were bigger and more powerful cogs at the top of the organization. This supported the social hierarchy of the time which had only one model of leaders – white, middle-class, middle-aged men. There was no need for leadership development from this perspective because leadership was seen as innate. A further assumption with the machine metaphor is that there will be a right answer to any problem, and as leaders have ultimate power and authority, they will know what is best and right for the organization – that is what they are paid for.

These ideas have morphed into the idea of the leader as hero, which still has significant currency and influence today. One researcher calls it 'a belief in the power of one'.[6] There has been no shortage of leaders willing to publish self-aggrandizing memoirs that fuel such a view. Management gurus, too, have furthered the notion of the heroic leader by introducing the idea of the transformational leader – someone who shares a powerful vision, is charismatic and inspires others to follow them. This view of leaders casts them as saviours when they turn around an organization's fortunes and also as utter failures when they don't. Serge Tchuruk, the Chief Executive of Alcatel, the French telecommunications company, said: 'In times of crisis, executives are seen as imbeciles. In times of euphoria, they are seen as geniuses.'[7] Examples of the rise and fall in the perceived stature of leaders are legion: Luc Vandervlede and Stuart Rose (Marks and Spencer), Kenneth Lay (Enron), Tony Haywood (BP) and Fred Goodwin (RBS). All found their personal standing rise and fall with that of their corporations. They were cast aside and replaced by a new leader, a new well-paid cog – to use the machine metaphor. However, as Chris Grey, a recent commentator on leadership, writes, 'by honing so relentlessly upon an individual, (this view of) leadership tends to blind us to the complex, social nature of particularly large organizations'.[8]

Given the emphasis on control at every level and the desire for predictability, change is inherently troublesome for those holding the machine metaphor view of organizations. Incremental improvements to efficiencies may be achievable, but the stress on predictability and control tends to make operating in organizations with the machine perspective quite inflexible in practice. Leaders may offer the mantra of 'thinking and acting outside the box', but, an extensive survey,[9] found that more than 95 per cent of organizational change in practice was small scale and incremental.

What is interesting is that although nobody claims organizations *are* machines, this continues to be a dominant metaphor that influences thinking and practice in many organizations today. Indeed, it is so embedded that it has the quality of Argyris' theory in use, because people act and behave in practice as if it *were* true (even though as a metaphor it cannot be true or false). It is there in the emphasis on formal structures and hierarchies, in the policies and standard operating procedures. It is evident in the language people use. Phrases like 'levers for change', 'drivers of change', 'roll out', 'scale up', 'set in motion', 'diagnose and fix the problem' and 'business process re-engineering' are all rooted in the machine metaphor. This has real, practical consequences for leadership and for change. And, although the origins of this way of thinking about organizations can be found in the early part of the last century, the implications ricochet and reverberate within organizations today and lie at the heart of why many change efforts fail.

The organism metaphor

Advances in biology, ecology, cybernetics and general systems theory led to new metaphors emerging for understanding organizations. These metaphors include seeing organizations as human brains; as organisms; as ecosystems. What these metaphors have in common is a shift in thinking from the parts to the whole; a growing focus on human relationships and the interconnectedness of people and processes. There is also an emphasis on the need for adaptability and responsiveness to changes in the internal and external environment. Through this metaphor, organizations are seen as complex networks that are mutually interdependent. Feedback loops enable the system to monitor and respond to changes in the environment, like a living, self-regulating organism with a movement towards 'stable equilibrium'. Emphasis is on understanding the relationship between an organization and its environment, which will include the relationship with other organizations, as well as the relationships between the parts and the whole. In practical terms, the latter manifests in the idea that organizational effectiveness is achieved through the alignment of individual and organizational purpose.

These ideas were supported by what became a significant research tradition from the 1940s onwards into psychology at work, in particular in employee motivation and satisfaction. Maslow[10] was influential with his theory that as human beings, we have a hierarchy of needs. These are often represented as a pyramid, with basic survival needs, such as food and shelter, at the bottom. According to his theory, these basic needs must be satisfied before higher-order ones can be met. Higher-order needs include affiliation and belonging through to self-actualization at the top of the pyramid. Maslow did not suggest that all these needs could be met through work, but his thinking contributed significantly to the notion that work is more than a basic necessity – it's essential for a sense of individual purpose and meaning.

A range of theories and practices emerged, often loosely grouped under the name Human Relations, and later Organizational Development, which shifted away from seeing people as cogs in the machine to envisaging them as thinking, feeling beings with complex desires, aspirations and emotions. Given the right conditions, the assumption was that people can learn and adapt, reflect back on events and problem solve. This eventually evolved into the idea of the learning organization. With the emphasis on interpersonal relationships and the importance of the social fabric in the healthy functioning of organizations, these ideas provided a humanistic challenge to the more extreme interpretations of the machine metaphor of organizations. An implication for leaders from all of this was an invitation to see their role as being in part about creating workplaces where people feel valued, are engaged and have their needs for growth and development met.

Seen through the organism lens, change within organizations and within the wider system is perceived as a natural phenomenon. So organizations, like other organic systems, are seen to have a natural life cycle of birth, growth, maturing, death and then rebirth in some new form. Key questions when looking at change through this lens include: What is needed for survival? What is needed for organizational health and well-being? How do we learn and adapt to the changing environment? An assumption with this metaphor is the importance of involving the whole ecology or system in change: hence, the phrase you may have heard organizational development people use of 'needing to have the whole system in the room' when planning a system-wide change. There is also recognition that different 'species' of organization may be required to suit different environments. Instead of one size fits all, ideas such as 'fit for purpose' and 'best fit' are used. This may mean that some parts of the organization need to be pruned for the greater good. 'Diseased' and 'dying' parts may need to be cut off to stimulate invigorated growth. Talk may be of the need to 'cut the fat', 'slim down', 'get fit' so that there is survival of the fittest at a system level.

As ideas about organizations evolved into to seeing them as living systems, ideas about leadership also changed and the two mutually reinforced each other. What became known as the Michigan studies[11] in the 1950s suggested leaders fell into one of two categories – those who had a concern for task and getting the job done and those who had a concern for staff. You can see here echoes of the machine model of organizations, as well as those that are consciously or unconsciously informed by the ecosystem metaphor. There was then an exponential growth in research and thinking about leadership, resulting in far more nuanced and complex ideas. The role of the context began to be taken seriously so that effective leaders were seen as those who could adapt their style appropriately. Just as different 'species' of organizational form were required for different environments, so different leadership styles were required for different situations. The most well-known exponents of this approach are Hershey and Blanchard[12] who coined the term 'situational leadership'. We now have the idea that leadership behaviour is something that is malleable and can be learned. Unlike leadership in the machine-based metaphor of organizations, where the leader is the same in all situations, here the leader chooses and adapts his or her style to fit the context. Researchers labelled this and other similar approaches 'contingency theories' because 'it all depends'.

Leadership was now becoming seen as a balancing act: the role of leaders was to monitor and notice what is going on in the internal and external environments, identifying threats and opportunities, as well as coaching and nurturing the learning of individuals and groups. This would provide the data and feedback loops, enabling them to adapt their style. Heifetz,[13] in his work on adaptive leadership, has a lovely, slightly different metaphor for this. He encapsulates this duality, of monitoring the horizon and being up close and personal, when he talks of leaders needing to be on the balcony and on the dance floor.

Organizations as complex responsive processes

In our experience, leaders sometimes find the last way of seeing organizations the most challenging of the three offered here. It encourages us to think very differently. However, perceiving organizations as complex responsive processes often resonates with people's lived experience of the sometimes bizarre and unexpected things that happen in organizations. It places far greater attention on the role and importance of human relationships and the process of relating than in the organism metaphor. It also emphasizes predictability and unpredictability. It should also be said that some theorists who subscribe to the complex responsive processes view of organizations claim that this is not a metaphor, but a description of how things *are*. We see it as giving us insight into a significant element of organizations, but that it only describes part of what we understand by them.

As you may have noticed, the metaphors we have used to look at organizations are in part informed or inspired by scientific thinking and developments. Looking at organizations as complex responsive processes is informed by a broad range of recent scientific thinking and discovery spanning quantum physics, biology and meteorology that are held together by the term complexity science. They all embrace unpredictability and unknowability. In complex systems, the connections between nonlinear relationships are so many and varied it is not possible philosophically or practically to predict the impact of one part on another. We cannot say that if I do X, then Y will occur with 100 per cent certainty and confidence. To take two examples of this from complexity sciences: in quantum physics, light has the possibility of being both wave-like and particle-like; in chaos theory, a small change in one state may lead to a much bigger effect elsewhere in non-linear, unpredictable ways: so a butterfly flaps its wings in South America, and on the other side of the world there is a hurricane.

Much of the school of thought that applies complexity thinking to organizations was developed by Ralph Stacey,[14] who was originally a strategic planner for Shell. He tried, and in his eyes failed, to do the job. He came to the conclusion that this wasn't because he was somehow bad at his job, but that the job of planning was an impossibility. There were too many unknowns; too much uncertainty. He came to see the plan as a comfort blanket for senior leaders, a defence against anxiety to convince themselves and others that they were in control. Stacey came to the conclusion that the conventional, machine model of organizations, with planning as a key function, was fatally flawed. He constructed a new way of seeing organizations as complex responsive processes.

The key unit of interest for Stacey is the interactions between people, the gestures we make and responses others make in return as we talk together in conversation. He invites us to see organizations as multiple individuals and groups of people who are interacting together to achieve particular tasks. Indeed, Stacey talks about organizing as 'an ongoing self-referencing process of gestures and responses between people'.[15] In fact, he suggests that it is unhelpful to think about organizations as spatial entities that somehow have an existence separate from the people who populate them. We often talk of organizations or departments as if they are living things; we ascribe motives and behaviours – 'the organization decided to expand into the Middle East', 'the department reacted badly to the news of layoffs'. Although this may be a handy way of talking, in his view this obscures the fact that organizations are ongoing processes of interaction, not entities. To quote another writer in this area, Patricia Shaw:

> Speaking, imagining, remembering, moving, feeling, designing, persuading, making connections, using tools, developing strategies,

> analysing situations, forming narratives, taking action in relation to others – this is what I mean by the "flow of my experience" and it happens through interacting with others.[16]

At the heart of this theory is the concept of how, when we interact with each other through gesture and response, we make meaning together. I speak to you; I have some intention behind what I say; you listen and interpret what I say based on your own context. I can influence, but not control, what meaning you make from my gesture. You respond and together we make some kind of meaning. To use a philosophical term, meaning is socially constructed.[17] The way we think and talk shapes the gestures we make to someone else and what we notice of how the other person responds. This then impacts on the meaning we make from that interaction, which may confirm or disconfirm our original meaning. As this is an ongoing process, this, in turn, shapes the next move we make or comment we utter. They may be what we see as significant gestures – getting up and leaving or saying 'I love you'; they be small – a slight shift in tone of voice or the raising of an eyebrow. These gestures may or may not be picked up the other person or interpreted in the way we intended – hence, the unpredictability of relationships. The same kind of process will be happening for the other person as they notice and interpret your gestures, perhaps paying attention to some aspects more than others so that they too are socially constructing meaning. This is an ongoing process.

In this complex system of people relating and interacting, some of the patterns of our interactions *appear* stable, some unstable. Stacey argues that people create the patterns and relative stabilities that are recognizable as 'organizations' in constant interaction with each other and their perceived circumstances. Change however is ever-present in the dynamic nature of the interactive process between people.[18] For example, there may always be a team meeting on a Monday; you generally take an optimistic view of any proposal that comes to the meeting, but it could be otherwise. A new boss could ditch Monday meetings; you could experience some criticism which makes you more pessimistic. So, while patterns may often appear stable and predictable, there is always the potential for a different response with intended and unintended consequences in the future. It is not possible to predict these patterns, but when we look back we can often see earlier signs that perhaps we didn't notice originally. Like watching a movie or play second time round, the action can seem far more inevitable and predictable than when you first watched it. This is why commentators such as Mintzberg[19] say that strategy is written backwards - we have strategic intentions, but because we cannot predict what will happen it is only when we make sense of it afterwards, and tell ourselves and others the story of what happened, that it looks more logical and inevitable than it did at the time. Similarly, through the stories we tell ourselves and others, we are socially constructing meaning together and may create the illusion that we were in control and directing the action all along, even if this is not actually the case. The stories leaders tell are particularly important because their gestures often have more attention paid to them than other people's because of the power others perceive them to have.

One of the tensions about relationships is that although you need them to achieve anything within an organization, they are also a constraint. Relationships aren't completely elastic and changeable. We can't, or rather don't, just do or say anything. We are bound by our own beliefs about the nature of the current relationship we have with someone and by what we see as cultural norms, social conventions and expectations around power dynamics. To use that more philosophical term, this is because of the way we have socially constructed them. As we have already mentioned in our use of metaphors to understand organizations, the way we see things, and talk and about them in our heads, impacts our beliefs and also has practical implications in how we behave.

To illustrate, let's look at the phenomena of self-fulfilling prophecies.[20] If you are my boss and I believe you do not rate my expertise, this will impact how I behave when I meet you. I may be a little withdrawn, holding back or I may over compensate with enthusiasm, telling you all the wonderful things I have been doing. You will make sense of this behaviour, i.e. my gesture, and this may well confirm your view that indeed you do not rate me. You may, therefore, barely acknowledge my presence the next time I see you, rushing past me to your next meeting. Through your gesture you confirm the meaning I was already making of our relationship - this becomes a self-fulfilling prophecy, or to describe it another way, a stuck pattern of relating.

Despite these constraints, when one of us chooses to make a different gesture, we have the possibility of changing the nature of our relationship. Through our different gesture, we are inviting a different response from the other person. In our previous example, you might have stopped in the corridor and given me a compliment and invited me to join a special task force you are setting up. Through this new pattern of gesture and response, we could have had the possibility of creating new meaning, of seeing each other and our relationship differently. We would have had the possibility of change.

Change through the lens of complex responsive processes

Looked at through the lens of complex responsive processes, change happens through changing conversations and relationships. We can shift what seem to have become stuck patterns. As the leader, you do not need to be in each of those conversations, indeed you cannot be. Your role is creating the conditions for others to engage in different conversations. In planned meetings and chance encounters, you may respond to and amplify what you are noticing or start something in motion, engaging with positive intent even if you do not know exactly how others will respond.

As organizations are complex responsive processes, your gestures are like the ripples on a pond. A core principle of complex responsive processes is that small differences can be amplified and become transformative patterns, or what Malcolm Gladwell[21] describes as 'tipping points'. Stacey says that complexity indicates 'the macro emerges in the micro'[22] – if you want to see the 'large system' you need to look at its small interactions.

> Complex systems display the capacity to change and produce new forms only when they operate in a paradoxical dynamic of stability and instability at the same time [...] small differences can escalate into major, completely unpredictable changes.[23]

Those who feel comfortable with control may feel alarmed at the idea of unpredictability. Those who feel trapped and stuck may feel liberated by the new possibilities of instability that this way of seeing organizations encourages. Stacey himself rejected the idea of trying to map patterns of stability and instability, however in our experience, leaders seem to find the grid in Figure 1.1 helpful to link these ideas with their own lived experience.

This grid represents those parts of an organization or system where there may be relative stability, as well as other parts where there may be much greater instability, or even chaos. In terms of change, relative stability would be characterized by a high level of agreement about what needs to happen and a high degree of certainty in the environment. This is bottom left on the graph. This may be because the change in question is one that has been done before, hence, the knowledge and confidence about what to do and how to do it. In the top right, there is much more uncertainty in the environment and far less agreement about what to do or how to do it.

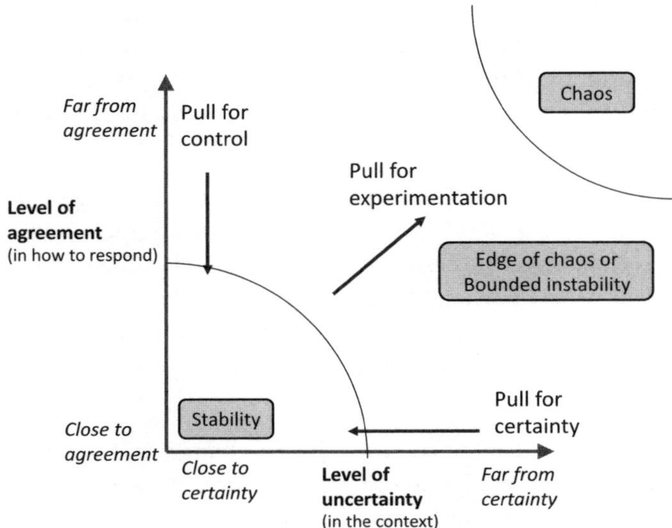

Figure 1.1 Zones of stability and instability. Adapted from the work of Stacey by Vanstone, Critchley and other Ashridge colleagues.

The top right zone of this graph is sometimes labelled 'mess' or 'chaos'. In this way of looking at organizations, mess and uncertainty are acknowledged and even seen as creative spaces with multiple possibilities for the new to emerge. An Executive Director at Marks and Spencer was overheard saying in a senior strategy meeting: 'It's really good we're confused about this. If we thought we knew what we were doing here we'd cock it up. We need some uncertainty to give us room to think.'[24] The CEO of Shell USA told his leaders at their conference: 'The world is a messy place. If we want to stay on top of the corporate ladder, we must plunge into the mess. We must learn to work with the mess.'[25]

What appear to be stable and stuck patterns can be a real barrier to change in organizations as, over time, gestures and responses between people have become socially constrained, reinforcing each other and becoming stuck. It can feel as though they have solidified into a pattern that is impossible to shift. Two colleagues of ours experienced this when working with the Board of a Professional Services company over a number of months. The Board were struggling to agree on a strategy to grow the company over the next two years. Despite various conversations, exercises and interventions, it still felt like wading through treacle. The CEO was super bright with a PhD from Oxford and a reputation for a phenomenal memory and killer questions. He talked a great deal. Privately our colleagues had several one to one conversations with members of the Board. In these conversations, people expressed their frustration with the lack of progress and their fear of saying what they really thought during Board discussions – apparently those who challenged didn't stay long in the company. Others remained loyal and in awe of the CEO. In this case, the pattern of interactions seemed highly stable and predictable. Our two colleagues started talking about the pattern being so embedded that there was a culture of group think[26] in which disagreement and challenge were tacitly forbidden.

On the morning of what was to be the last contracted session with the Board, one of our colleagues admitted to the other that she was dreading the session. She was already imagining how she would feel drained and frustrated at the end of the day, as once again she was sure no progress would be made. Her mental model of the situation would have impacted on the gestures she made with the group. Fortunately though, her colleague reminded her of Stacey and unpredictability. 'Don't assume nothing will change,' he said, encouragingly. 'We need to stay alive to the possibility of something different emerging from their interactions'. After lunch, one of the eleven Board members suddenly found his voice. It was only one sentence and it was quietly addressed to the CEO. 'I don't feel as though you trust me, or indeed trust any of us,' he said. There was an attentive silence and with those words something shifted in the room. This is what Stacey calls a 'gesture'. Others spoke out and for the first time ever that group began, tentatively at first, to have an honest conversation about what was really going on. This is one of the strengths and indeed liberating aspects of the complex responsive processes view of organizations. It encourages us to see that through conversation, there is always hope. The unpredictable can happen: life and fresh air can be breathed into a stuck and overly stable pattern when a different gesture breaks the pattern and is noticed and amplified by others.

In a different case, it was the leader who made a gesture that started shifting the conversations. John was the CEO of a retail bank where everything was organized according to the assumptions of the machine metaphor of organizations. It was a very macho, fear-based culture. No sign of weakness was permitted. At the annual leadership conference, the communications team had put much effort into planning every detail: the dinners, the slides, the speeches, the key messages. But in the evaluation forms, one gesture was mentioned by nearly everyone as their main 'take home message' and, to their surprise, it wasn't in the plan. The CEO had been asked a question and had simply responded: 'I don't know.' And *that* was what people remembered. It was a new and totally unexpected gesture that was the start of a new way of talking, a new culture emerging. It was suddenly permissable to admit a lack of knowledge because the man at the top had done so. This enabled people to break out of the charade of cultural norms and stuck patterns and to start talking about what was really going on and what was really needed.

This latter example illustrates that not all gestures are equal. We often liken being a leader to living in a glass elevator. A lot of what we say and do is seen by others, so our gestures as a leader will often carry more weight. What we choose to amplify, what we say, what we do counts; but because the responses of others cannot be predicted, we are freed of the burden of feeling that everything falls to us to sort out, to decide, to control. Instead, what is required as a leader is to act with a sense of intention and direction, to guide without being enslaved by a desire for certainty and a belief that we know best about everything. Leading instead becomes about creating an ongoing story or narrative that helps people make sense of what it is they have been, and are experiencing and where they might be going. The narratives leaders and others tell create some stability and sense of direction.[27] The stories people tell about who the collective 'we' is and where we are going guides people and will shift as new possibilities emerge. Weick writes that stories give some sense of stability and coherence to the transience of moment-by-moment lived experiences: 'Stories are [...] the products of previous efforts at sensemaking. They explain. And they energise.'[28] Such narratives can be the scaffolding that holds and structures some of the uncertainties for people and gives a sense of direction.

The complex responsive processes way of looking at organizations offers different ideas about what is required of leaders, and also takes the spotlight away from them. Leadership becomes less about the person in charge and more about how the collective is jointly engaged in conversation and action.[29] As organizing is a complex (in the sense of the Complexity Sciences) process, no one, including leaders, is able to predict exactly or control the direction of these multiple complex processes of gesture and response, hence, the emphasis on unpredictability. Even though leaders may be given ostensible responsibility by others, Stacey thus suggests they are in charge, but not in control. This way of seeing organizations thus takes away some of the huge burden of responsibility, pressure and loneliness leaders often experience when the way they think is predominantly informed by the machine metaphor. 'As a leader trying to change performance of a charity or a business or a hospital, do you really need to pretend to be Nelson Mandela?' asks leadership writer and researcher George Binney.[30]

This allows you to recalibrate your expectations of yourself as a leader. However, from this perspective, self-awareness and reflexivity become important attributes. Leaders also need to be ready to embrace what emerges and to notice and respond choicefully to what is happening in the moment. This is what Stacey refers to as 'practical judgement'.[31]

How seeing organizations differently informs relational change

We do not believe that any single metaphor or theory for understanding organizations captures the complexity of organizations. As Gareth Morgan,[32] a specialist in this area, writes, 'all theories of organization and management are based on implicit images or metaphors that lead us to see, understand and manage organizations in distinctive yet partial ways'. The metaphors we have considered are all in evidence in how people think and talk about different aspects of organization today. The machine metaphor, though, continues to dominate. And there are some theorists, such as Stacey, who would argue that the complex responsive processes is not a metaphor but represents how things are in reality.

However, it is worth noting that as these three different ways of looking at organization have evolved in time, there is an increasing emphasis being placed on the importance of relationships. There is also increasing acknowledgement of the existence and impact of uncertainty, as we represent in Figure 1.2.

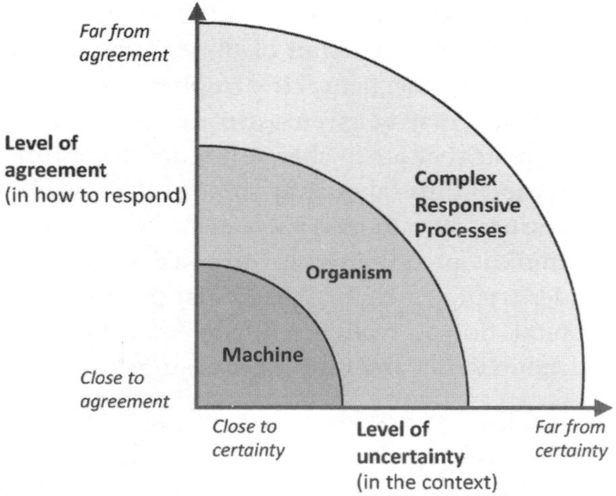

Figure 1.2 Boundaries of usefulness. Attributed to Smallwood, Marshall and Atkins.

The acknowledgement of uncertainty may account for the increasing interest in thinking about organizations as complex responsive processes which sees leaders as being in charge but not in control. The recent growth of social media and social movements are certainly good examples of changes that are neither controllable nor predictable. The macro social, geopolitical, economic environment is also highly unpredictable. Indeed, the acronym VUCA (volatile, uncertain, complex and ambiguous) was first used by the US military but is increasingly being used to describe the current global environment.[33] It may also be that on a more personal level, the complex responsive processes view of understanding organizations speaks to people's own personal experiences of the sometimes unexpected and bizarre happenings that occur.

A relational approach to change draws on aspects of organizations that are illuminated by each of these three ways of looking at organizations. Here we outline some of the key principles of a relational approach to change that are drawn from each, and are then developed further and made practical in subsequent chapters.

From the machine metaphor:

- Planning plays a helpful role in creating a shared sense of understanding of what is intended.
- Plans serve in part to contain the anxiety that uncertainty evokes. However, in terms of relational change it is important to be willing to flex plans to respond to what emerges.
- There are tangible aspects of organizations such as organization charts, buildings, reserved car parks, uniforms and job titles that constrain some relationships through beliefs and practices related to power dynamics.

Prompted by the organism metaphor:

- People, processes and place are interconnected.
- The context or internal and external environment is important, and it is imperative to fit approaches to change to the context rather than forcing so called 'best practice'.
- Growth, development and creativity through people is possible and desirable.

- It is important to create the conditions for learning and for new ideas to emerge.

Prompted by the complex responsive processes perspective:

- The uncertainty and unpredictability of the world is accepted, with patterns of stability and instability emerging which are not predictable.
- The fundamental dynamic between people is that of gesture and response and the creation of shared meaning, with change happening through conversation.
- The way people think and talk has practical consequences
- Leaders are in charge but not in control. Their gestures are often amplified because of the power dynamics in the system and the impact of the stories they tell.
- Leaders need to create enough certainty so there is just enough structure and control for dialogue, innovation, and new conversations.

Your role as a leader taking a relational change approach is to create conditions for those around you to make sense of what is happening and what next steps to take together. You might have plans, but you recognize that there is no guarantee that these describe what will necessarily happen, although they guide and signal intention and direction of travel. You're on the lookout for opportunities to adapt and change direction as the future emerges. In his book, *Living Leadership*, Binney[34] describes how leaders work best in complex circumstances when they are connected to themselves, so they have insight into their own behaviour and actions, and are connected to those around them so they can relate to others and engage them in change through conversation. They are also connected to the environment and context in which they are working so they can spot opportunities, encourage experiments to see what might be possible and create a narrative with others that allows people to make sense of what is happening.

As we have seen, viewing organizations as a machine, as an organism or as a complex responsive process draws attention to different aspects. In working with leaders, we use a device to help visualize these different features as existing, metaphorically speaking, 'above and below the waterline'. This is illustrated in Figure 1.3.

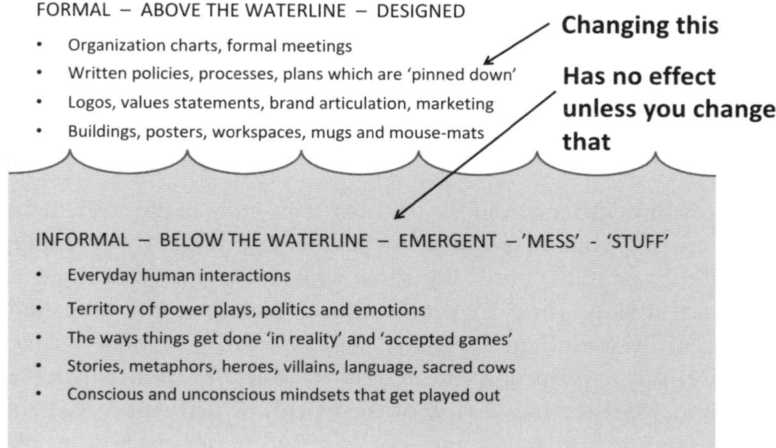

FORMAL – ABOVE THE WATERLINE – DESIGNED
Organization charts, formal meetings
Written policies, processes, plans which are 'pinned down'
Logos, values statements, brand articulation, marketing
Buildings, posters, workspaces, mugs and mouse-mats
Changing this
Has no effect unless you change that
INFORMAL – BELOW THE WATERLINE – EMERGENT –'MESS' - 'STUFF'
Everyday human interactions
Territory of power plays, politics and emotions
The ways things get done 'in reality' and 'accepted games'
Stories, metaphors, heroes, villains, language, sacred cows
Conscious and unconscious mindsets that get played out

Figure 1.3 Paying attention to what goes on above and below 'the waterline'. After Caryn Vanstone, WL Gore and colleagues on AMOC.

Some aspects of organizations are visible and tangible; other aspects are more intangible, invisible and unpredictable. Structure charts, standard operating procedures and job plans exist 'above the waterline'. The machine metaphor of organizations would draw attention to such features. Other tangible and physical features that exist above the waterline are things like buildings, branding and publicity material. However, the meaning that people ascribe to them is not tangible and is likely to vary and to depend on what is going on below the waterline. Below the waterline are the multiple informal interactions between people; the gestures and responses and the meanings made together; the ebb and flow of feelings about the work, colleagues, the organization; the interplay of power and politics that is manifest in stories with heroes and villains; the gossip round the edges of meetings, and the collective and individual sense making about what happens, what is 'really' going on and what it might mean. This territory is much more unpredictable. It is this territory that the complex responsive processes view of organizations draws attention to, and it is what gets ignored in the machine metaphor.

The relational approach to change emphasizes the importance of paying attention to what is going on above *and* below the waterline. In our experience, the area below the waterline is generally underplayed by leaders.

A postscript for those who like philosophy

The words 'modernism' and 'postmodernism' may make some people dive for cover. If you are one of those people, just ignore this paragraph and read the rest of the book. For those who are interested or intrigued, we are advocating what in philosophical terms would be called a pluralist, multi-paradigm approach. This is because we believe that in some cases it is appropriate and helpful to adhere to modernism (i.e. a Newtonian, machine-based view of the world), which embraces beliefs about reason and progress and, consciously or unconsciously, plays down other views, particularly those that reflect ambiguity and uncertainty. Postmodernism, on the other hand, emphasizes the uncertainty of life in general, including organizational life. A multi-paradigm approach potentially offers a new look at this modernism vs postmodernism duality. Whereas use of a single paradigm can produce a valuable but narrow view, multi-paradigm inquiry may foster 'more comprehensive portraits of complex organizational phenomena'.[35] In our view, it should not be surprising that when it comes to matters as complex as organizational change, as human beings 'we are capable of believing that different approaches and metaphors are valid as perspectives on how organizations work and how change may come about.[36] Indeed, in our experience, it is perfectly possible, and sometimes effective, to have an eclectic approach, a bricolage, a kind of unaware pluralism which enables flexibility and context-appropriate approaches without ever unearthing the theoretical underpinnings.

We believe that as human beings we have the capacity to hold a pluralist view. Only by holding and using *all* of them do we get the fullest possible range of understanding and action to cope with the complexity and challenge of modern organizational life.

Questions for further reflection

- Looking at your own organization, through each of the three metaphors, which different features are highlighted?
- What aspects of the machine metaphor are you attracted to and how do they inform how you see change and your role currently?
- What about for the organism/ecosystem metaphor of organizations?
- The complex responsive processes view of organizations is the one that leaders sometimes take a while to get their heads round. Which aspects of this way of looking at organizations and change do you personally find interesting and which leave you feeling alienated or confused?
- How much do you pay attention to what goes on below the waterline?

Chapter 2

Seeing change differently: The art of choosing your approach

In this chapter, we start by exploring ways of seeing change. We then look in more detail at two approaches to this that envisage very different roles for you and others. With directive change much of the responsibility stays with you as the leader; with facilitative change, however, the contribution, ideas, experiences and energy of others is actively sought and welcomed. We look at the continuing legacy of the machine metaphor of organizations, with its emphasis on plans. Plans have many merits but holding on to them too tightly can mean the focus is on what you *think* ought to be happening, blinding you to what is *actually* going on. This is where the complex responsive processes view of organizations is helpful. It encourages you to connect to what other people are seeing and experiencing from the myriads of conversations and interactions they participate in daily. It also encourages you to pay attention to your own experiences and feelings. These, in turn, enable you to notice the emergent and unpredictable metaphorically 'below the waterline', so that you can choose how to respond, rather than ignoring all of it. This flexibility is a core aspect of relational change in practice.

Relational change is thus a balancing act and thus we introduce the idea of working with polarities. We conclude by advocating why we believe change is an art rather than a science.

Multiple perspectives on change

Take a piece of paper and draw your view of change. This might sound a bit of an odd thing to do but do give it a go anyway. Use colour. Use shapes. Use images. Try, if you can, to avoid using words.

What have you drawn?

Sometimes, when we ask leaders to do this exercise, they draw something that looks like a plate of dropped spaghetti, with lines of different colours swirling all over the place. Others draw masses of splodges and mini explosions like a Jackson Pollock painting. These types of representations suggest change is messy, complex and chaotic.

Another frequent image is of change as a series of steps, sometimes drawn going up in neat orderly progression; on other occasions, the steps, at the beginning, are higher thus suggesting that it can be more difficult to get things started. Sometimes, people draw a line like a wave or a heartbeat, with ups and downs to indicate successes and setbacks.

Then again, there are people who focus on the emotional aspects of change. We've seen pictures with smiley faces, big suns shining with lots of bright yellow, cheerful rays and others featuring grey rain clouds, lightening zigzags, sad faces, thumbs up, thumbs down, stick people dancing and jumping and people with a big red cross drawn through them. And there are others who draw formulae and bags of money which suggest business cases and a commercial imperative to change.

We have also seen organic images, such as a picture of seed, a sapling and a tree; or a rough drawing of a tree in each season. Such pictures seem to be emphasizing the idea that change is a natural phenomenon or something cyclical. At the other extreme, we see pictures which look more like production lines or an engineering sketch, with arrows and pulleys, cogs and boxes. Such pictures are more suggestive of change as a linear process with different steps and little to do with people.

And others still some draw the unexpected – roads that suddenly divert and snake off in another direction. We recently ran a session where someone drew an octopus in a string bag to represent what she saw as the impossibility of managing change: every time you have wrestled one arm into the bag another one pops out somewhere else.[1]

As no doubt you will have already noticed, many of these pictures have echoes of the different metaphors of organizations already explored in Chapter 1. This exercise shows in a very simple way the variety of assumptions and interpretations individuals have about the nature of change. Whenever you embark on a change programme or initiative, you will be encountering people starting from very different places. Individuals' perspectives, including your own, will be shaped by many factors, including recent experiences of how change has been handled. How people feel about the current situation will play a part, too. Those bored with, or frustrated by, the status quo may view change as an opportunity and a source of novelty, innovation and excitement. Conversely, those who feel they have seen too much change recently or who have significant change taking place in their personal lives may yearn for stability.

We often start workshops on change with this drawing exercise. The props required are simple – just some pieces of paper and pens. Rather than getting caught up in words and semantics or trying to define change, this simple exercise shows the multiple perspectives on change in a very visual way. Asking people to share their representations of change invites them to think about their own assumptions and perceptions. It also demonstrates the range of views out there and surfaces the idea that change is rarely a simple process. Bringing all these things to people's attention can be a very helpful way of starting off a piece of change work with any group.

Introducing directive and facilitative approaches to change

If you see organizations through the lens of the machine, the likelihood is that you will expect change to be a linear, step-by-step process. Back in the 1950s, Kurt Lewin[2] introduced what was probably the first official model of change, comprising three stages:

Unfreeze present state → Move → Refreeze in desired new state

A plan appealing in its simplicity and unambiguity. All the people in the drawing exercise who portrayed change as a series of linear steps are describing a directive approach. This is an approach which is underpinned by a number of assumptions – that there is agreement about what needs to change and that the future state is known and achievable; that nothing unexpected will happen to interfere with this smooth forwards movement; that there will be no significant challenge to the end point or the approach; that a leader can direct and control what happens. Variations of this continue to be the dominant orthodoxy in most organizations today.

The benefits of plans are no doubt obvious to you. Plans ensure that which resources are needed, when and where, are specified. When working at a scale where many people are involved, plans are a way of communicating and attempting to align the activities and energies of everyone. Plans also appeal to our rational and logical selves and suggest that someone, perhaps ourselves or a group of other people, have thought about what is required, considered the different options and identified the best way forwards. Psychologically, plans are often reassuring for both the people who create them and those on the receiving end.

The problem with directive change, however, is when those adopting this approach assume that change will happen in the way the plan says. However, 'stuff happens'. A cartoon showed three daleks, those Dr Who villains who glide across the ground on small wheels shouting 'exterminate, exterminate!'. They were facing a flight of steps. The caption underneath read, 'We need another plan'. In directive approaches, this kind of unexpected situation is sometimes acknowledged with the creation of risk registers, but this is trying to predict and manage uncertainty, rather than work with it; it is trying to wrestle potential mess and disruption back into the plan.

Some of the unexpected comes from changes in the external environment: a major client goes out of business so there is a profit shortfall and planned investment is put on hold; a competitor introduces an innovative new product; a crop failure means raw material prices are much higher than expected; or the government introduces new and unexpected regulations, for example.

Other unexpected things may happen within the organization: a powerful group of people actively challenge what has been proposed; the senior leadership changes; people don't take any notice of the 'corporate message' and continue as they always have done, and so on. When we use phrases like the 'best-laid plans of mice and men', we acknowledge the regularity of the unexpected.

The limitation of directive approaches to change on their own is the assumption that the world is static while the change is taking place, but very often the context is changing at the same time as the particular change is being undertaken. One leader we worked with[3] was fond of saying that what he and his team were doing was akin to building a new motorway while the traffic was still moving. He would then show a picture of a dead hedgehog with the yellow line going across it – easy to become road kill in such circumstances. A further assumption with directive, linear models of change is that change takes place as singular events. However, often other changes start before the first one has finished, and then before that has finished, multiple others have been initiated too. Here, too, lie sources of significant unpredictability and complexity. And people, whether part of the internal or external environment, can be a source of unpredictability. The night before the Battle of Waterloo, the Duke of Wellington's second-in-command plucked up the courage to ask him about his plans for the following day. Wellington is said to have asked: 'Who will attack first? Bonaparte or I. On that depends my plan.'[4] The list of 'stuff happening' is endless. So if we acknowledge that plans serve a useful function, but at the same time know that 'stuff' happens, what are the implications for us as leaders of change?

We have found extreme adherence to THE PLAN and a directive approach is highly problematic. Should there be a high level of certainty about the end point and the steps required, the environment is relatively static and well known and everybody affected is in agreement about the 'change' then directive approaches alone might work. However, it is rare for all these factors to be in play in anything other than some theoretical, 'in principle' sense. Key to a relational approach to change is paying attention to what is *actually* happening in practice as a result of people working with each other, rather than being enslaved to beliefs about what you think *ought* to happen and what is inscribed in the plan. We encourage leaders to actively notice and inquire into what is happening in the internal and external environment and, rather than ignoring it, to work with it. Alongside this is a need to resist the temptation to sound as though you know it all or are 100 per cent certain of the outcomes. Believing your own rhetoric risks setting yourself up as the hero, which will make it harder for you to respond and change when inevitably the unexpected happens. This means holding plans lightly enough to make adjustments.

For instance, when Unilever began outsourcing transactional HR activities to Accenture in 2005, there were many among the 100,000 employees who were unaware of, or not in favour of, the change. However, there was enough certainty and agreement about the current and future state at senior levels in the organization for a plan to be created. Given the scale of the endeavour, a plan was vital as it served to hold and align activities. This was the biggest outsourcing programme globally that had ever been attempted. In the 180 countries in which the company operated, there were different HR policies, from holiday arrangements to the use of a company beach hut and employee entitlements for rice. Migrating and aligning all of these policies was a mammoth task and the plan was the thickness of a telephone directory for a medium-sized town. Updating the plan and monitoring the status of each item using the classic RAG (red, amber, green) rating was in itself a massive communication and management task. And, of course, unexpected events did occur – there were far more HR policies in some countries than in the original estimates; a few key individuals left the project team; the costs of setting up call centres were higher than predicted; there were differences of opinion between the Unilever people leading the team and those from the outsourcing partner; Unilever business leaders in some low-wage countries argued HR was going to cost them more after outsourcing, so cross-charging adjustments needed to be made; outsourcing in Unilever's fourth-largest market, India, was delayed by eighteen months because of a change to Unilever India's legal status, and so on. Although this outsourcing was achieved through a predominantly directive approach to change, some re-planning and adjusting of time lines, activities and cost savings were still required. The reality was quite a bit messier than the simplicity of Lewin's model suggests. The change leaders had to adapt the plan and create a story to make sense of those adjustments, while also holding true to the original intent. Another juggling act.

More recently, writers such as John Kotter[5] offer versions of a directive approach to change which build on Lewin's idea with more sophistication. However, the approach is still very linear, a hallmark of directive change. It also remains rooted in the machine metaphor of organizations. Kotter is much quoted with his neat **eight-step plan of action**:

1. **Create a burning platform to establish a sense of urgency.**
2. **Form a powerful guiding coalition.**
3. **Create a vision.**
4. **Communicate the vision.**
5. **Empower others to act on the vision.**
6. **Plan for and create short term wins.**
7. **Consolidate changes and instigate more change.**
8. **Institutionalize new approaches.**

The leader plays a very central role in this approach, with many of the steps comprising activities that he or she should be driving; hence perhaps its appeal to some. It is also often associated with the language of transformational change led, therefore, by implication, by someone who is a transformational leader. Again, this language may appeal to some. Certainly the emphasis is on those who have formal power in the hierarchy clubbing together to create a powerful guiding coalition and then later empowering others.

In terms of the dynamics of change, the leaders tell everyone else what is happening. Empowerment means others are then given discretion within the framework that has been decided by those who are more senior. The need to acknowledge and work with power is one of the helpful aspects of this model; however, as we explore later, in Chapter 5, Kotter has a rather narrow, hierarchical definition of power. The model, like all directive approaches, offers reassurance to those in charge as it purports to provide confidence and rational certainty that the change and everyone involved can be managed and controlled.

Privately many leaders admit they are uncomfortable with the central role envisaged for them by Kotter. It can feel burdensome and lonely. They admit to feeling inadequate when faced with the expectation that they know best or feel they should do so. It can be daunting to believe you should create the right vision and have the charisma to communicate that vision so that staff are excited and enthused, even if you are more of an introvert. In many respects, this approach can set leaders up to fail, as it implicitly suggests that if the change doesn't happen as planned somehow the leaders have failed – the burning platform was not articulated well enough, the vision was not exciting enough, the guiding coalition was not sufficiently aligned. We could go on.

Given that the directive view of change puts a huge burden of responsibility for the change onto the leader, when things do not go to plan two responses tend to occur, neither of which are helpful. Either the leader feels he or she has failed, and perhaps, to add to their woes, others further up the hierarchy suggest that is the case too. Or the leader may turn the blame onto others around them – people didn't listen, didn't do what they said.

In our view, the fault lies not with the leader trying to follow this model but with the model itself. It presents what is still an idealized and sanitized view of change. It air brushes out the messy reality of people working together and assumes that the leader can be in control, directing proceedings. It assumes that all that matters is what is above the waterline and ignores what is emerging below. While more sophisticated than Lewin's approach, Kotter's eight-step model remains wedded to a machine based view of organizations with all the limitations this brings.

If we are not advocating a directive approach, what are we advocating in terms of relational change? The art of relational change is being able to work with both directive and facilitative approaches depending on what is going on in the moment in the internal and external context. However, because the dominant approach to change in organizations tends to be directive, we have found that leaders generally need to put much more emphasis on facilitative change, creating the conditions for people to notice and work with what is emerging in their context. With a directive approach comes a tendency to overplay control and stability, whereas a facilitative stance emphasizes the complex nature of organizations as constantly evolving social processes. It accepts that 'stuff' happens and also the inherent un-knowability and un-predictability of the future. As Myers, Hulks and Wiggins write:

> Directive change emphasises the managers' deliberate intentions to achieve organisational change, with a clearly defined start and end point for change. Facilitative change emphasises the view that, whether or not change is intended, organisations are in fact, constantly evolving. It focuses on creating the conditions for change

to occur, to enable change through continuous ongoing processes of organisational experiment and adjustment, with no defined end state.[6]

The ramifications of sticking to a purely directive approach is something a CEO encountered when he embarked on a change programme to improve profitability. The core business of the medium-sized, privately owned company was running clinical trials for pharmaceutical firms. The CEO created the plan for the change programme himself with limited involvement from anyone else. The plan included controls on the maximum salaries for hiring new statisticians. Senior leaders warned the CEO that this figure was 20 per cent below the market rate in the US and 40 per cent below market rate in India, but he kept to his plan, arguing that it was always possible to find enough people who could be hired at a lower rate and that his staff just needed to try harder. New statisticians were, indeed, hired for two large new projects, but, as a result, at these lower rates, those hired were junior, inexperienced in the sector or just not very good. Senior people found themselves having to work even harder to compensate to make sure client deadlines weren't missed. They kept flagging their concerns to the CEO, but he was not up for changing his mind. He was the CEO, he told them; it was his company and he had decided. Their job was to make things happen.

So, the CEO continued to act in accordance with his plan, failing to pay attention to others' views and experiences, unconnected to those around him, wedded to his directive approach and confident in the rightness of the approach and the end game. However, the plan didn't make sense to his staff. Some of those who had been around longer wondered if he was trying to maximize profitability as a prelude to selling off the company. Given his forceful or, in his own words, 'forthright' management style, most didn't dare ask him directly. The few senior people who did were given short shrift. Within a month of each other, two of the CEO's most senior leaders resigned. Both had worked at the company a long time and were well-regarded internally and by clients. The CEO hadn't expected this: his attempts to persuade them to stay failed. Several months later, another senior leader left. The cumulative impact of such departures was to make some employees wonder if they should go, too: what did the senior people who had left know that they didn't? None of this was in the CEO's plan. Still, he blamed others; not the plan.

Each individual employee noticed different things that made them feel unsettled and less sure of the company's future or their own place within it. People talked to each other of course, each person making sense of what was going on through the lens of their own needs and anxieties. Staff turnover began to increase significantly and, that year, for the first time, the company failed to meet revenue or profit targets. Two important new tenders were lost to the competition. The CEO's response was to work harder and harder himself and demand the same of others. He was furious, but never stopped to consider whether his own behaviour and approach to change had contributed to the current situation.

It would be wrong to say that the change plan *caused* the senior people to leave, or that their departure *caused* the subsequent wave of resignations and the loss of the potential new pieces of work. There could have been many reasons for all of these events happening, none of which may have been connected or all of which may have been connected. As the complex responsive processes view of organizations reminds us, what we call organizations can be seen as multiple networks of individuals interacting with each other in conversations, face to face, on the phone, through email, gossiping, wondering as well as talking about the task at hand. As people interact, individuals are continuously involved in making sense of things together. In the company above, some individuals may have been paying more attention when the first two senior people who resigned. Perhaps they had worked closely with them and really liked and admired them. Others may not have not given such departures much thought until a couple of their colleagues talked about them or there were further resignations. All of this is going on 'below the waterline'. Nobody can control this because it is inherently unpredictable. We can neither predict with absolute certainty what is going to happen nor unpick the past to try and isolate some causal flow of events.

Had the CEO listened and paid attention to what was going on, inquiring into the reasons for his senior peoples' concerns with some belief and trust in their perspectives, talking to them to see what modifications his plan might need, it is possible that the outcome could have been different. This would have meant changing to a more facilitative approach to change. He could have made some different gestures that demonstrated to people, his intention to modify the plan. Some staff may have believed him, some may not, depending on how much individuals trusted him or personally wanted to believe that all would be well. Different stories about what was happening may then have been told among his employees. Some of the senior people may have stayed. We cannot run a controlled experiment to see what would have happened.

What we can learn from this story, is the importance of leaders paying attention to what is *really* happening around them rather than holding steadfastly to the plan, rigidly ploughing on, regardless. Working with others, listening to their perspectives, noticing what is going on, asking people questions and reflecting on what they say means taking a more facilitative approach to change. Doing so will give you the data and evidence to support or challenge your own sensemaking about what is going on in practice, as well as the general direction of travel. It means holding a plan lightly and flexibly enough to embrace emergence and adapt the plan, thus acknowledging the insights of the complex responsive processes view of organizations.

As the leader, it may mean giving direction with confidence for now, but with the humility to acknowledge it may need to be modified, continually involving others, showing that their input and views are genuinely welcomed. This is what Stacey, on whose work we draw, in his later works calls, 'practical judgement'.[7] It means believing that you do not need to have all the answers, but that you can work things out with those around you. And at certain moments, you as the leader who is in charge, even if not in control, may need to make some explicit choices or decisions about what next.

Working with polarities

The differences between directive and facilitative approaches to change can be usefully explored using Barry Johnson's[8] idea of polarity management. Polarities are paradoxes to which there is no simple 'yes' or 'no' answer; they are tensions which are inherently unsolvable because both poles have strengths and limitations. You cannot choose one side as a 'solution' because that would mean neglecting the other. The objective of polarity management is to get the best of both opposites, while avoiding the limits of each, so that we can see as complete a picture as possible of the whole situation, an idea that comes from the ecosystem/organism metaphor discussed in Chapter 1 (see pages 10–13).

Faced with a polarity, a very practical way of surfacing or unpacking the strengths and limitations of each extreme is the creation of a polarity map. We've used this technique with groups needing to collectively explore all manner of polarities that they need to work with. To create a polarity map, you mark out four squares, as in Table 2.1 opposite. Although this can be drawn on a flip chart, we have found that it works even better when marked out on the floor using masking tape, so people can physically move round the map as they think and talk.

Taking directive and facilitative approaches to change as the polarities, the left-hand side represents one pole – in this case, a directive approach to change – and the right-hand side represents the opposite pole – in this case, a facilitative approach to change. The upper squares represent the strengths of both poles or the positive outcomes that result from focusing on that pole. The lower two squares represent the negative outcomes that result from focusing exclusively on that pole and neglecting the opposite pole.

There is no 'correct' order for filling out the polarity map. Start wherever you or the group want or split the group into four and give each group a quadrant to discuss. When people have considered all four, the whole dilemma with the strengths and limitations of both poles can be seen. As this is a polarity or dilemma to be worked with, not solved, there is a natural movement or dynamic which creating the polarity map makes apparent. Johnson likens this to an infinity loop – the movement being continual from quadrant to quadrant.

Working with these dilemmas is an ongoing process of balancing and rebalancing. Over-focusing on the strengths of one pole leads to its limitations becoming more apparent, which can then require a shift to focus more on the other pole. In our experience, what tends to happen

Positive outcomes from focusing on a directive approach to change	*Positive outcomes from focusing on a facilitative approach to change*
• Gives clear direction and milestones • When there is a stable context and agreement about next steps and end point, can be the most efficient and pragmatic approach • Everyone knows what is meant to be happening • Reassuring to everyone that we know who is doing what, when and where we are going • Allows scheduling of resources and cost control and can do so at a large scale • Gives people confidence to act with intentionality	• Encourages openness to new possibilities and ideas • Pays attention to what is emerging and what is really happening • Ensures everyone feels they can contribute, as it's not fixed • Allows activity to be flexible to take advantage of the unpredictable • More congruent with the messiness of stuff happening in reality
DIRECTIVE APPROACH to CHANGE	**FACILITATIVE APPROACH to CHANGE**
Negative outcomes from focusing on a directive approach to change	*Negative outcomes from focusing on a facilitative approach to change*
• Too rigid to be helpful and responsive when the unexpected inevitably happens • Ignores what is happening between people 'below the waterline' • Overly restrictive so can't accommodate new ideas or experiments • Assumes we know and can predict what is going to happen when this doesn't fit with messiness of reality • Can encourage fixed views	• Can be anxiety provoking for many as they don't know what's happening when • Doesn't allow for scheduling of resources and is harder to budget • Harder to do on a big scale • Can be time consuming • Requires well developed relational skills

Table 2.1 A polarity map looking at working with directive and facilitative approaches to change.

is that some people may be drawn into anticipating the downsides of the present pole, which they identify as the 'problem'. Others may be attracted to the upsides of the other pole, which they identify as the 'solution'. However, in explicitly identifying the strengths and limitations of both, the whole picture is transparent to everyone which encourages productive conversation about how to maximize the strengths and limit the downsides of both poles. This helps everyone see that there is space for both perspectives rather than getting drawn in to believing one is 'right' and the other 'wrong', so 'both and' rather than 'either or'.

Relational change as art not science

We suggest that working with both directive and facilitative approaches to change is more akin to art than science. When situations are stressful and times are tough, we recognize the very human yearning for predictions rather than possibilities, for templates rather than tentative suggestions. However, as we have already explored, this will rarely serve you well in practice. While there is much theory and research to guide and inspire, we cannot call the study and practice of organizational change a science. Context really matters because organizations cannot be sanitized and sucked of life to become controlled experiments. This is why predictive social sciences have such a poor track record. There is no linear, causal relationship that if you do 'x' then 'y' will result. Equally, unlike laboratories, conditions in organizations can never be fully specified or replicated. They are 'messy'. Rather than universal solutions, an element of contingency thinking – 'it all depends' – is inevitable and wise.

There is much to be learned from best practice and research, but 'the challenge is to deal with the paradox that much scholarly knowledge is framed in universal terms, whereas practical problem-solving requires specific solutions'.[9] The specifics of your own preferences and style and your own organizational context mean that offering a silver bullet, a tool kit or single technique would be disingenuous. At the end of the day, you, as the leader, will need to make a choice about what to do next, to make a judgement call based on what you and others know and what feels appropriate and helpful at that moment. This is why relational change, while very practical, is more of an art than a science. Being a leader is more like being a jazz musician than a member of a classical orchestra. You need to have learned to play your instrument and studied music, but you don't slavishly follow the music. You experiment and improvise with others. There may be the odd squeak but something new emerges. Another leader described relational change as more like sailing – recognizing the importance of scanning the horizon, understanding local weather conditions and tidal flows, knowing your boat and your crew and then working together to tailor what everyone does to suit the local conditions.

We also need to let go of any expectation of guaranteed linear relationships of cause and effect. The 'if we do "x", then "y" will inevitably follow'. Here, too, organizational change sits more comfortably with arts subjects. Looking forwards, we cannot know with any certainty what will happen next. Looking backwards, we may try and ascribe causation but it is often impossible to disentangle cause and effect. Even if, eventually, we settle on one cause as the most significant, this is a matter of judgement, rather than a sure fact.

Take Shakespeare's Othello. What led him to murder his beloved Desdemona? We could say it was the maid stealing Desdemona's handkerchief with its embroidered strawberry; Iago showing it to Othello; Iago's suggestion that Desdemona had been unfaithful; Othello's own anxieties about his unworthiness or his jealousy – 'the green-eye'd monster'. All of these factors contributed to the unfolding drama. While we watch, we hope for a gesture that will reverse what seems to be happening, but we cannot isolate specific events as being causes which all will agree on. Similarly, with relational change, we are not operating in the realms of linear cause and effect.

Take a further example – the causes of the First World War (1914–18). We could identify the immediate trigger as the assassination of Archduke Ferdinand in Bosnia-Herzegovina in June 1914; the build-up of the arms race between Britain, France, Germany and Russia; the competitiveness fuelled by economic envy and empire; the constraints of the Schlieffen plan; a treaty signed seventy years before in which Britain promised to protect Belgian sovereignty. This illustrates the complexity and impossibility of trying to identify causes. In many cases, we can never know for sure what they are.

What tends to happen with historical events, with life in organizations and, indeed, with our own personal histories, is that we individually and collectively create stories which we understand to be 'what really happened and why'. The more frequently we tell those stories, the more convinced we become of their 'truth'. Some versions become more dominant and believed than others, but none of them will have the status of scientific proof. Stories play an important role in organizations and there is more on this subject in Chapter 10. The point here is to recognize that change is not about trying to identify a linear causal relationship; hence, it is more helpful to see working with change as an art form. The invitation we are making here is for you to see yourself as an artist – creative, innovative, influential, experimenting and making choices to see what happens. Novelist Julian Barnes writes, 'In all the arts there are normally two things going on at the same time; the desire to make it new, and a continuing conversation with the past'.[10] This could also apply to you as a relational leader of change.

The leader needs to make choices. So does the artist.

In 1819, the French artist Théodore Géricault created a painting, *The Raft of Medusa*, inspired by the stories surrounding a famous shipwreck that had occurred three years before. This wreck was well known to audiences at the time – accounts of cannibalism and mass murder among survivors on a life raft both repelling and attracting the public. There were many things that Géricault could have painted and didn't – the Medusa striking the reef; the mutinies in the night; the cannibalism or the moment of rescue. Instead, he chose to paint the moment when the survivors on the raft wave in the vain hope of attracting the attention of a boat on the horizon which is sailing away without seeing them. In making choices about what to paint, Géricault emphasizes a particular aspect of the story. You, too, will have many choices as you decide what to do next. Just like an artist, you need to give yourself time to think about what is important to you and to others, to consider what you want to emphasize, what gestures you want to make.

Subsequent chapters here are designed to give you a significant range of ideas and possibilities for seeing and acting differently so that, as an artist, you have more ideas to draw upon. Our intention is also to enhance and develop the skills and self-awareness that we think are needed to lead relational change well, your artistic sensibility, if you will, which will help you be choiceful in the moment.

Questions for further reflection

- How clear is the current stage of the change you are involved in?
- How clear and predictable is the end game?
- How well does the notion of an 'end-game' serve you?
- How much agreement is there around where you are and how you wish to proceed?
- What is really going on? Who could you listen to in order to find out?
- How can you and others pay attention to working with the ongoing emergent change in parallel with your directive change initiative?
- What is the minimum amount of planning required that will give people a chance to make sense together of what is happening and to contribute to what happens next?
- How does it help you in this change to see yourself as an artist?

Chapter 3

The dynamics of relational change: To push or to pull?

Relational change is about developing an awareness of how even small shifts in the way you ask a question or make a comment can engage others in conversation or close them down; can create movement and energy or remain predictably and ritualistically stuck. Thus, in this chapter, we make practical the different behaviours and gestures associated with a directive approach to change and those associated with an approach that is more facilitative. Choices range from telling others your own views and ideas to ways of encouraging them to share theirs. We invite you to consider the impact such choices have on yourself and on other people. We explore what is needed to create dialogue and what keeps people caught in endless debate or colluding in superficial harmony. In exploring the differences between push and pull, between advocacy and inquiry and between debate and dialogue, we hope to stimulate you to experiment with new gestures and approaches to involve others, as well as to reflect on why the type of gestures you have made in the past may have led to certain outcomes. Your choices will impact the rhythm and feel of change. They will affect the type of movement, momentum and energy experienced by both you and others - enthusiasm or withdrawal, excitement or stasis, a step more involved or a step away; hence, our use of the phrase, dynamics of change. In this chapter, we introduce several models that we believe are helpful. We close the chapter with some observations to explain the role we see for theories and models in our exposition of relational change.

The old rhetoric of engaging others in change

When we have asked leaders why they shy away from involving other people in change, they often give a number of reasons that may well resonate with you:

- I've not got enough time. It's easier to just tell people to do things.
- Other people won't understand what we are trying to do so are unlikely to have anything to add.
- I know what needs to change; I'm the boss and it's my job to know the answer. People expect those senior them to know what to do and that's what I'm paid for – to do the strategic stuff, decide what needs to change and make change happen. Those lower down need to play a role but it's more about implementing the change not shaping it.
- People don't like change so it's much better to just tell them once it's all sorted, otherwise they just get anxious or distracted from focusing on the day job and business as usual.
- I've tried engaging people in change before. It's one of those politically correct buzz words, all soft and fluffy 'HR/communications' speak. You just get nodding dogs, silence or the normal suspects saying what you expected.
- I'm uncomfortable about asking others their opinion and involving them in change as I think it will make me look weak. Those reporting to me or peers would expect me to know.
- It's politically naïve to engage other people in change – much better to keep your powder dry and then present them with a fait accompli.

These are all understandable positions, based perhaps on negative past experiences or unexamined fears and assumptions. Yet we believe this way of thinking can trap you in traditional and ritualistic ways of seeing engagement, closing off the valuable role others can play in change, especially in working with what is actually happening. There are a wide range of possibilities when it comes to involving others, some effective when adopting a directive approach to change; others more suitable when taking a more facilitative approach, so for those occasions when you want to genuinely work with others to understand their perspective as well as to enable them to appreciate yours.

Introducing 'push' and 'pull'

You have probably caught yourself occasionally in mid-sentence, knowing that what you are about to say is not going to sit well and have the impact you want. We all have. Yet, during organizational change, when there are often tensions about what might be happening and raised emotions, it is important to think about the way you ask questions or make comments. This can have a considerable impact on the answers you receive. It also impacts how you relate to others, how others relate to you and whether or not they will share with you what is really going on and work with you to create the future. There are similarities here with what physicists refer to the wave–particle duality of light. If a scientist conducts an experiment in which the beam of light is measured with a particle detector, because the question assumes light is made up of particles, then the light will hit the detector as a stream of particles. If a wave-like question is asked and light is measured with a wave detector, the light will hit the detector as wave-like interference. In the same way, how you ask a question and what you ask will impact the response you receive. Ask in an aggressive voice, assuming someone has deliberately made a mistake and you will get an aggressive response back. Ask with a real curiosity to find out what happened and the likelihood is the response will be more conciliatory or illuminating. Ask a project manager a fact-orientated question, such as, 'Are we on plan in terms of budget and time?' and the response will be to give the facts – 'yes' or 'no'. Ask a more open question, such as, 'What is going well with the project and what are your main concerns?' and you may get a more reflective response, with the project manager sharing his/her gut feel and intuition.

John Heron,[1] a pioneer in the field of participatory research methods, was fascinated by the impact of different ways of asking questions and commenting in one-on-one conversations. He developed a model that is a useful way to explore the different styles open to us when we interact with each other. He began his research looking at how GPs interacted with their patients, but later looked at interactions between people in numerous work settings. He identified what he referred to as six different intervention styles. By intervention he meant ways of asking questions or making comments, indeed anything that could be called a move, or what Ralph Stacey,[2] from the perspective of complex responsive processes would call a 'gesture'. Heron characterizes three of the styles as directive, 'push' styles and the other three as more 'pull', or facilitative styles.

For many leaders, the behaviours that go with a directive approach to change are familiar, as they tend to fit with the dominant machine metaphor view of organizations and the idea of the leader as someone who tells others what to do. Some people feel that if they are leading, they ought to be telling others what to do. We once overheard a leader saying, 'Surely the push styles are what is meant by being "leaderly"?' The word 'leaderly' made us smile and he is undoubtedly right that this fits in with traditional views of the leader both in control and in the know. However, to work with people in ways that pay attention to what is going on below the waterline and create the conditions for innovation, it is vital to develop and use the pull styles. The 'pull' behaviours required to adopt a more facilitative approach sometimes need a little more attention and practice.

To experience what it feels like to be 'pushing' or 'pulling' and, equally, how it feels to be on the receiving end of such gestures, we often ask leaders to do something that may at first seem a little alien to them. It is a simple exercise that allows people to experience the differences between push and pull at a somatic and emotional level.

We ask people to pair up, holding both hands up in front of them and touching their partner's hands palm to palm. Then, without talking, one person in each pair is asked to push their partner round the room. We reverse the exercise so that both people have a chance to experience pushing and being pushed. We then do two more iterations, this time asking each person to experiment with how it feels to pull his/her partner around the room, again without talking, although this usually results in quite a bit of laughter.

When pushing, some people enjoy the sense of being in the driving seat. They enjoy the control. Others dislike the sense of being responsible for the other person. Some people notice how tiring it is to be always on the alert, feeling you need to make sure that everything is all right for the other person, that they don't bump into any of the other pairs moving round the room. For those who are being pushed, some enjoy the fact that they don't really have to do anything or take any responsibility. It's an easy ride. Others hate it and find it hard to trust their partner. We see them desperately looking over their own shoulder to check that they are not about to hit any of the pairs moving round the room.

When pulling, people often talk about the way this feels much more collaborative; there is less sense of one person being totally responsible for the other. One person is pulling, but as they are moving backwards they are sharing control with their partner who can see where they are going. Pairs generally move around the room much quicker when they are pulling.

This exercise illustrates very simply individuals' different responses to pushing or pulling, or what Heron also called being directive or facilitative. Personality, job roles, professions, other people's expectations, our upbringing and family norms, all contribute to our personal preference for pushing or pulling. It demonstrates in a very physical way the different energies and dynamics created by whether our gestures are pull or push.

Most of us have a preference for two or three out of the six intervention styles and because they are our preferences, we will, through habit, have become pretty good at them – so good perhaps that it is easy to forget that there are other gestures we could make. There is a questionnaire at the back of the book which allows you to self-assess your preferences (see Appendix 1). None of the styles listed is inherently good or bad. However, as a relational leader of change, it is helpful to have the skills and ability to adapt and flex your style, depending on the situation. Otherwise you are, from a conversational perspective, in the situation of the workman for whom every problem is a nail because he only has a hammer in his toolbox.

Push

Prescribing: When prescribing, we draw on our own expertise, knowledge or authority to give direction, advice or recommendations. The assumption we make is that our views as to what should happen will be accepted by those on the receiving end. In other words, we are also assuming or taking a level of control. This is an intervention style that fits well with the machine metaphor of organizations and the concept of the leader as hero who does not invite discussion or the sharing of different views. Such a style is particularly appropriate when there are legal or safety issues that are non-negotiable or during an emergency where people need to be told where the nearest fire exits are.

In terms of change, a prescribing intervention may be helpful at the beginning when setting out key parameters of the project, such as savings target or timelines that are non-negotiable. It may also be needed when attempts to create dialogue have been tried for a long time and time has run out. However, there are risks with this style of taking over and imposing solutions, over-controlling and creating dependency. In terms of relational change, this is not an intervention to use too often as it closes down dialogue and other people sharing their views.

Informing: Informing interventions have a less authoritative tone than prescribing ones. As the label suggests, with this style, comments are made with the intention of sharing expertise or knowledge. However, in this case there are no implicit expectations that the information or advice will be acted upon. They are gifts offered without strings attached. Informing interventions suggest you have information or experience that may be relevant to the other person, but you view and treat them in all other respects as an equal. You are intervening because you believe you have something helpful to say but without making assumptions that you are right and certain. In terms of change, an informing intervention during a project team meeting might be showing where to find extra information; supplying missing facts; explaining what has just happened, without making any judgement calls; sharing your own experience. Risks with this style include overloading people with too much information, using too much jargon, or not articulating why some information is important.

Challenging: Challenging suggests this style is rather adversarial in nature but it does not have to be so. This style is useful: (1) to draw attention to the assumptions people may be making; (2) to raise their awareness of the consequences of their actions; (3) to draw attention to what you may have noticed going on below the waterline and you think they haven't. Asking a team to articulate its assumptions about what is both in and out of scope for a new product development or drawing a colleague's attention to the positive feedback you'd heard about his/her presentation, would be challenging interventions in the sense that you are drawing others' attention to things that may have escaped their notice. And challenging interventions can be more confronting and uncomfortable, such as giving a colleague feedback about how you felt belittled when, as the only woman in the room, you were asked to take the minutes. Observing a colleague's shift in body language and asking him/her what that was about would be a challenging intervention, too, and could be very helpful to surface his/her thoughts or feelings.

For others to be able to respond and truly 'hear' and learn from what is being said, such interventions needed to be worded thoughtfully. They also need to be spoken gently, rather than in a voice edged with anger or judgement. We find it is useful to develop certain phrases to signal the nature of what is coming so that the other person is not catapulted into defensiveness. You will need to adapt this to create your own form of words, but helpful phrases include: 'Do you mind if I just share something with you?', 'Can I check out something with you?', 'I've noticed something that I'm curious about: can I just share it with you?'

Pull

The three pull interventions differ in tone and intent. They are all used to encourage others to open up, to share their thoughts and feelings about what they notice is going on, to become more aware of what they believe or know, to give more of themselves, to be engaged. Such interventions put others in the driving seat in terms of directing the content of a conversation or discussion. They are, therefore, particularly helpful when adopting a more facilitative approach to change and when you are wanting to find out what others are noticing and experiencing. Being open, listening well and genuinely being curious are important here. There is more detail about this in Chapter 8.

Discovering: Discovering interventions are an invitation to others to talk, to open up. We might also call them open questions. Used by a leader involved in relational change, they are a vital way of learning about what others have to say, what they have experienced, what they have noticed. In terms of change, such interventions can be as simple as 'Tell me more about …'. It might be 'tell me what customers like about our service?', 'Tell me what you enjoy best about working here' or 'your experience of "X"'. Alternatively, they may be open questions that encourage others to share their ideas – 'If you could change one thing about our billing system what would it be?'

Releasing: Releasing interventions help others to talk about and acknowledge their emotions, in contrast to discovering which is enabling them to voice their thoughts. In your workplace, the expression of emotions may not be the cultural norm. However, a key reason why change is often problematic is that it triggers emotional responses in people which, when unacknowledged, have the potential to fester. Working with the emotions stirred up by change is explored in more detail in Chapter 6. Shifts in the other person's body language, tone of voice or use of particularly vivid metaphors often indicate the presence of strong emotions and the need for empathy, active listening, and this type of intervention. In terms of change, examples of releasing interventions would be, 'From your tone of voice, I have the impression that you don't agree with this. What does it trigger for you ....', 'How does this make you feel?' An essential skill here is to be able to sit with some silence to give the other person time to answer. You also need to judge how deep to go, how long to linger. This is not about becoming a therapist. Very often in the workplace being able to express emotions and have those acknowledged can be very helpful in allowing people to move on from negative emotions.

Supporting: Supporting interventions build other people's confidence, reminding them about what is going well and encouraging further learning and taking of responsibility. Expressing your appreciation, being specific about what has gone well, giving permission to experiment and make mistakes are all supportive interventions. Here, too, tone of voice is vital. These interventions need to be genuine and authentic, otherwise there is a risk of sounding patronizing. Overdoing it will also sound false.

Most people, when they complete the self-assessment tool that accompanies this model, find that they use two or three intervention styles a great deal and one or two rarely feature. Those that you use infrequently are the ones to consciously practise and add to your repertoire or watch out for other people using them to see what response their gestures invoke in others. The pull styles are particularly useful to practice, as they allow for much more facilitative approaches to change.

In live conversations, there are clearly a mix of these six interventions in play at any one time and they will not appear neatly and discretely differentiated in the way described here. However, in identifying these six different styles, pulling them out for inspection and giving them a label, our aim is to help you notice the different choices available to you and when each might be appropriate. As Stacey[3] reminds us with complex responsive processes, we can never predict with certainty the meaning that another will make of our gesture and what response they may make in return. However, this model allows you to consider your intentions and the impact they may have with greater awareness of the choices you are making. In addition, it is worth considering the existing culture and power dynamics in your local context. For instance, if people are not used to being asked their views, they may not be immediately forthcoming. They may wonder why you are suddenly changing the type of gesture you are making so there will need to be some adjustment from their side. If you make a different gesture and it does not immediately get the response you were hoping for, we'd encourage you not to give up and think this doesn't work. Instead, engage in some inquiry, share what your intentions were; ask them how they experienced you and what would have made them feel differently. This can then be a source of learning for the future.

Creating dialogue or allowing debate

What else is required to adopt a facilitative approach to change? As explored in Chapter 1, a complex responsive processes view of organizations emphasizes the way that change takes place through multiple conversations. Some leaders find this idea reassuring and liberating; others are more sceptical and want to know more precisely what sort of conversations are helpful. Bill Isaacs[4], a leading researcher into dialogue, talks about creating conversations with a centre and no sides. What does this mean in practice?

We rarely think about how we behave in conversations, but we all know that they can feel very different depending on what we are discussing and with whom. Some will have the cut and thrust, parry and counter-parry of a duel or a sword fight; in others, comments can feel like billiard balls banging into each other and then shooting off in different directions, a dynamic of collide and repel; some can be more akin to a gentle meander; or they can feel awkward and collusive, everyone skirting around an issue that no-one wants to name as everyone would rather not disturb the peace.

When did you last have a good conversation at work? And what was it like? When we ask people how they would describe a productive conversation at work, they tend to mention the following:

- An energy and vitality in the conversation.
- Time going quickly.
- An empathy and connection with others that wasn't there before.
- It becomes apparent why a situation was more complex than they first realized.
- The emergence of new ideas, surprises and creativity.
- An openness and honesty about what is not going well and a willingness to work out what to do about it together.
- An understanding of what is clear as well as what is still unknown, messy or undecided.
- Feeling that others are speaking authentically, without excessively filtering what they say, and being able to do the same.
- Feeling alive.

This type of conversation is rare because often people are too busy, agendas too full or people don't have the skills required. When conversations don't go well, leaders talk about the following happening:

- One person after another puts forward their perspective, with no-one really listening to anyone else: parry and counter parry; point scoring.
- People stay polite and formal with no one saying what needs to be said.
- Anything vaguely controversial is shut down so important stuff is never dealt with.
- People talk in jargon, giving set-piece justifications or stories you sense they have told many times before that somehow don't ring true.
- There is no sense of movement - a conversation or meeting feels like empty rhetoric and ritual.
- Nobody shows any interest or curiosity in other people's views and perspectives.
- Time drags and you'd rather be somewhere else.
- You leave feeling drained of energy and frustrated.

In the UK, much of our education - and indeed our political system - emphasizes talking, advocating, the 'tell'. Debates in the Houses of Parliament are characterized by one side advocating a particular position, followed by others advocating the opposite. A key writer on this topic, Chris Argyris,[5] distinguishes between 'advocacy' - stating your own position, and 'inquiry' - exploring and being curious about others' positions. Without inquiry, we have debate that is adversarial, with each side assuming it is right and failing to listen and there is generally little movement or progress. Research into productive conversations suggests this is rarely the best place to start. Instead, what is needed is to approach others with an open mind and genuine curiosity. In our work with leaders, we have found that this often leads to a number of benefits:

- You learn from others' perspectives about what they think is important and why they hold such views. This can often lead to surprising insights for yourself that prompts fresh thinking and will give you a more rounded appreciation of the issues.
- People respond well to being genuinely listened to, perhaps because in the general busyness this is rare. If you have listened first, people are much more likely to then listen to your perspective. This may not result in immediate agreement and a shared view, but is much more likely to lead at least to some mutual empathy and respect.
- A word of caution though ... people will only open up and share their views, if they genuinely believe you want to hear them. We all have an internal authenticity barometer, so if you are doing this ritualistically and going through the motions but don't really think you will learn anything then you won't. It will become a self-fulfilling prophecy. Give yourself an honest talking to before embarking on inquiry conversations and if you are really not able to participate with openness, save your time and your colleagues and don't have the conversation.

One of the main researchers and writers in this area is Bill Isaacs. He focuses primarily on the patterns of conversation that contribute to dialogue. Creating dialogue requires you to:

- Inquire with curiosity and listen respectfully.
- Cultivate and speak your own voice, skilful advocacy.
- Suspend assumptions, judgements and certainty.

The word 'dialogue' derives from the Greek '*dia*' which means 'through' and '*logos*' which translates as 'words' or 'meaning'. Dialogue is literally, therefore, a flow of meaning. Isaacs[6] talks of dialogue allowing people to think together, avoiding false harmony and the going over of well-rehearsed positions. Dialogue seeks to harness the collective intelligence of a group by creating settings where people can safely and consciously reflect upon their differences through inquiry and listening to each other. By asking inquiry questions such as the discovering and releasing pull interventions described earlier and then really listening to the responses, people begin to loosen the grip of certainty they might have been carrying. Isaacs introduces the important idea of suspending. By this, Isaacs means letting go of, for the moment, our beliefs and assumptions. Instead, in dialogue the encouragement is to attend to the present rather than reliving and re-seeing through our memories of old hurts, slights, beliefs and stereotypes. This, in turn, allows people to begin to see things from new perspectives, and then new ideas and understanding emerge in unexpected and fruitful ways. This shared inquiry becomes a way of thinking and reflecting together – and 'from shared meaning, shared action arises'.[7] This generative process of dialogue is likened to a seed that does not contain the tree but contains the potential for a tree. People hold between them the potential to create something valuable together.

A powerful and yet simple way of creating the conditions for dialogue with any group of people is to start with placing chairs in a circle. When there are literally no sides and no barrier created by a table, it is surprising how an atmosphere is created which enables a different quality of conversation. Such an arrangement breaks the pattern of conventional meeting places at work and harks back to the Native American tradition of circles round campfires and sitting round in the chief's tent or to the majlis (parliaments, essentially) in the Arab world. You can also have a 'check-in' which is when people are invited to say a few words about how they are feeling about being at the meeting; ideally every voice needs to be heard. After this, people can then really start talking about what really needs to be talked about.[8.]

Such symbolic gestures as changing the seating and having a check-in start to change the expected and ritualistic dynamic of work-based conversations. (See Joe's story in Chapter 12.)

In terms of creating movement in dialogue, Isaac draws on the work of Kantor,[9] who was a clinician working with dysfunctional families.

He developed his four-player model of the different actions that are needed in a productive conversation. They are relatively easy to discern – and to make this real and useful for yourself, you might want to deliberately observe different meetings or conversations to spot these different patterns. You will no doubt also be able to discern the impact when the actions are out of balance.

When someone makes a move, he/she is initiating an action – perhaps proposing some next steps. At that moment, the focus of the conversation is on that person. Someone else listening may agree and, therefore, in terms of position, is at that moment a 'follower'. A third person may think that there is something missing in the proposal or have a different idea, and so becomes the 'opposer', symbolically standing between the other two. Finally, a fourth person who has been watching the whole dance, makes a comment on what they are seeing and hearing from a more neutral perspective that can help others appreciate the whole; this latter role Kantor called the 'bystander'. Kantor's research suggested that in a productive conversation all four of these actions need to be used in balance, with people taking it in turns to occupy any of the four positions. These positions are fluid. There are no hidden or official rules. Rather this represents another way of looking at what happens in generative conversations. If there is not enough bystanding or following we can be back to debate or the billiard ball model of conversation where there is a stalemate of to and fro. Following can give energy and impetus to a particular view. Opposing can make sure that there is sufficient thought and consideration rather than groupthink. And, of course, sometimes, in practice, the positions are blended as in someone may make a follow and then an oppose – 'I like what you are saying but I have a problem with it because ...'.

As Peter Senge says, 'Most of our workplace conversations are characterized by rigid roles: by all movers pushing past one another to champion their views; by disabled bystanders, paralyzed at not being able to bring their voice, or by cowed followers, fearful of offering anything but the meekest agreement to the voices of authority'.[10]

Some leaders use this model to help them notice the patterns in different conversations to which they are party; some deliberately

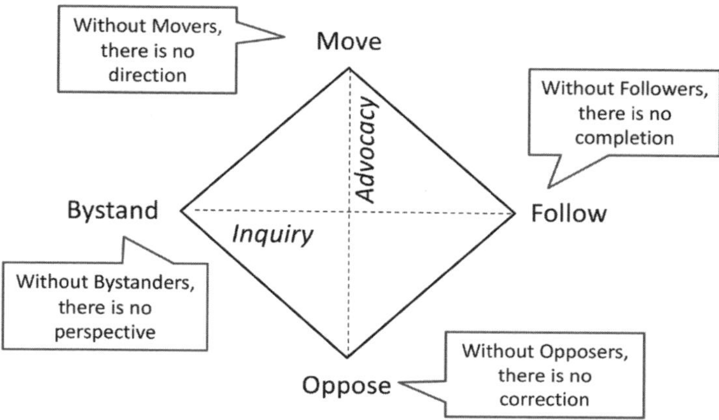

Figure 3.1 The four player model. Adapted from Kantor and Isaacs.

share the model and vocabulary with their teams. As a leader, you can make different gestures to create an opportunity for dialogue rather than debate. This can help you recognize the differences between negotiation, which is about trading an agreement between parties who differ, and dialogue, which is about reaching a new understanding so that together people dissolve rather than solve the problem. This is an alternative to the debate or billiard ball model of conversation in which people are separate from one another, colliding and bouncing off without being in relationship, without creating understanding or generating new ideas. More detail on the practice of dialogue is covered in Chapter 8.

The physical setting, as well as the moves you make linguistically, play an important role, too. We are back to Stacey's[11] ideas about the importance of gestures that effect the response you get. If you are more senior, summoning someone to your office is likely to make them feel like they must come; you may not have intended this, but such a gesture suggests that you are exerting your power in the hierarchy. For more details on the way that micro gestures can moderate the power dynamics between you and others, see Chapter 5.

Some of you reading this, may already feel that as a leader you do pay attention to these small gestures. For others, it may seem odd to be encouraged to think about such micro gestures. As a leader, aren't you supposed to be thinking big visionary thoughts, brokering large deals and holding people to account? Yes, that might be part of your job, *and* creating the conditions for dialogue is vital, too, if you want to hear what people really think, if you want to connect, if you want to be in touch with what is emerging below the waterline. There is more detail on the impact of small gestures and creating the conditions for dialogue in Chapters 7 and 8.

Creating zones of safe uncertainty

As well as creating the conditions for dialogue, you may also need to consider how much uncertainty is bearable for groups or individuals at a given moment. Barry Mason[12] asks the people he works with whether they see uncertainty as mainly the path to creativity or mainly a path to paralysis. Some uncertainty is needed to create edginess and excitement that stimulates new thinking and creativity. Too much and the sense of the unknown can leave people paralysed with fear.

Steve Chapman, who describes himself as a change and creativity consultant, describes the idea of safe uncertainty in the following way.

> **Safe uncertainty** is the fertile ground where creativity, innovation, adventure can grow and flourish. Safe uncertainty is about being comfortable with the world of *just* enoughness. It is about having *just enough* structure, *just enough control and just enough* planning to mitigate only the biggest of risks whist leaving enough fluidity, spontaneity and freedom to welcome new possibilities. In organisation terms, a culture of safe uncertainty is one where folk are encouraged, within negotiated parameters, to try something new and if it doesn't work to then fail happy and learn from the experience.[13]

There are distinct parallels here with 'Stacey's' grid,[14] shown in Chapter 1 (see page 18). Of course what counts as safe or risky will depend on the context and on your own preferences as a leader, as well as the people you are working with. There is no way of telling in advance what will feel right. Rather it is a question of trying something and paying attention to the responses, asking people if you have given

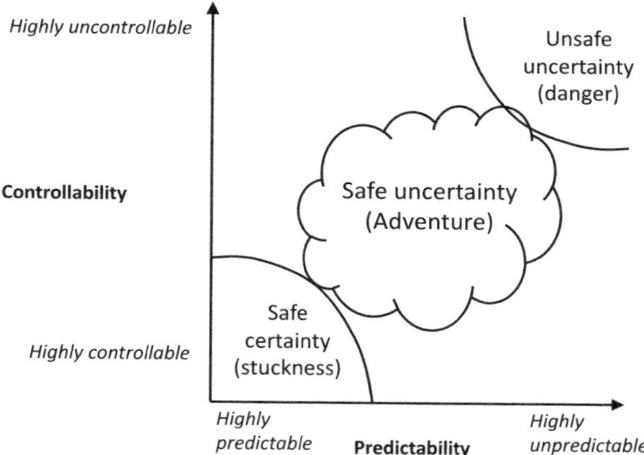

Figure 3.2 The zone of safe uncertainty. Adapted from Mason, Chapman, Stacey, Vanstone and Critchley.

them adequate structure or if they need more clarity or direction. The art is thus to engage others in conversation to explore what constitutes an area of 'safe uncertainty' at that moment.

An example of this is when we worked with a group of thirty Organization Development people from across a range of public-sector organizations, introducing Action Research to them as a means of understanding more about their practice and gathering insights into a significant change programme. Most had never done Action Research before, so there were many questions about how to do it, who they needed to involve, how to record the data, what counted as data, etc. As we listed the questions on the flip chart, we could feel anxiety levels rising. Some 'informing interventions', to use Heron's[15] terminology we introduced earlier in the chapter, reassured some. In addition, we suggested people self-organized into trios in the room. This created enough structure for the next part of the process as suddenly people felt that they were not alone. In addition, people were given a date for the next meeting, but were encouraged to hold off answering any longer term questions and implications for the moment. Thirdly, we framed the next phase as 'experimenting', encouraging them to give Action Research a go without having to feel that they were now committed to being part of this research group. With these interventions, excitement rather than anxiety returned. This example illustrates the way that, as a relational leader, paying attention to what is going on for a group of people, in the moment, allows you to modify what you were intending to do or say. You can make a different gesture, use a different intervention style, blend some pull and push gestures. These will all affect the type of movement, momentum and energy experienced by both you and others, hence our use of the phrase, 'dynamics of change'.

A word about theories and models

In this chapter, we have drawn on several different models to explore some of the dynamics of relational change: Heron's model with the six different intervention styles; Isaacs' model of dialogue; Kantor's four-player model for looking at the different moves required in a conversation and Barry Mason's concept of safe uncertainty. We, therefore, think it worthwhile to pause and explain the way we draw on theories and models throughout the book.

Our assumption is that if you are in the thick of change, you are interested in what to do in practice so don't want too much theory and research, but you do need enough to understand the rationale for what we are proposing. You want to be convinced why relational change works as well as to understand what it involves. Kurt Lewin[16] wrote 'there is nothing as practical as a good theory'. Sadly though, much academic theory and research is written for other academics, making the language often inaccessible and the links with practice hard to fathom. In this book, our aim is to draw lightly on key ideas from theory, explaining them in everyday language so that you can see the sources of the thinking that underpins and forms the bedrock of relational change.

We also introduce various models that derive from academic theory and research. These can direct your attention to particular aspects of your work world and the phenomenon of change that you were not fully conscious of, but had perhaps been on the periphery of your awareness. There may, we hope, be a delightful moment of recognition when a model speaks to something that you have experienced and felt – 'Ah yes, that's what I've seen'. There can also be reassurance

– 'So it's not just me that's wondered about that'. In helping you see things differently, models can also provide you with a new language, a particular vocabulary to talk about a specific aspect of change. New words allow us to think more precisely, giving us greater possibilities for action; they also enable us to have different conversations with colleagues, as you can jointly talk and explore with the help of a more nuanced vocabulary. Indeed a leader said to us recently: 'I wasn't sure what to do next but I used a model to start a conversation with a colleague and together we worked it out. The model provided a spring board for our thinking together.'[17]

However, models do have some drawbacks. We have been emphasizing the messiness of change and the unpredictability and complexity of organizational life. In simplifying and airbrushing out the lumps and bumps of lived experience to create a neat, tidy model we can easily lose sight of this. Another academic wrote that: 'All models are wrong but some useful.' Models are wrong in the sense that they are not the same as the experience, and can seductively fool us into forgetting this. When surrealist René Magritte painted a picture of a tobacco pipe, he wrote in beautifully loopy writing above it, '*Ceci n'est pas une pipe*' – 'this is not a pipe' – drawing attention to the difference between a picture as a representation of reality and 'reality' itself. The phrase, 'the map is not the territory', similarly draws attention to the at once obvious and not obvious, that the map and physical reality are different things.

The map is very helpful for navigating where you want to go. It functions as a guide, by drawing attention to certain features of the landscape we are experiencing. In doing so, though, it doesn't tell us everything about that landscape at any point – whether we think it's a good spot for a picnic or who we might meet when we're there. The models we discuss similarly act as a guide to direct your attention to certain features. Some of the models may complement each other and you may see connections between them. Others may seem contradictory. As mentioned at the end of Chapter 1, in philosophical terms we are pluralists who are guided by what is pragmatic and useful, accepting that there will inevitably be contradictions and paradoxes given the complexity of organizations and change. Relational change is a mix of what is useful rather than an attempt to create one coherent theory. The models we share are those that we have found helpful even though they are simplifications that can suggest a cause and effect, a linear relationship that does not exist in the messiness of lived experience.

Questions for further reflection

- What would be your reasons for using more 'pull' approaches, and with whom?
- Which of the Heron styles could you do with practising?
- What energy do you notice in yourself and others when you take a directive or facilitative approach?
- With which individuals or groups where you currently have debate might you want to experiment with creating dialogue?
- What steps would you need to do to initiate this?
- With which groups of people might you try to create a zone of safe uncertainty to encourage more creativity?
- Who might be your ally in trying out some new ways of approaching change?

Chapter 4

Organizational agility: Working well with politics

Mention the word politics to a group of leaders and there is often quite an extreme divergence of opinion. Some people see it as an inevitable part of making things happen in organizations. Others view politics as a rather murky activity, often unseen and potentially self-serving. They tend to say they would rather have nothing to do with it. In our experience, developing your ability to understand and operate well within the political landscape of your own context is a vital part of relational change because it is about recognizing and working with the different interest groups that exist. These differences are often amplified in times of change when there is anxiety and uncertainty. In this chapter we offer several models for thinking about politics and political activity to help you enhance your political skills and awareness for the good of the whole rather than for self-serving ends.

Why are politics inevitable in organizations?

If you listen carefully to the speeches of CEOs or other senior leaders, they often talk as if the whole organization thinks like them and wants the same as them. There is probably much use of the personal pronoun 'we'. They talk as though there is a collective view of the strategic direction of the business or the growth targets, a view which completely aligns with their own ... and there may well be much agreement. Yet, this kind of rhetoric often represents an idealized hope for unity, when in fact there are many views and opinions. Indeed, the way we all use language as a shorthand, referring to organizations as a 'generalized other', can give the appearance of uniformity, obscuring the multiplicity of differences that exist. This is the point made by Stacey when he challenges us to think of organizations as being constant multiple interactions between people rather than an 'it'. Consider, for example, the way politicians and newspaper headlines generalize about 'the NHS' as if it was a unified homogenous organization. Yet think how different your experiences have probably been at your GP surgery, your local A&E or perhaps the hospital where your Dad had his hip done. And in each of those locations, your experience of the NHS will have varied depending on whether you were engaging with the receptionist, nurses, doctors, porters or a manager. Each professional group will have different views about how the NHS is run, what should be changed and what should be prioritized. And this is the same for all organizations. They are all political because of the different views and interests that exist among people.

The word political comes from the Greek word '*polis*', which denoted the Greek city states, where politics was the art of resolving difference through the act of talking. It is an inherently relational and human activity which means recognizing and working with people's different interests to find a way forwards. Within organizations, different interest groups arise for a multiplicity of reasons. History, location, professional groups or identities all tend to shape the way people in particular parts of the organization see the world, the stories they tell about both the past and the future and what they see as important. Dividing people and the work into different units through departmental or divisional structures is a legacy of the machine view of organizations. It may make sense in terms of clarifying responsibilities and yet it can also create conflicting goals. For instance, in marketing, the prime purpose may be maximizing sales through offering customer choice; in the production department it may be keeping costs down by minimizing variation.

The existence of different interest groups can cause adversarial politics and conflict. Beth and James started a company which delivered training on interpersonal and communication skills. The company grew to over forty people, with a good brand name and reputation. After ten years, a third director joined to establish a consulting arm offering talent management and culture change support, tapping into and developing the contacts the business already had with HR Directors. Those who joined consulting tended to be on higher salaries than those in the training division. The consultants saw themselves as non-conformist, creative, free spirits, offering bespoke solutions to their clients, in comparison to what they saw as the lower end of the food chain, the commodity business of training. Those in the training arm saw the consultants as elitist, arrogant prima donnas who swanned around while those in the training division continued to solidly turn out the results that kept the business afloat.

In this story, there are multiple opportunities for politics to arise, as you can undoubtedly imagine. The two divisions have different histories. In one, loyalty, longevity and solid performance have been valued, in the other the value is in selling skills and winning clients. The consultants are allowed time to develop the thought leadership and client relationships, so have lower utilization rates than the training people, which makes sense to the head of consulting but is a source of aggravation to the head of training. When it comes to making decisions on bonus distribution across the two divisions or pricing in a client where both consulting and training are trying to win new work, both groups will want different outcomes. Overt and covert political activity will ensue as the leaders of the two divisions seek to argue the merits of their views.

Differences also arise as departments or units receive different sets of information. This means employees literally see world through their own department's perspective of what they measure and pay attention to – customer comments or patient stories, market share data or cost of sales. Yet all units within an organization are also dependent on others to achieve their own deliverables or targets. This interdependence, which is emphasized in the ecosystem metaphor of organizations, results in groups and individuals becoming very concerned about what others are doing. Lastly, there is always a scarcity of some resources which means competition for who gets what, whether that is money, talent or time with the CEO. As one commentator writes, 'conflict arises whenever interests collide';[1] so organizational conflict is not just a matter of misunderstanding and miscommunication, it is an inevitable consequence of different interests at play and therefore politics is an unavoidable part of organizational life.

There is clearly a need for some means of resolving such differences. Of course, you may say, that is why we have annual budgeting and the planning cycles. In fact, there are few more political activities than setting budgets and objectives, because this involves trading for resources to meet different targets or outcomes. In change, too, there are always different interests at play and the stakes are high. Some will want the status quo to continue; others will yearn for the new order. And there will be varying interests in the possible shape that the future takes. Another writer talks about, 'A cacophony of complementary and competing change attempts, with managers at all levels, joining the fray and pushing for issues of particular importance to themselves'.[2] Much of this is going on below the waterline, which helps illuminate why change is inevitably complex, messy and unpredictable and yet engaging in politics is vital.

A survey[3] of 428 managers found that over 75 per cent believed that successful executives need to be good politicians. At the same time, 55 per cent felt that organizational politics was unfair and unhealthy. This suggests a quite widespread view that politics is both necessary and unpleasant. These different responses tend to be triggered by people's assumptions about organizations and beliefs about how things ought to happen, as well as their experience of what happens in practice. In our experience, what is important is the intent with which people engage in political activity.

To explore how political activity plays a part we turn to an additional metaphor that we have found really resonates with leaders.

Introducing the front stage and back stage

A helpful way of thinking about political life in organizations is to compare it to the theatre, with two separate areas of activity[4]. There is the front stage, where the play is seen by the audience, and the back stage, where preparation and rehearsals take place, out of sight. As a leader, you need to be active on both the front and back stages. Both serve important purposes, but the back stage becomes especially important in times of change.

The **front stage** in an organization is where activities take place in formal, open settings. Regular meetings and committees with published agendas, minutes and often elaborate governance structures would all be examples of front-stage activities; so would Board or divisional management meetings, budgeting and target setting processes, which often have their own label or acronym. There may also be specific meetings focused on the change in hand, with the grand term of 'Programme Architecture' to describe the suite of project or programme management meetings and processes for approving business cases, gaining approval and monitoring progress.

Focusing on the front stage encourages you to identify and use existing processes and meeting structures to legitimize the change or gain agreement for the next stage. The public performance of rational, logically phased change recognizes the need for plans, milestones and project governance that all resonate with the machine metaphor of organizations. These activities remain vital because they are a form of communication, keeping others aware of what is going on and of progress. However, from a psychological perspective, such front-stage meetings are doing something equally, if not more, significant. Such meetings are the accoutrements of comfort and anxiety reduction for senior leaders. They satisfy people's unconscious need for 'structure hunger',[5] to know enough of what is going on. The mess and uncertainties are airbrushed out into powerpoint slides or a thick document and activities are given a colour – red, amber, green, as with the Unilever story in Chapter 2. The plan can make everyone feel that things are under control or at least known. The front stage thus gives reassurance and confidence to allow change to continue. Given the anxieties and uncertainties and unpredictability of change, this is important and necessary. But it is not sufficient.

Back-stage activities, which take place out of sight of the masses, would include having a quiet word in someone's ear before a meeting; going to talk to an influential decision-maker to find out their concerns or aspirations; drawing someone's attention to particular benefits of a proposal, or a particular risk when you catch them at the end of a meeting; making sure an individual is aware of some of the background history. It might also be about building a coalition in support of a particular decision or agreeing to some kind of deal or negotiating a trade-off. Back-stage activities can be deliberately planned but, more often than not, they are about taking advantage of an opportunity – when you just see someone in the corridor or walking to the car park.

There is significant research evidence that decision-making is rarely as rational as we might have hitherto thought.[6] In large group settings it is also often hard to explore what people really think and feel as group dynamics, power and ritualistic patterns often dominate rather than there being genuine dialogue. So although the front stage is important, decisions are often the outcome of back-stage activities. Focus on the back stage encourages you to have different and often more honest conversations. Greater honesty is possible as it is psychologically safer for both you and the other person. You are both out of the public eye, away from the spotlight of others' expectations, which means you can explore where someone is really coming from, 'off line'. In the language of Heron[7] (see Chapter 3), working on the back stage is an opportunity to 'pull', listening to find out what people are really thinking and to inquire into their perspectives. This may give you the opportunity to modify the plan or, through conversation, you may help them make sense of the change so that differences are less likely to harden into resistance. You may also use a back-stage conversation in a 'push' capacity, connecting with senior people or influential colleagues to ensure that they are aware of important facts or ideas. Or you may want to share something of the work with them so that they feel, and indeed are, better informed and prepared when the change initiative is discussed in the more public and exposed front-stage arena.

It is also worth noting that if a change impacts the whole of an organization, perhaps during a merger or an enterprise-wide re-organization following the arrival of a new CEO, there is likely to be an increase in back-stage political activity generally. This is because there will be more anxiety and uncertainty which can only be voiced safely in private. People will also be unsure about the rules of engagement on the front stage as they will be unsure who now has power and influence. This will mean more corridor conversations and less reliance on the front stage, formal meetings. With information scarce and rumour rife, talking to others is a means of trying to find out what is happening, as well as perhaps seeking to influence what might happen.

Reasons for engaging in back-stage conversations, therefore, include:

- Inquiry to gain important new insights and ideas that may be vital to the success of the change and yet could have been missed or overlooked.

- Inquiry to find out others' knowledge, hopes and concerns. You may also discover that others often have more nuanced views than you may have assumed when you lumped them together as 'managers' or 'salespeople'.
- People who feel listened to are generally going to be less resistant as people generally appreciate being asked their views.
- Allow you to test out your own thinking, rehearsing the story of how you want to talk about the change, hearing which of the benefits you've described really make sense to people and where further thinking is required.

The degree to which such back-stage activity is required is a matter of personal judgement, the time you have available and the opportunity you have to bump into people spontaneously. It is much harder to do if you work from home most of the time or are rarely in the same building as the individuals with whom you want to have some back-stage conversations. However, in our experience, the need to actively engage in this is often underestimated. When coaching senior leaders, we've heard people say things like:

- This back-stage activity isn't real work is it?
- It all sounds too time consuming
- How do I know that it is worth it?

Here again we are in the realms of relational change as an art form rather than a science. It may depend on how contentious your change programme is; you may need more of it at the beginning to get things started or when things have become a little stuck. However, we see some back-stage activity as an essential part of change efforts, as well as a requirement for leading more generally. You probably already engage in some back-stage activity, even if you haven't called it this. Our encouragement is to pay it more attention and consciously notice and use opportunities as they arise.

Reframing politics as organizational agility

Your reaction to the idea of engaging more in back-stage activity may depend on your attitude to organizational politics in general. We know from working with leaders that the word politics is loaded.

When we ask people to think of negative associations with politics they tend to come up with words or phrases such as: 'politicking', 'playing politics', 'managing upwards', 'brown nosing', 'manoeuvring', 'manipulating', 'being underhand', 'sneaky', 'Machiavellian', 'untrustworthy', 'lobbying', 'bribing', 'blackmailing', 'threatening'. None are complimentary.

When asked about positive associations, words or phrases include: 'persuasive', 'good at influencing', 'encouraging', 'good at selling', 'advocating', 'wise', 'smart', 'astute', 'savvy' – all words you would probably feel comfortable with if they were used to describe yourself. In our experience, we have found these attributes are critical to successful, relational change.

Microsoft has 'organizational agility' as one of their competencies, this being the ability to navigate an organization, to know who to talk to, who has influence and power and how to reach that person in order to ensure things happen. This beautifully describes a positive and productive view of political behaviour. In its competency framework, Microsoft has descriptions of overdoing each competence. In the case of organizational agility, overdoing it is described as 'politicking', which we refer to above. The difference is in the intent and, indeed, other people's perceptions of the intent and motivation behind engaging in a particular behaviour. Organizational agility suggests making things happen behind the scenes for the good of the organization. Politicking suggests engaging in such behaviour for personal or self-serving ends.

But what does this mean in practice? Politically competent people do not expect everything to be plain sailing so they are attuned into what is really happening. They are opportunistic when there is a chance encounter that enables them to listen or share their own perspective; they make careful selective moves to seek out and talk to particular people, to listen and to adapt their plans accordingly in their attempts to get things done. They are thoughtful about what is helpful to discuss front stage and back stage to support the change effort.

So, being politically active ensures you use your back stage influencing to support your change work, using both inquiry and advocacy, pull and push. It means you use the front stage to share and legitimize more broadly aspects of the change. In doing so, you will have different conversations and, although you will never know exact cause and effect, such activities help you create the conditions for change, even if sometimes in unexpected ways.

Who you need to influence and how: Stakeholder mapping

Given organizations are political systems with competing interests and agendas and decision-making is never purely rational, you can't rely on the facts and the evidence doing all of the job for you. So who do you need to influence? Rather than relying solely on gut instinct, or the people you already know, the 'usual suspects', creating a stakeholder map can be helpful. This involves taking a systematic approach to identifying, in advance, different groups or individuals in your organization who are likely to impact what you are trying to do. However exciting you believe the change to be, not everyone out there will have the same stake or interest. Some groups or individuals may be affected significantly by the new approach; for others only minor adjustments to how they work may be required. Mapping these different groups and individuals requires putting yourself briefly in their shoes and thinking

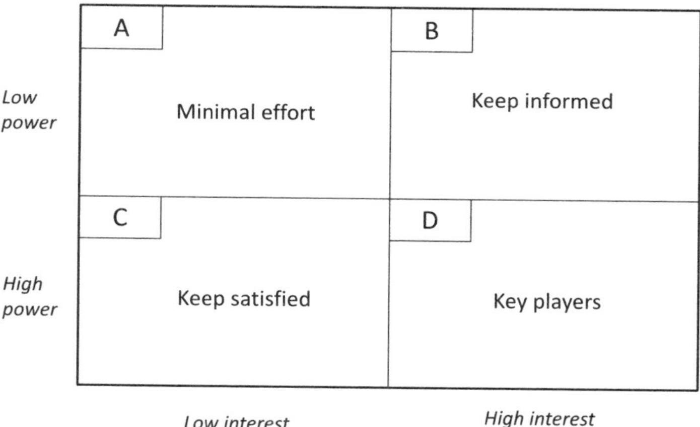

Figure 4.1 Power-interest matrix. Adapted from Scholes.[8]

analytically about what they might think, their potential motivations and power bases, their willingness and ability to help or hinder the change. The mapping also helps you think about communication. Rather than blasting everyone with the same message or ignoring some groups, mapping stakeholders means you can target who needs to know what, when, and how. This is far from an exact science, but investing some time and energy here can save considerable time, as well as hassle and aggravation, later.

A simple but useful tool is the power-interest matrix, as illustrated in Figure 4.1 on the previous page.

On your own, or in conversation with a few trusted colleagues, populate the matrix above with names of individuals or groups in relation to the change you are working on. Some top tips when doing this:

- Keep in mind that the focus is not the general power of a group or individual but their power in relation to this particular change.
- Challenge yourself to go beyond stereotypes of 'managers always think x', the sales teams never want to do x'. When we lump everyone together into the 'generalized other' it can be easy to forget that such groups will be comprised of individuals where there may well be a range of responses. (For more on this, see Chapter 9.)
- If you have no idea what potentially important individuals or groups think about the change, the mapping exercise has perhaps already served its purpose by prompting you, or others, to go and talk to some people in those groups to find out. This in itself can create engagement and support as the very fact you are asking will be appreciated. Do approach this genuinely – you'll get a lot further if you mean it!
- Avoid plotting long lists of stakeholders who 'in principle' or 'potentially' could have influence – stick to the ones that will – otherwise the map will be over populated and unmanageable!
- Subdivide groups if there are different levels of interest within those groups. This may be something you only realize once you have engaged in conversation with them.
- Do remember that key stakeholders may be outside your organization – the regulator, the local council, suppliers.
- Aim for 'good enough' rather than the perfect map. The latter

doesn't exist and, in fact, it is the thinking and the conversations that are prompted by creating the map that are in some respects more important than the 'finished' article.

Once you have done the analysis and created your stakeholder map, the next stage is to use it to help consider who needs to engage whom and how. One of the benefits of creating this plan is that it allows you to make visible what influencing jobs need to be done so that you can delegate some of these tasks to other people in your team. Some people like to give this the grand sounding title of a stakeholder management strategy. Basically, what's required is some thought about tactics in relation to the different stakeholders and to decide who is responsible for implementing the activities in relation to each group.

What different tactics do you have to choose from? Generally both front-stage and back-stage activities described earlier are required, with the balance depending on your context and your judgement. Some stakeholders may be influenced through formal project management processes, such as quarterly project reviews, which may already exist; others may require you to deliberately arrange a 1:1 conversation; with others it may be less time critical and more a case of a light touch comment if you happen to bump into them by the coffee machine.

The approach will depend on which quadrant in Figure 4.1 people occupy.

A: Low power – low interest. *Minimal effort*

Groups or individuals in this quadrant have little interest and little power so you can pretty much cross them off your to do list. You may just want to keep monitoring them to make sure nothing changes which might suddenly make them metaphorically shift to a different box.

B: Low power – high interest. *Keep informed*

People in this category are probably going to be most efficiently served through regular 'broadcast' communication. Broadcast communication is useful, relevant and informative, but it does not require much tailoring for specific audiences. Neither does it need to be face to face or interactive. Emails, copies of minutes, notice boards may all suffice.

C: High power – low interest. *Keep satisfied*

With this group, you need to do more than communicate *to* them. You need to interact *with* them. You need to listen to them, checking out what they know about the change, what they are thinking and feeling about it. You need to ensure that they feel that their interests are being taken care of or if not, to understand why. From your interactions with this group you may well find you need to be flexible and change your plans to incorporate any useful ideas resulting from conversations with these people, so taking a facilitative approach to change.

D: High power – high interest. *Keep engaged / keep warm*

This is where you will need to focus your efforts and energies because the individuals and groups you have placed here have much greater interest in what happens and they have the power to act as enablers or barriers. This doesn't mean that lengthy and frequent meetings are required with each person or group. It will to a certain extent depend on the context and personalities of those involved but you might want to consider the following:

1. Engaging them at the beginning
   Early on in the programme arrange to meet and give a *brief* outline of your intent with the change. The notion of brief is important - you are there to inquire. Our encouragement would be to spend most of the time listening and probing to find out their views, their concerns, what they would like to see, so you really understand what is driving their views. Adopting this facilitative approach will enable you to find out about their perspective rather than to promote your approach, so resist any urge to sell, defend or argue. You might also want to find out what level of involvement or communication they would like during the change. Asking them 'What would you find useful?' is a really helpful question. Later on you will need to keep them updated in whatever way you have agreed, so do put that into your plan. Sometimes you may want to just pop into their office or catch them at a meeting or in the corridor to give a short update on whatever aspects you now know are particularly of interest to them. If there is something difficult or contentious

coming up, you might want to send them a short update so that they are forewarned. You might want to let them know how your plans were shaped by what they said, as a courtesy.

2. Keeping them engaged
   The key thing is to keep them on the radar and keep checking in with them so that you know that they are still on side. Don't forget them ... although this is easier said than done. If you see them by chance, take a moment to remind them of how things are progressing – or not. This is opportunistic back-stage activity is highly effective. It is also an example of the emergent, spontaneous nature of change. If they have issues or concerns about particular aspects of the change programme, ensure you keep them in the loop. Proactively let them know what is happening so that they know that their interests are recognized and respected. This in itself can often reduce potential aggravation.

Identifying and engaging with stakeholders is an important aspect of relational change. However, it is worth noting that we are referring here to a rough map rather than anything as definite and predictable as a plan. People do sometimes talk about managing stakeholders, indeed we heard one person talk of massaging stakeholders! However, the key is to engage with people authentically, recognize that this is about influence, creating favourable conditions and allowing you to engage with what is really going on.

Understanding your own – and others' – political style

Many of the more intangible and complex ideas in the area of relational change can be helpfully understood by resorting to metaphor, as we have already seen. This is also very much the case when thinking about your own behaviour patterns and tendencies when it comes to engaging with politics. Two researchers, Baddeley and James,[9] explored political behaviour in local government and then rather colourfully described the four different styles that emerged from their research by using animal characters. They plotted them on a matrix depending on whether or not they are politically aware and whether or not they act in the interests of the organization or out of self-interest (see Figure 4.2 below).

Both the fox and the owl recognize who knows, who can and who cares. In other words, both are politically adept and hence above the horizontal axis. However the reasons they engage in political behaviour are very different.

The fox is someone who is politically aware but tends to act in his or her own interest, often engaging in what is seen by others to be game playing. Machaivelli would have been a fox and it is fox behaviour that gives politics a bad name. Foxes like to be seen as powerful. They enjoy manipulating others; tend to create winners and losers and are superb at the subtle put down, cleverly tripping people up, wrong footing them, landing them in awkward places but all done without it being obvious, especially to people further up the hierarchy. Whenever there is trouble, they aren't there. If there is a really tricky piece of work, they will duck out of it by flattering someone else and suggesting they would be better suited to the task.

Foxes tend not to display *true* feelings spontaneously, and while they can be aggressive this is often well masked with a charming veneer. So you never quite know where you stand with the fox, which is of course

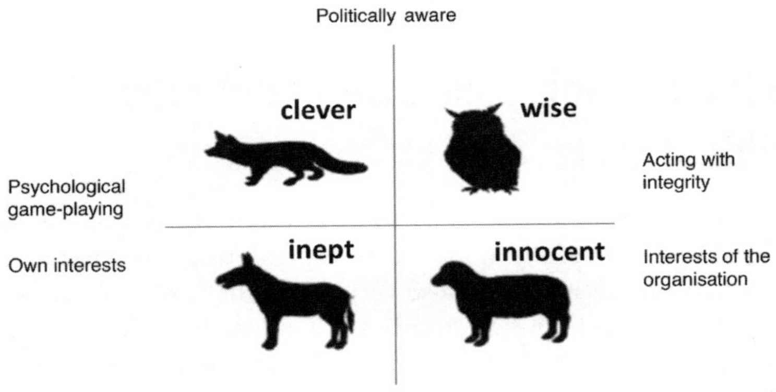

Figure 4.2 A framework for exploring political behaviour. Adapted from Baddeley and James

part of the reason they are powerful. They will deny, with all innocence, that they ever received that email you say you sent. They will confidently claim that they have discussed a matter with everyone who they say is supportive when you are pretty sure that isn't the case. You could call them Teflon man or woman ... nothing seems to stick. No doubt you've met a few foxes where you work.

The owl is also politically aware and knows how to navigate the organization or wider system. However, owls' intentions are perceived to be for the good of the organization, rather than personally self-serving. Their interest in power is seen to be because it allows them to influence organizational purpose rather than purely for reasons of status or power. They tend to be assertive, tactful and emotionally literate. They are excellent listeners, so are skilled at inquiry, interested in and aware of others' viewpoints. This means they also tend not to be defensive, to be willing to learn from mistakes, reflect on events and be open with information and how they feel about things. As a result of these interpersonal skills, they tend to be good at building coalitions around them to get support and when they negotiate, they attempt to create win-win situations, but can cope with being disliked. The relational leader of change aims to be owl-like.

In this schema, there are two groups of people (or animals, to keep to the metaphor) who are absolutely unaware of politics, who do not pay attention to power, to 'sensing the mood' or noticing the organizational direction of travel. As a result of this, both groups are the last ones to have their CV ready should redundancies be on the cards. **The donkey** is often characterized as inept or awkward, perhaps hired originally for their technical competence but lacking in interpersonal skills. They may want to be nice but they don't really know how. Their focus is on themselves. They may well try and play psychological games but when they do so it is often obvious to everyone else even if not to themselves. As they are focused on themselves, they are poor at reading others and tend not to pay attention to others' feelings, to cultural or organizational norms or to consider what might be diplomatic in the moment. Their assumption is that it is acceptable to call a 'spade a spade' – it's their right after all – and then they are often angry and surprised when people get upset by their behaviour and things don't go their way. This lack of self-awareness and failure to understand their personal impact makes a donkey tricky to performance manage if you have one in your team as they rarely get the message from feedback!

The fourth animal is **the sheep** who, in the model, is labelled as 'innocent', or perhaps more unkindly as naïve. Sheep tend to rely a great deal on authority, assuming that those who are further up the hierarchy will be right and that decisions are based on rationality alone. They are, therefore, very compliant, good workers who put their trust in organizational procedures so they would not even consider that building a network or finding support might be necessary. They share information openly with anyone who asks, wanting to be helpful and do the right thing for the organization, especially as described by those with expert or positional power. The sheep would not really consider that others were acting with ulterior motives, so while the sheep listens, he or she misses double messages or nuances and sees things as 'either–or'. Asking them to help you create a stakeholder map would be a waste of time. They would want to help you but because they are politically unaware, they wouldn't have the insight into why you were doing it or see the nuances in motivation and power between different interest groups.

We have found the model very helpful in stimulating people's thinking about their own behaviour. One of us had a coaching assignment with a psychiatrist who was a leading researcher in his field and an impressive clinician who was suddenly promoted a very senior leadership role. He and the CEO started to have serious run-ins as he challenged her in the fortnightly leadership meetings. He had not thought about the difference between the back stage and what they could discuss 1:1 and what was appropriate front stage in the large group meeting. He realized he had been behaving like a sheep even though she had seen him as being a bit of a donkey. These ideas helped him rethink how to modify his behaviour in this new role. However, as with all models, this one comes with the health warning that it is easy to stereotype and label others. For instance, you may have labelled someone a fox, but keep an open mind when you go and speak to them to find out their story. Equally be aware that you may intend to be acting as an owl but others may perceive you as being like a fox.

Politics is neutral: It's all about your intent

Rather than seeing politics and political activity as good or bad, as something to engage in or avoid, we see political activity as neutral and a reality of organizational life. The difference is the intent with which we engage in it – for our own personal advancement or to knock down someone else? Because we care about a particular issue or to build our own empire? Rather than dismissing politics and political activity, we believe that engaging with it is both helpful and important, especially when done with good intent. It can:

- Stimulate debate and helps ensure that all sides of an issue are aired and debated.
- Be a critical source of dynamic energy.
- Keep conversation about change 'in play' ensuring proponents of change hone and refine their arguments.
- Increase involvement of key political players and other people, increasing their engagement and ownership.

The amount of time you can, and need, to devote to this will depend on your context. Our encouragement is to be an owl, not a fox; to give attention to back-stage activity; and to identify those with an interest in the change you are working with and actively engage them in conversation. In doing so, you will be being politically competent and organizationally agile.

Questions for further reflection

- How do you engage in political activity and for what ends?
- Who are the key stakeholders who are likely to have an impact on the change you are involved in and how are you giving them the kind of attention and involvement they need?
- How much attention do you give the back stage and the front stage?
- What prompts you to take on which of the four animal roles when?

Chapter 5

Symbolic acts and small gestures: Recognizing and shifting power dynamics

In change, nothing happens unless power has in some way shifted. Until then, there may be talk of change, but there will be no real change in practice. There may be much rhetoric around the new vision, the new strategy or the restructure. However, if the old ways of working continue then the chances are that embedded patterns of power have remained untouched and unchallenged.

In this chapter, we explore two types of power. The first is power as a relational and multi-dimensional phenomenon between people, which serves to affect how they think, feel and behave towards one another. In this sense, it is closely related to the idea of influence and can be relatively fluid. Understanding your own potential sources of power and being aware of the gestures you can make to moderate the power dynamic between yourself and others is a core skill in relational change. It can help create the energy, attention and interest that provides the momentum to shift power which exists at the system, organizational or unit level. In changing the story, you tell yourself about your own power, you may also give yourself the courage to be ten per cent braver in the moment.

The second type of power is that which is embedded in the status quo in each organization's culture, structure, policies, procedures and norms. In introducing any change, the current orthodoxy and way of doing things is being challenged. There will be those who have a vested interest in things staying the same because their own power, status, comfort and sense of who they are derive from what is currently the norm. Shifting embedded power requires a mix of both deliberate actions and spotting and amplifying signs of the new as they emerge or as you create or encounter them.

Understanding the way power is constructed

In engaging others in change, you will no doubt have already found yourself needing to persuade, encourage, influence, cajole or request people to give their time, energy and perhaps resources to participate in the change process. You may have been asking for a considerable time commitment from people if you want them to join a multidisciplinary change team. It might have been a less time intensive request – coming to an away day, agreeing to meet you for a conversation, or giving you a slot on their meeting agenda. You may feel confident that you are already pretty effective at this type of activity. For others, getting people to say yes and commit, rather than saying 'yes' to fob you off, can feel like hard work. Exploring the power dynamics between you and others will help you understand and shift what might be going on.

However, people are often uncomfortable talking about their own power. When running leadership programmes, if we ask participants to line up in order of how powerful they each think they are relative to others in the group, there is an extreme amount of embarrassment and discomfort. Power is, in many ways, a subtle and mercurial phenomenon. It can shift, moment by moment, in the push and pull of a conversation. Traditionally, power was seen as fixed and immovable; something people possessed, rather as if power was a personality trait like being tall or having red hair.

More recently, power has come to be seen as socially constructed, which means it does not exist out there as a tangible thing, like an object or a person. Instead, it is an aspect of the relationship between people that we individually, or often collectively, construct because of our perceptions of the other person, and what we then tell ourselves about them. These perceptions may stem from certain facts we know about a person, such as their job title, how we have experienced them in the past, how we have seen them behaving with others, or indeed the stories and gossip we have heard about them. From this we consciously, or often unconsciously, construct a story of whether we are more or less powerful in relation to them. This then influences how we behave when we meet them. When we see organizations as complex responsive processes, although in principle anything may happen, in practice we and others are often constrained by our social constructions or beliefs about power relationships.

In Chapter 1, we looked at the way our mental models of organizations affect the way we act. Our social constructions of how we see our power in relation to others also makes a significant difference to how we behave. For instance, our perceptions of power impact on the decisions we may make in a meeting to speak up or stay silent in the presence of someone we see as powerful. If I believe you are powerful, I will act in a way that treats you with a great deal of respect and deference. I let you speak first; I do not challenge you. In relation to me, at that moment, you are indeed powerful as this is how I have constructed or envisaged our relationship. You, in turn, because of my behaviour towards you, will construct yourself as more powerful than me, so reinforcing my original construction of the relationship. In this way, the stories we tell ourselves create the phenomenon which we then act into, as if it was reality. In doing so, we then confirm to ourselves what we had constructed, validating our perceptions and making us feel: 'I'm right. This is indeed how it is.'

In socially constructing power relationships, we don't just rely on facts about the other person or what we have heard others say about them. We are also influenced by the voice in our head, what in Transactional Analysis is called our 'script'. This is explored in more detail in Chapter 8, but suffice to say here that sometimes a voice from the past which we have internalized (one of our parents or a teacher, perhaps) keeps telling us that we are not worthy or not clever or that we shouldn't be such an upstart as to think we are equal with others. If we continue to listen to this inner voice, we can unwittingly diminish our own sense of power, agency and ability to influence others and amplify, instead, in our heads, the power of others.

These ideas can be 'discombobulating'.[1] However, once you get your head around social constructionism, it is wonderfully liberating. We base our social constructions on what we see, hear and notice and then make particular interpretations as a result. It is these interpretations that we can change. When we do so, we can suddenly see things differently, which can be exciting. We create new possibilities. In other words, we create change. If we can modify the way we see others and ourselves, we can create different ways of being, acting and talking together. This can suddenly make you think, 'Why was I worrying so much about that?' This is why in coaching people talk of having a 'eureka' or 'light bulb' moment – or what Erik de Haan, a leading researcher on coaching, calls a 'critical moment'.[2] This is one way in which we can create change through conversation.

To give an example of the way power is socially constructed, if I know that the other person has the title Senior Vice President, has an office and secretary and is the CEO's heir apparent, I will draw on these tangible facts to create a story to myself of this woman being more powerful than me. I may also have an inner script that tells me to be quiet in the presence of my elders and betters (an oft-repeated message in my childhood). I will have constructed a power difference and then acted on this as if it were true, as if differences in power were facts rather than a social construction. However, things do not have to remain this way. If I am running a workshop on my specialist topic and the same person is a face in the audience, I may see myself as having greater power than her at that moment.

If you were momentarily surprised to read the word 'woman' there, you would not be alone. We also base our social constructions on assumptions and norms that operate at a societal level. We are, thus, likely to assume that someone with the attributes described is more likely to be male. This is one of the ways that inequalities in power continue to play out between men and women, between white and non-white people, between those with a posh accent and those without. This is where power as a relational phenomenon between individuals links to embedded patterns of power discussed later in the chapter.

Power dynamics shift when we are able to see a different power relationship between us and another. This can modify the previous relationship. This does not have to be reciprocal. Power, like love, does not exist as a finite quantity. So, just because I suddenly see myself as more powerful than you, it does not automatically follow that you will see yourself as less powerful than me. There is no balance or weighing scale where if one becomes more powerful, others must automatically see themselves as less so.

In summary, power is not an attribute or a possession that we have or don't have. Instead it is a socially constructed aspect of the relationship between people. Our social constructions are based on what we know and perceive about the other, as well as the stories we tell ourselves. We then behave in ways that are congruent with our mental models of ourselves and others.

Understanding your own sources of power

Research by French and Raven[3] identified six main sources of power which individuals and groups may have in relation to each other. These are described below. As just discussed, other people's perceptions of whether you have these sources of power in relation to them, or indeed others, will be social constructions based, in part, on facts, in part, on their experience of you and, in part, on how they make sense of this all at any given moment. They will also be influenced by the culture and norms operating in the organization and within the wider society in which they live. Similarly, the way you personally construct how you see your own sources of power, and the story you tell yourself about this, will influence how powerful you feel in any situation.

1. **Position power**
   Many sources of your power as an individual within an organization stem from what is known as 'position power', the authority that comes from the job. The job can give formal access to organizational resources that can then be used to reward or punish others (see below) and can legitimize making subordinates feel responsible to you as the boss. Position power is enhanced by gaining control of departments which are bigger, more profitable or have expertise that is critical to the functioning of the organization. However in many change projects, especially those that cut across different disciplines and units, position power may have less impact and relevance.
2. **Reward power**
   This is the power to give rewards to those who comply with your requests and do what you ask. Your ability to reward others may come from your position power. You would have 'reward power'

over some people if you control resources such as the bonus pool or promotion decisions. (Note – what is important here is others' perceptions of whether or not you control these decisions, even if in reality you need to consult with HR or others further up the hierarchy.) You would also have reward power if you are able to give someone an interesting and high profile secondment or the opportunity to sit next to a senior executive at the sales conference, or to present to the Board. Overuse of reward power can stimulate extrinsic motivation, i.e. people doing things for the reward rather than for intrinsic motivations, and expectations of special rewards from you every time you want them to do anything new or unusual.

3. **Expert power**
   This is based on the fact or impression that you have significant relevant experience and expertise compared to others. Comments and actions that you make which turn out to be helpful or successful will tend to increase perceptions of your expert power. Expertise can be consciously acquired by systematically seeking specific experiences or gaining qualifications. However, it is often easy to undervalue your own 'expert power' because there are things that to you are now second nature and obvious, forgetting that others may not have had that same exposure and experience. Women are rather more prone to this than men. In relation to change, there can be a number of shadow sides stemming from being seen to have expert power. Others may assume that you know the best course of action in a given situation, deferring to you rather than really thinking for themselves or helping think together; they may not challenge you to road test your ideas as they assume you are the expert; it may be hard for you to encourage others to contribute innovative ideas unless you deliberately and expressly welcome this. If we think about the different political positions explored in Chapter 4,[4] the fox would want to preserve and amplify the perceived value around their expert power, avoiding careless statements and rash decisions to maintain the mystique. They would never make anything look easy. The owl, in contrast, would recognize the strengths and shadow sides of their expert power. They would be willing to draw attention to

it when there was a need to perhaps move things forward that had got stuck, or when a decision was needed, but would 'sit' on their expertise to allow others to really participate in dialogue to co-create an innovative solution.

4. **Information power**
   This resembles expert power except that those with 'information power' are not presenting themselves as an authority on a particular topic but as people who have information not possessed by others. There are two aspects – gaining information and using it – both of which affect how influential you are. To gain information you need to position yourself in networks through which relevant information flows, including networks outside the organization. Without these you are isolated. Important information may be technical or about the organization's social system; it may be specific to the change process or include broader knowledge and understanding of what is going on in the wider system with customers, suppliers, regulators. Some people have information power because of their job role – those who have client contacts for instance, and can speak for the client, or who negotiate with the regulator; others have this power because of the networks they join, the breadth of the journals, websites and papers they access. Still others may have information power because of where they sit physically or their proximity to others who have power – think here of the CEO's PA or those whose desks are on the same floor as the Board. In terms of organizational metaphors, information power is a key element of the ecosystem/organism way of looking at organizations as it is the means of monitoring what is going on in the external or internal environment, hence it is a source of power. Even if you do not rate your own information power, you may want to ensure that there are those in your change team whom you trust and who do have this source of power. Owls and foxes both recognize the power of information, especially given the anxiety and uncertainty that accompany change. However, they differ in how and when they disclose the information they hold – to help others make a good decision or to ensure the decision goes their way.

5. **Referent or personal power**
'Referent' or 'personal power' refers to the loyalty of one person for another, based on liking, friendship and a desire to please. It is derived from your personal qualities and the relationship you have with an individual. Unlike other sources of power, it is not related to your job but increases when you are considerate to others, show concern for their feelings and needs, treat them fairly, and defend their interests when dealing with superiors and outsiders. It is also based on an individual's attraction to you which itself is a function of your friendliness, gregariousness, honesty, candour and integrity. Your poise, wealth or confidence may also lead them to identify with you. Foxes, for all their charm, may try to increase their referent power through flattery and seeming to listen to others. However, most people are wired for authenticity and can 'smell' such tactics a mile off.
6. **Coercive power**
This is the power to punish. Within organizations the use of 'coercive power' may be brutal – shutting factories, withdrawing from markets, firing individuals. It can also be quite subtle, but is no less powerful for that. Physical and mental pressure, public shaming, passive aggressive punishments such as exclusion, strict adherence to policies and procedures would all be examples of coercive power. The use of coercive power does not build commitment. It engenders compliance, causes resentment and often leads to some of the more difficult aspects of change – resistance, sabotage, strikes, work to rule, which are in themselves examples of coercive power. A relational approach to change would advocate only using this as a last resort, where there is no alternative remaining or when there is a perceived need for speed and decisiveness. If you have to draw on this source of power, the general advice is to do so quickly and uniformly. Here, too, there is a link between the coercive power individuals are believed to possess and the embedded power within an organizational culture. Individuals or groups may socially construct the coercive power of the Board or a particular leader or supervisor based on their own experience or what others have said. This can then create fear, with people deliberately keeping their heads down below the radar, creating a stuck, self-perpetuating pattern of interacting.

Analysing your own sources of power in relation to different people

To make this practical and personal, you might want to consider your own sources of power in relation to key individuals in the change in which you are currently involved.

Source of power	Individual 1	Individual 2	Individual 3	Individual 4	Individual 5
Position power					
Reward power					
Expert power					
Information power					
Referent / personal power					
Coercive power					

Table 5.1 Considering your sources of power relative to others.

What does this analysis tell you about yourself? Are there any sources of power you would like to increase? How might you do that? Are there certain relationships where you seem to have little power? What might you want to do having now noticed this? And what power do those you have listed have in relationship to you?

The greater the range of power bases available to you, the greater your choice of gestures. Note that only expert and personal power are likely to produce commitment. Position and reward power are likely to elicit grudging compliance, while coercive power is likely to generate resistance.

Shifting and moderating power through small gestures

A core premise of relational change is the importance of dialogue, of finding out others' views and experiences, engaging them in a way that is of mutual benefit. To engage well with others requires us to pay attention to the power relations between us and them and sometimes we might need to make a proactive gesture to modify this for a good conversation to occur. Complexity theorists such as Stacey[5] and Shaw[6] describe the way that through talking, through conversation we create new ways of seeing the work and the world. However, this only happens if the opening gestures we make signal to other people that we genuinely want to inquire and explore with them. So how do you signal that you want to be facilitative rather than directive? To pull rather than push? The answer is to pay attention to the micro gestures you make signalling your intentions. You cannot guarantee how others will interpret such gestures, but in making them you increase the likelihood of modifying some of the power relations that may get in the way of dialogue. In doing so you may be unsticking some stuck cultural patterns.

Working with leaders we have heard many different stories of how they modified the power dynamics between themselves and others through small gestures to enable genuine dialogue. You will doubtless have your own examples, but here are some offered in the spirit of stimulating your own experiments.

- If you are more senior than the other person, consider meeting in their office or somewhere neutral like the coffee shop rather than in your office, thereby diminishing the physical trappings and reminder of your position power.
- Admitting that you don't have the answer, or sharing your own feelings, can help create the conditions for encouraging others to talk honestly about what they are seeing or experiencing rather than just telling you what they expect you want to hear. There is of course a balancing act, relational change being an art. You need to judge how much to share. Over-disclosing may unsettle other people. Instead what is needed is thoughtfully sharing in a way that

is authentic and at the same time 'holds' the anxiety. So it may be sharing the fact that you don't have the answer but that you have confidence in the skills and knowledge of the team.

- When there are significant position or expert power differences in the room which you want to minimize, you may choose to start the meeting by getting people to give their name and share their hopes for the meeting, rather than asking them to give their job title which immediately brings position power into the room.
- Other small gestures include asking people to discuss their views in pairs first so that those with more perceived position or expert power do not dominate with their views from the start. (More on this in Chapter 7 on re-imagining meetings.)
- You might want to include specific mention of power in ground rules for your change meetings. We worked with an ambulance trust where the first ground rule was 'leave rank at the door'. This enabled people to challenge, in a legitimate way, those senior leaders who had greater position power. This in turn modified the way the ambulance staff and the leaders socially constructed their mutual power relationship, breaking some stuck patterns as well as allowing them all to discuss what was really going on in the service.[7]

It is equally important to think about some of the small gestures you may wish to make when you are about to meet someone whom you perceive has more power than you.

- Suggest meeting somewhere where you feel comfortable.
- Take a moment to remind yourself of your own power source in relation to them - you may know more about the change than they do, i.e. have significant expert and information power.
- Remember they are human too and engage with them at a personal or human level - an assumption of equals, both with contributions to make to the conversation.
- If you are speaking to them on the phone, stand up to make the call. It will lower your voice so that it has more gravitas and make you feel more grounded.
- If you have done media training, you will have undoubtedly come across the importance of identifying in advance your three key points and practising them, so that you have honed how and what you say. Such rehearsing can be really useful in any high-pressure

situation, as it allows you to become clearer about what you really want to say beforehand rather than having a few false starts in the crucial meeting. The fact that you have prepared will also make you feel more confident to improvise your response, should you be asked something unpredictable. (See Chapter 8 on honest conversations.)

Once we recognize that power is dynamic and constructed in relationship with others, it gives rise to the significant and exciting possibility of you being able to shift and moderate power during the change process through the gestures you make. This is core to a relational approach to change. However, what is vital here is your intent. If you make a move to shift the power to allow proper engagement and dialogue, the chances are that you will create a different conversation. You are being an owl. If your intent is to win one over someone else, to score points, then others will perceive you as a fox and the previous power dynamics will be reinforced.

Embedded power

One of the most significant aspects of your own context will be the culture where you work. Over time, certain ways of organizing and 'being' will have become habituated so that they are seen as 'the way we do things round here'. This is what is meant by the culture of an organization or department. There may be aspects of that culture that support the changes you are wanting to encourage. However, in our experience two scenarios are more likely:

1. **Aspects of the current culture may themselves be what need to change. (For instance, in our work with organizations we often hear people talking about wanting the culture to be more customer orientated or more pacey or more innovative.)**
2. **Change remains superficial and on paper only as the culture and embedded power remain untouched, hence the phrase 'culture eats strategy and restructures for breakfast'.**

As a relational leader of change, working with power means being aware that power is not just a property of relationships between people. Power is also embedded in many aspects of organizational culture and inherent in the status quo. For change to really occur, there will generally be a need to challenge and shift some of the existing power relationships and assumptions embedded in cultural norms. This can then create the conditions for something new and different to emerge and symbolize that change is real and is happening.

The power of an existing culture is often most apparent when you or others unwittingly transgress a cultural norm. When you start a new job, you will have arrived with certain assumptions and expectations, based on your previous experience elsewhere and to a certain extent what you noticed during the recruitment process. However, no doubt in the first few days and weeks others will have corrected you when you 'tripped up' and said or did things that they perceived as counter cultural. As the newcomer or the external consultant, you are often blissfully unaware of the proverbial elephant in the room or sacred cows. 'Oh no. That's not our role; you can't claim that as an expense; you can't park your car there; you need to ask permission for that; we don't sit there.' There will be a litany of things to learn about 'how we do things round here'. In those mild or more extreme 'ouch' moments, you will have experienced the power of the dominant culture and the pressure to conform. This is what we mean by embedded power: tacitly understood ways of behaving that constrain what is seen as do-able or discussable in the collective minds of the majority. In Moira's story (Chapter 11), she transgresses unwritten rules by sharing Board-level discussions with her own more junior team, thus eliciting the wrath of the Chief Operating Officer as a result.

Although things could in theory be structured, organized or valued differently, people act as though only the current ways of being, thinking, seeing and behaving are possible. This results in a social stratification of groups within organizations and more broadly within societies, with some enjoying more privileges than others. These power structures are often organized along lines of class, race, gender or professional identity and are then legitimized through the use of symbols, language and rituals so that they become the norm, the assumed, the taken-for-granted ways of doing things.

Understanding culture in more detail

Early researchers into culture, in particular Edgar Schein,[8] suggest culture is comprised of different levels. Artefacts such as buildings, furnishings, dress codes, mission statements, stated values and other objects on display are visible and exist above the waterline. Behaviours and behavioural norms also exist above the waterline. Behavioural norms might include conduct in meetings: Is it OK to be late? Who gets to talk? Is the purpose to review documents or have dialogue? They may include how conflict is handled. Is conflict acknowledged in public or avoided? The signs can be quite subtle. A colleague of ours working in the very formal culture of a government department overheard a senior civil servant saying to a colleague, 'Couldn't you see I disagreed? I raised an eyebrow ...'.

The meaning of artefacts and behaviours may not always be apparent and multiple interpretations may be possible. These, too, are socially constructed, which is why culture is not a 'thing' that can be managed and controlled. For instance, if a leader keeps his door open is this a sign of a culture of informality or a sign of a culture where leaders want to check up on what employees are doing? The only way of finding out is talking to people and noticing patterns that together build up a picture of what seems to be the culture. In some organizations, it doesn't matter who you talk to, you still tend to hear the same stories and phrases and people behave in similar ways. Such organizations are said to have strong cultures. Detractors might even say that they resemble more of a cult. In other places, there may be diversity with a higher tolerance for different ways of doing things, or micro cultures at a department level or site level. The latter can be easier to work with in terms of change, as there are already different ways of doing things in the current culture.

Leaders' gestures may reinforce the old culture or may affirm and amplify the new as part of shifting old patterns. However leaders' gestures may sometimes be taken to mean something very different from what was intended. We worked with a leader of a medium-sized firm who bought broken biscuits for the staff kitchen because they were good value and the business was under financial pressure. Employees interpreted this gesture as her not caring about them. In another organization, the new CEO cut down the trees outside his office. The corridor conversations were that this was an example of his ruthlessness and his lack of respect for the past. He told us that the pine trees had a disease and needed to be cut down for safety reasons, but without this knowledge the alternative story became part of the culture. So, as a leader, you need to be aware of the stories that circulate about your own gestures and welcome the opportunity to have conversations so that you can explain your intentions and give your own voice over to amplify or offer an alternative interpretation to what others are saying and the meaning they are making.

Below the waterline, out of sight, are the basic underlying assumptions and world views held by employees. These are largely unconscious and taken for granted beliefs that are often the ultimate sources of values and action. They often need to be inferred from what you observe. Many have their origins in the early history of the organization and, as such, encapsulate the values, beliefs and experience of the early founders. Such assumptions may relate to the organization's position in the market, perhaps that it will always be number one or have a particular technology at its heart. A core assumption within Xerox was that there would always be a market for photocopiers; a core assumption in Kodak was that cameras would always need photographic film. Assumptions can also relate to core beliefs about the external world – that it is a dog-eat-dog world out there and everyone must fight for themselves; or that partnership and collaboration are the best ways of organizing.

Such assumptions can blind everyone to what is going on in the external environment. In hindsight, people find it hard to believe that they could have held onto their beliefs for so long.

As we saw in Chapter 2, early ways of understanding change took the view that what was needed was to disturb the current way of seeing the world so that the system was unfrozen. However, changing culture is problematic because these core assumptions are generally unconscious and therefore unseen and unnoticed by the majority. This is why they are powerful. Artefacts and behaviours can also be open to multiple interpretations, so the idea that leaders at the top can manage and reshape the culture in predictable ways is a chimera. However, what you can do is encourage different ways of imagining the future, creating different types of conversation which will create an energy to discover new ways of working. As an employee who is introducing some kind of change, you are both part of the culture yourself and also wanting to disturb the existing habits and taken for granted routines. Caryn Vanstone,[9] an expert on culture change, talks about the need to challenge everyday assumptions, by drawing attention to the way things are now done and the need to change. At the same time, you need to stay part of the club and not cause too much conflict with long standing internal rules. Too much disturbance and you risk being rejected; too much collusion and there will be no change. So here again, a real balancing act required and change as an art form.

It can be helpful to create enough disturbance to generate an acceptance of the need for change. A phrase that Kotter[10] introduced, and we mentioned in Chapter 2, is that of 'creating a burning platform'. Sometimes external events provide the burning platform – the loss of a major contract, the emergence of a new competitor. Sometimes data in the form of falling sales or share price, or patient or customer stories shock people into recognizing that things have to be different. However, challenge and shock need to be balanced. If the anxiety created is too great, there is no energy or appetite for creative thinking. There is panic and paralysis. It was said of Napoleon that he was a great leader because he gave his people a vision of reality as well as a sense of hope.

An alternative is to create a burning ambition, to help others see that there could be different ways of doing things. This may be through focusing on what the organization is currently doing well; it could be by visiting other organizations to see what they have done; it could be using some Appreciative Inquiry techniques which are explored further in Chapter 6.

As the French writer Antoine de Saint-Exupéry is reputed to have said, 'If you want to build a ship, don't drum up the people to gather wood, divide the work and give orders. Instead, teach them to yearn for the vast and endless sea.' And then, as people change the nature of the conversations they have and change becomes talked about, change is already happening and the old ways already exert less hold. However, because a new culture is not a thing that exists out there in tangible form, it cannot be controlled or prescribed in advance. Your role as a leader is to amplify and encourage the emergence of the new. As Patricia Shaw says, rather than trying to wave a 'magic wand to change the corporate Cinderella into a bright and successful princess overnight'[11] [...] what everyone does and says matters in unexpected ways. It is important to stay alert to that, to notice what keeps unfolding. That is how the culture of this new company is already being created moment by moment.'

As well as engaging in conversations about change, you also need to consider how your own behaviour and actions might signal the new. If you have just arrived as a new leader, your very arrival will signal the possibility of change. People expect the newly appointed to want to change things to the extent that it is almost seen as odd if they keep things the same. Your early moves about who you choose to meet, and where you meet them, will be scrutinized and stories created, so it is worth considering whether you just want to meet the normal suspects who have traditionally held power or do you go and spend time with the front line people, with customers? With those who work outside head office? Such gestures are, in themselves, symbolic acts which can signal your intentions.

You may also want to change some artefacts to signal your broader intention for change, to show that you are different from what has gone before and are not constrained by the power of history. Sometimes those perceptions of power shifts are deliberately intended. For example, when the retailer Sainsbury's renamed their London head office the Store Support Centre, they were deliberately signalling to staff – and, indeed, other stakeholders – that the powerhouse of the firm was in the stores where the customers were, not with the grey suits of corporate planning and finance. Recently two new leaders also made similar statements: Nicola Sturgeon, the first female Minister for Scotland, and Clare Marx, the first female president of the UK's Royal College of Surgeons, independently of each other both commissioned large photos of women they admired and placed them round their offices. In doing so, they replaced the portraits of uniformly male and elderly predecessors, marking a highly symbolic break with the past.

On their own, such symbolic acts are never enough. However, their importance is that they are a public and visible sign of the new and the future. They play a part in unhooking people from the old and creating a new narrative. Such symbolic acts also generate conversations that start to challenge people's assumptions about how things are and how they might be. What symbolic acts might you choose to make where you work?

So what is the role of a leader in shifting, challenging, throwing a spotlight on patterns of power that are embedded in the culture? There are a number of actions you might want to consider as a leader:

- Encourage conversations about new ways of doing things. The very act of talking about different approaches, even if not everyone is in agreement, starts the process of detaching from one world view.
- Make symbolic acts that signal something different, and engage in conversation with others about why.
- Avoid 'splitting', i.e. suggesting that somehow what was done in the past was 'bad' or 'wrong' and that the new is 'good'. People will have invested their time and energy creating what you may now be calling the past. So, rather than 'trashing' the past create a narrative for people that acknowledges that how things were organized in the past worked for then, for the purpose and context at that time. They are just no longer fit for purpose now. Such phrasing is important as it both acknowledges the past with respect and gives a story for why things need to be different now. More of this in Chapter 6.
- Pay attention to being the change that you want to encourage. If you are about encouraging innovation then how you approach everything needs to be congruent and therefore innovative. This can be hard, so working with a colleague or an external person can be really helpful in giving you feedback on how you are doing with this. More on this in Chapter 10.
- Amplify the new through what you pay attention to and discuss. A leader was concerned that one unit was always so busy they never stopped to consider alternatives; there was a manic energy about the place. He started to change the culture by changing the way the leadership team meetings began. He asked each person to take five minutes to check-in and reflect on what they had learned since the last meeting. When some people commented on how helpful

they found it to stop and think, he amplified those comments by sharing his own experiences of why this was beneficial. He made sure such points were noted in the minutes so that a new way of being emerged.

- Talk about and celebrate signs of the 'new' emerging. Research has shown that the most prominent event that contributes to how engaged we feel at work is a sense of making progress, yet in a worldwide survey only 5 per cent of managers used 'progress' as a motivator.[12] You will have no doubt heard the phrase 'create short term wins'. We too would agree with Kotter[13] that communicating and talking about small steps is vital to create energy and momentum towards the new, which shifts belief towards the future and in doing dissolves aspects of embedded power.
- Bring in some new people, chosen with care, who can offer alternative ways of seeing things, who can bring confidence, experience and belief that creating something different is possible in your organization, too. Care is needed to ensure that they do not arrive thinking they know better, suggesting they are superior to current employees and starting every sentence with, 'When I was at Company X'. Nothing is more likely to turn people off.
- Encourage the creation of alternatives, pilots and experiments. We particularly like Martyn Brown's idea of Trojan mice.[14] These are small, fast and under-the-radar experiments that do not attract the attention of the Powers That Be. However, they generate great learning and confidence in what might work, whether successful or not.
- Engage people in scenario planning. This was an approach to strategy development undertaken first for Royal Dutch Shell. Exploring different scenarios and possibilities allows people to be more creative and it is less threatening for those currently in power as it creates a sense of choices rather than only one way forward.
- Consider working in a pair. Work with an organization development person, coach, supervisor to help you reflect on what is going on and explore different moves you may wish to make. More on this in Chapter 10.

The power of numbers

We are often asked questions such as, 'How many people do I need to engage in the change? How many can I afford to have sitting in the middle? Do I need to have everyone on board?'.

Let us start by being reassuring – you do not need everyone on board. If this was an aspiration of yours please drop it immediately, otherwise you risk beating yourself up for what is undoubtedly nigh on impossible. For change to happen you need to create enough critical mass so that there is sufficient energy and momentum for things to move forward, for different approaches to be explored, pilot schemes and small-scale experiments to be undertaken. The more these things happen, with different people involved, the more you create energy. Malcolm Gladwell, in his book *The Tipping Point*,[15] gives a number of examples where trends suddenly take off without there being a specific magic number. Here again we are back in the realms of change as an art rather than a science.

This is where power and politics come together. It is probably not helpful to spend too much effort trying to convert those who are firmly against the change. This can be time consuming and de-energizing. In Chapter 9, we reframe resistance as ambivalence and show that people's motivations are generally far more nuanced and complicated than a simple binary for or against. As a change leader, you don't need to be a hero who converts a hundred per cent of the people to start shifting embedded patterns of power.

Questions for further reflection

- How do you see your own sources of power in relation to key individuals involved in your change programme?
- What gestures might you make to modify some of those power dynamics?
- How might you want to change the script in your head when you are about to go and give a difficult message to someone you see as having greater position or expert power than yourself?

- What embedded patterns do you notice in your organization that need shifting as part of the change effort?
- What opportunities might you create to start changing such embedded patterns?
- What gestures might you want to be looking out for so that you can amplify them to continue shifting those patterns?

Chapter 6

Recognizing and working well with emotions

We're all human and many factors will influence how we feel about what's going on during change: our current role, our previous experiences of change, what we may gain or lose from this change, as well as what is happening in our personal lives. Being able to recognize and understand your own emotions, as well as those of others, is helpful as a leader. It is even more important in leading change. Yet emotions are often ignored in the work place. In this chapter, we explore why this might be and then offer a way of understanding your own personal drivers which will affect how you respond to change. This increased personal awareness can give you more choice about how you respond to the emotions and behaviours of others, rather than relying on your default mode.

Much of the latest thinking about the emotional responses to change has its roots in what was ground-breaking research into bereavement undertaken by Swiss psychiatrist Elisabeth Kübler-Ross[1] in the 1960s. We share two different but related frameworks that can help you make sense of the emotions people are likely to experience at different times during change and transition. We then introduce some very practical ways that you as a leader can support others to help them move on from the past.

We conclude with an approach to change called Appreciative Inquiry which involves engaging others in inquiring into what works well and using these strengths as the foundation for change. This can help you shift the emotional context in which you are working by offering an alternative to the deficit, problem-based way of going about improvement which can leave people feeling everything is in the 'too hard' or 'why bother' box. Appreciative Inquiry can transform the emotional subtext of doom and despondency into one of real, but grounded, energy and excitement for the new and the future.

The role of emotions in change

Research from boardrooms to project teams has consistently found that people's emotional responses, personal biases and feelings significantly influence decision making in organizations, albeit often unconsciously. Psychologists such as Kahenman[2] and management theorists such as Andrew Campbell[3] show that we are not nearly as rational and logical as we may like to believe. Yet the world of work tends to privilege reason, logic and numbers. Within some professions, such as engineering, banking and accountancy, this pattern is often particularly pronounced. We recently overheard a finance manager refer to people as costs on two legs. Human capital is another phrase that invites us to see people as assets, as sources of value rather than individuals with what Mary Beth O'Neill calls, 'backbone and heart'.[4] In Chapter 1, we looked at the way that seeing organizations through the machine metaphor tends to de-people it so that the organization becomes a faceless and feeling-less construction, and the people who work there can be seen as cogs in the machine. This makes it easier to ignore the fact that those who show up each morning to process those invoices, plan that marketing campaign, hire those new nurses are people with emotions, feelings and moods.

However, like it or not, change is nearly always accompanied by strong emotions. This is because the content of the change - *what* is actually going to be different - can impact people's sense of identity, challenge deeply engrained habits and disrupt familiar patterns of relationships. This is why people rarely feel neutral about what is happening. The process of change, in other words *how* the change is introduced, also affects people's emotions. If people feel they have had a say in what happens, that they had some choice and some level of control, they are likely to experience less extreme emotional reactions than those for whom this has not been the case. Where there has been no choice, no engagement and limited communication, the loss of control and autonomy psychologically can put them in the role of victim.

Interestingly, many leaders, when we introduce the topic of emotions and change, immediately assume that we are referring to the more negative ones such as anger and denial, rather than positive ones such as excitement and enjoyment. Perhaps you did too? This might explain some of the reasons leaders often approach this topic with some trepidation. We've also heard comments like:

- We don't talk about emotions here. That would be seen as a sign of weakness.
- We're an engineering company. Need I say more?
- Emotions belong outside of work don't they? I deal in facts and figures.
- I'm a bloke so of course I don't deal with emotional stuff. Ask my wife.
- I'm a woman so I don't talk about emotions at work. I don't want to conform to the stereotype of women dealing with the soft, fluffy emotional stuff.
- I wouldn't know what to do if someone cried in front of me.
- Oh no - definitely not. Too tricky. Too unpredictable. Too time consuming.
- I'm not a psychotherapist so what on earth would I need to do?

First of all, some reassurance. We have worked with many leaders who were initially fearful about their own abilities in this area or were sceptical about the need or value that working with emotions might bring. However, after being exposed to the ideas in this chapter, they realized that there are simple actions that can be taken which make a significant difference. Much of this is about allowing ourselves to be human, to connect with others, and to give them space and time to connect with their own feelings. Context plays a part, in that industries and organizations have different 'emotional display rules' in the sense of norms around the expression of emotion. Cultures that emphasize the formal, the professional, and are very polite tend to be less comfortable with the expression of emotions. Yet, whatever your own context, the research and our own experience suggests that acknowledging and working with emotions can prevent change processes foundering and prevent individuals getting stuck. On a more upbeat note, creating the conditions for positive emotions to flourish can increase energy, innovation and motivation, and understanding your own emotional response can enable you to be more grounded and choiceful in how you respond to situations and other people's 'stuff'.

Understanding your own Personal Drivers

As children, we are subject to numerous exhortations, encouragements, reprimands and cajoling to try and shape our behaviour so we fit in and meet our parents' expectations of how we should behave. Phrases such as 'Be a good girl and do as you're told', 'Boys don't cry', 'Hurry up or you'll be late', 'Pull your socks up/tuck your shirt in/try and look smart', 'Don't grab' and 'Do your best' are phrases we are all familiar with. We may well have uttered something similar to our own offspring. And it's not just parents and carers who repeat such messages. So do other grown-ups around us when we are small. Over time we hear these social messages so often that they become internalized. They become part of us and the way we orientate ourselves in the world. Psychologists use the term socialization to refer to this process of learning to conform, or at least fit in, with society.

Kahler and Capers[5] categorize these social messages into five headings: Be Perfect, Be Strong, Hurry Up, Try Hard and Please People. These social messages are probably all recognizable to you, but the likelihood is that some will have greater personal resonance than others because you were exposed to them more frequently or perhaps some came with far greater rewards or sanctions attached. The term personal or behavioural drivers is apt because there is often a driven nature to the way people respond to these social level messages. This is because they carry a powerful conditional subtext from childhood – 'You are only OK and only acceptable if you are like this'.

Leaders have told us that the notion of personal drivers has helped them catch themselves in the moment, understand other people's emotions and explain occasional strong emotional reactions they experience. However, although our personal drivers can be helpful for us as adults to navigate our way in social situations, we often act them out automatically. In leading change, they can prompt us to respond in a default way, rather than pausing to think whether this is a helpful response right now or remember that each has a shadow side.

Let us look in more detail at each of the five drivers and explore how they may play out in change situations.

Be Perfect If you have a Be Perfect driver you are the sort of person who believes things should be the very best they can be. You strive for high standards and expect the same of others and you pay attention to detail to make sure that things are presented well. You get annoyed when documents have typos or the percentages on a graph don't add up to 100. With this behavioural driver, it can be difficult to delegate, as it can be hard to trust others to do as good a job as you would do. People with a Be Perfect driver can sometimes be seen by others as intense and picky. The messiness and unpredictability of change can be particularly stressful for those with this behavioural driver. There will also be a tendency to want the Rolls Royce solution when exploring options and it can be hard to trust others to come up with good ideas.

Be Strong Those who have a Be Strong driver are able to stay calm under pressure and are the people you want around in a crisis, as they remain emotionally detached, are great at problem solving and are reliable. Many doctors have this driver. The shadow side is that people with this driver can find it hard to ask for help or to admit any difficulty. Such people can therefore seem very private, uncaring, non-communicative or withdrawn. Their greatest fear is that if they show their vulnerabilities they will be scorned or rejected by others. In terms of change, the default for those with this driver can be to try and solve all the issues themselves, but in doing so they risk alienating or excluding others who can and would like to be involved.

Hurry Up Those with a Hurry Up driver love being busy and thrive when there is lots to do. They tend to be fast workers who respond well to short deadlines. The shadow side of this is that they will often delay starting something until it is urgent, and may then make mistakes if they are in too much of a hurry or have treble booked themselves – a fairly frequent behaviour in those with this driver. They find people who take a long time to get their words out rather annoying, and dislike silence or having nothing to do and too much time to think. Others can find such people frenetic, agitated and annoying when they make demands on colleagues to hurry up. They can also have the unfortunate habit of finishing people's sentences for them. The challenge for those leading change who have a Hurry Up driver is to slow down and recognize that others need time to think, to explore, to get up to speed with what is under discussion.

Try Hard People with this behavioural driver tend to be enthusiastic and put a great deal of energy and effort into projects. They are particularly great to have at the beginning of projects as, along with this enthusiasm, they are often creative and have a broad outlook. The shadow side is that they can sometimes put in much effort without necessarily achieving a great deal, and can create mountains out of proverbial mole hills, or easily get distracted. Their greatest fear is being told they haven't tried or are irresponsible. Others can see such people as sulky, rebellious, taking on more than they can handle. If you have a Try Hard driver, it is helpful to have others around you whom you trust, who will help you stop and evaluate whether the effort you are putting in is productive.

Please People Those with this driver like harmony. They are good team players who will try not to ruffle feathers unduly; they will be empathetic, helpful and encourage good relationships among others. However, this can mean that they are not always sufficiently assertive on their own account and can sometimes take on other people's issues. Being rejected, criticized or ignored are their greatest fears. Others can see such types as people who are unable to say 'no', get overly involved emotionally, and help others in order to feel better about themselves. The challenge for people with this driver, is to recognize and accept that when instituting changes it is impossible to please everyone, however uncomfortable that may be. A level of disagreement is inevitable, and the important thing is to neither avoid tough conversations nor take them personally.

A self-assessment questionnaire to help you identify your dominant drivers is included in Appendix 2. Questions to ask yourself include:

- When you are at your best, how do your dominant drivers manifest themselves?
- When you are under stress, how might these drivers create difficulties for yourself and others?
- Given what you have read and experienced, what aspects of change are you likely to enjoy and which are likely to trigger a stress emotional response?
- Thinking about someone you work closely with, how might thinking about their drivers and yours give you some insight into what sometimes causes tension in your relationship?

Your behavioural divers will have become integral to who you are, but being more aware of them means you are more likely to recognize when you are feeling strong emotions that have been triggered by one of your drivers so you no longer need be enslaved by them. You can use this knowledge productively to make alternative choices.

The change curve – the emotions evoked by loss

The death of a close relative is for many people one of the most painful experiences they ever encounter. In all societies, the display of strong emotions at such times is both accepted and expected, even if other rituals differ. It may seem incongruous to be talking about the death of a loved one in a book about change, but, in fact, research into the emotions of the bereaved led to the development of a framework for thinking about the emotional responses in work situations where there is a change and loss, all be it of a different kind and magnitude.

Elisabeth Kübler-Ross,[6] who we mentioned earlier in this chapter, noticed a predictable pattern of responses to the pain of losing a close relative. At the beginning there is shock and denial. A part of the bereaved person cannot believe that his or her relative is no longer alive. So he or she will still automatically set the dinner table for two; will see someone in the street that that person momentarily believes is the dead relative; will still buy the loved one's favourite chocolate.

Such responses, to someone not involved in the situation, can seem odd and illogical, but they are entirely normal for the recently bereaved. Shock and denial then develop into anger. This anger is often projected onto the person who has died. Phrases such as, 'How could he have left me? He knew I can't cope without him', are common. The anger can equally be turned in on the self, blaming themselves for not making their relative stop smoking or visit the doctor earlier. The anger, too, may be irrational in the sense that what happened was not the grieving person's fault, but, psychologically speaking, the anger is very, very real.

After anger comes grief, the low point, which can sometimes turn to depression. Then, sometime later, individuals begin to accept what has happened and integrate the reality of the situation into their identity and understanding of themselves. This does not mean that they return to how they were before the death, rather than they learn to adapt and live with the absence. This movement and the different emotions experienced are often mapped onto what is known as the change curve. See Figure 6.1 overleaf.

Kübler-Ross's extensive research found that this cycle of emotions was highly consistent. The vast majority of individuals emerge from the low point of grief to eventual acceptance of the situation. However, she found significant individual differences in the speed with which people moved through the cycle of emotions and in the depth of the low point – for some people sadness, for others depression, for a few suicide. In addition, a further difference was that some people went through the cycle in a relatively straightforward order, one might almost say text book fashion; others 'cycled back' to re-experience the emotions associated with earlier stages. She theorized that these differences were related to variables, such as whether the bereaved individual had access to a strong support network and the individual's own

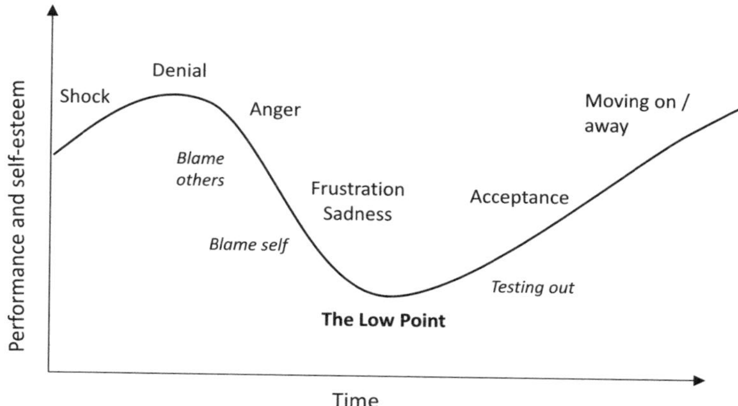

Figure 6.1 The change curve. Adapted from Kübler-Ross, Sugarman et al.

psychological resilience prior to the death: if the bereaved person had been made redundant or lost other relatives recently, he or she was far less resilient psychologically and was more likely to stay longer in the grip of negative emotions.

Subsequently, researchers found that this same cycle of emotions is triggered by life events in general and triggered by positive as well as negative events.[7] Being promoted would generally be seen as a positive event but it can still be accompanied by shock – 'I can't believe they've chosen me' – and some denial – 'Surely there's been a mistake. Bill is much better than me.' When you find out that the salary increase is less than you thought or that a key team member has a new job elsewhere, the emotional accompaniment can then become one of anger and frustration. However, with time, individuals move on, accept the situation, test out the new role and then integrate it into daily life so that they no longer consider it a change.

We could imagine the same cycle of emotions for an individual prompted by news of a restructure. There may be shock when it is announced because the last one was only nine months ago. This may later be followed by denial that your mentor, Derek, can really be going ('Surely not?') and that the CEO's protégé could possibly be given such a massive promotion ('No way!'). This can quickly turn to anger: 'Derek going will mean you won't have that senior level access anymore'; 'Derek didn't breathe a word of this when you saw him recently' and 'you really don't like that protégée who is arrogant and too clever by half'. Then, after further communication, it becomes clearer that you are going to have a new boss and that your product-based sales team is going to be split geographically. So you're still angry, now because you weren't involved in this decision-making and you have put in so much effort to build the team which is now going to waste. You are now also sad: you like your sales team and don't want to see half of them go over to your colleague, whom you don't rate. You've got a new boss, too; this will evoke more emotions depending whose stories you believe and your own assumptions about her. Two months on, depending on how your meeting with the new boss went and what you and Derek talked about, you are likely to be in a different place emotionally while still able to say, if asked, how you felt at different times since the announcement.

This story illustrates the complexity of emotions experienced by all of us at particular moments during change. It also shows that emotions rarely fit exactly as the model suggests, but the change curve is a useful reminder of the general pattern we all experience. It also attunes us to our own emotional responses, as well as to that of others.

It is perhaps worth saying a few additional words about the denial stage, which sometimes confuses people. Denial can last hours, days, weeks or even months. Kübler-Ross herself writes that denial 'functions as a buffer after unexpected shocking news'[8] until the individual can mobilize other resources. In the context of organizational change it tends to mean turning a blind eye to the full implications of new developments or hesitating to accept the personal implications. One researcher uses the term 'minimizing':

> 'It's a mistake', 'it could be temporary', 'this wasn't deliberate', 'I don't believe they'll go through with it', 'I can't believe it', 'this isn't happening!', 'it won't have a big impact', 'it won't affect me', 'it's still the same job'.[9]

Practical actions to mitigate the risks of ignoring emotions

In our experience, there is much you can do as a leader of change to support people through the emotions of the change curve, even though you cannot prevent them experiencing the feelings. Before we explore this, it may be worth acknowledging that we've heard other leaders say:

- I get the change curve and all that, but why do I need to get involved in this?
- Surely, everyone is an adult and they just need to get on and deal with this emotional stuff themselves.
- This really isn't my area – we have HR for this kind of thing.

Chances are that if these thoughts were going through your mind, you may have a Be Strong driver – you wouldn't ask for help so why should you need to give it to others? You may have a Hurry Up driver – can't we just get on with the task rather than faffing around with all this emotional stuff? You may have a Be Perfect driver – I wouldn't know enough about emotions to feel competent to deal with all of this, so better to leave well alone. You may have a Please People driver and dislike the idea that you won't be able to make everything fine for everyone.

There is significant research evidence that suggests ignoring the emotional aspects of change can have a detrimental impact on the success of a change programme and the future energy and creativity of people within the organization. This is in addition to ethical considerations related to the well-being and humane treatment of employees. Prolonged restructuring, retrenchment and down-sizing can lead to a predominance of depressed employees who see no future within the organization and develop ingrained negative emotions, often referred to as **toxic emotions**.[10] Employees can also experience **change fatigue**.[11] These and other negative feelings can perpetuate and spread because of a further phenomenon which researchers refer to as **emotional contagion**. This is the idea that we are all affected by the emotions experienced and expressed by others around us. If most people around us are angry, this can keep our own anger alive too. Treating people well by acknowledging and helping them work through their emotions can also reduce the likelihood of '**survivor syndrome**',[12] where those who remain after redundancies experience guilt and other negative emotions.

You may well be asking what you can do as a leader to acknowledge and work with emotions. In this next section, we offer a range of ideas.

1. **Share the change curve with others**
   Share the change curve with people so they can make sense of their own emotions, rather than trying to second guess them yourself. We have sometimes drawn the change curve on the flip chart or, even better, given out paper copies and asked people in pairs to discuss where they are now, where they were and to think about what has helped them move on in similar situations in the past. Sometimes we create a large change curve on the floor using string and sticky tape to mark it out. People can then be encouraged to stand where they are feeling now, where they were, say, a month ago, etc. If a group knows and trusts each other this more public conversation works. If you are unsure, or you think some people may feel anxious talking about emotions, the paired conversation may be psychologically safer. It is important to give individuals a chance to say as much or as little as they want to. As a leader, your role is to listen and acknowledge the emotions expressed. If you have a Please People driver, it is important not to try and make them feel better, tempting though that may be – chances are that is not in your gift anyway – and if you have a Be Strong driver resist the temptation to judge. Sharing, briefly, your own emotional responses to the change may also be helpful in that it may legitimize talking about emotions and show that you are in this too.

   The benefits of sharing the change curve include:

   - It reassures people that it is normal to experience emotional responses to change.
   - It can subtly shift assumptions about the acceptability of emotional expression at work.
   - It can reinforce the message that change is really happening, which may be a helpful nudge for any who are still in denial.

- It signals to staff that you understand what they may be feeling.
- The notion of movement through stages emphasizes the point that employees will be experiencing different emotional reactions allowing individuals to own where they are rather than feeling they need to conform to group norms.

This last point is particularly helpful if you are working with some people who are closer to the change than others. Managers for instance may know more about impending changes than their staff and will have had longer to adapt to it. A metaphor we often use with leaders is that of a train entering a tunnel. Those leading the change are often out the other side in the sunshine while everyone else is still in the dark. It is, therefore, important to remember that how you feel right now may be because you have had longer to acclimatize to the change, and others will need time.

2. **Identify the different places people might be on the change curve so you can adapt your gestures accordingly**
The change curve can be used as a rough guide to where other people might be emotionally, if you pay really good attention to how people are talking and behaving. To make this easier, we divide the change curve somewhat arbitrarily into four quadrants.

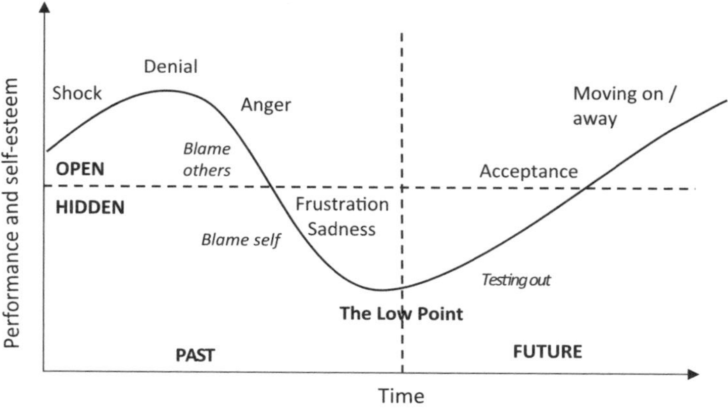

Figure 6.2 Analysing the change curve in more detail. Adapted from Wiggins.[13]

When individuals or groups are to the left of the midpoint on the curve they are still rooted in the old world, the 'as was'. If you listen carefully you will notice that their conversation tends to be dominated by reference to the past and how things were. They are likely to speak in the past tense, reminiscing, starting sentences with phrases such as 'When Fred was in charge ...,' 'We used to ...'. You may think that they are looking at the past through rose-tinted spectacles, but your role here as a leader is to notice where they are rather than challenge or rebut. When people are on the right hand side of the curve, their orientation, and therefore the way that they talk, is much more future orientated; they will talk in the future tense and use verbs such as 'will', 'could' and 'might'.

The curve can also be bisected horizontally. When people are in the top half of the graph, they will talk more openly about how they feel, whereas when they are in the bottom half their emotions are likely to be more hidden. The real danger zone for individuals – and indeed organizations – is lingering too long in the bottom left hand corner where it is hard to reach people and where, from an organizational perspective, resistance can sometimes harden into sabotage. This is also where, from an ethical perspective, depression can take on a more clinical and worrying nature, even leading to suicide.

3. **Listen and communicate when news of change breaks**
If people are in the top left quadrant, two things are really important – giving information and listening. Communicate, communicate, communicate is one of the key requirements. Communication means both giving what information is available and crucially also listening to people's reactions. When news breaks, it is often done in large group meetings to ensure that everyone hears at the same time, but people rarely remember much of the detail.

In our experience, leaders are often frustrated when they are told they need to keep repeating the rationale for the change or the key milestones. 'But I've told them all before', they wail. Yes, you might have told them before but this does not mean that everyone has heard. Rather than listening to the leader, what often happens is that people are listening to their own inner worries. This is where the acronym WIIFM comes into play – 'What Is In It For Me?' People's immediate concern will be the personal implications – 'Will I lose my job?', 'Will I be able to pay the mortgage?', 'What will I say to my wife?' In such circumstances, people literally will not be able to hear what else is being said.

Later, even when there is no new news, it is vital to communicate that nothing has yet been decided or that you don't know yet what will happen next. This is much better than saying nothing, as an information vacuum creates more unease and rumours. For more on how to listen well, see Chapter 8.

4. **Offer support to individuals and toxic handlers**
When individuals are in the bottom left quadrant emotionally, it is likely that the news of the change has sunk in but they may still be experiencing a number of difficult emotions – anger, sadness, etc. Generally, what is required at this point is support. This is much more likely to be in one-to-one conversations than group sessions. However, let's be honest, as individuals we vary in our capacity, available time and willingness to listen to others' pain and support them. So, while you may be able to do some of this, the likelihood is that other people will also emerge who are able to fulfil this role. One researcher has named such people '**toxic handlers**',[14] who can be from any level in the organization. They emerge as the person that everyone goes to talk to. As this is an unofficial rather than a planned role, toxic handlers are rarely acknowledged or supported formally. They often themselves then suffer from stress due to their efforts on colleagues' behalf. So another important intervention you might want to make as a leader is to explicitly offer recognition, appreciation and encouragement to individuals who support others. You may well need to listen to the grapevine to find out who they are.

5 **Engage others in the future**
When people are in the left hand quadrants, they are not ready emotionally to hear about the future. When they are in the right hand quadrants, it is different. This is where being involved

and engaged in thinking about and shaping change can be enormously helpful in accelerating people out of the negative emotions of the change curve. Designing sessions, such as those covered in Chapter 7, can be helpful. You may also want to pay attention to what researchers call reframing.

6 **Reframe**
The way you talk about change will impact people's belief and confidence both in you as a leader and in the future. We are not suggesting that you need to become an orator along the lines of Winston Churchill or Martin Luther King, That style of oratory allows for no co-creation of meaning. Neither does the delivery of a vision by the single heroic leader. For the relational leader of change, what is needed is a story that gives enough confidence and meaning to the change that others want to be part of it, while staying grounded, authentic and open to adapting to what emerges. Reframing is acknowledging, not denying their experience, and inviting them to see it differently. This is 'sensegiving' as opposed to 'sensemaking' activity for a leader. It can be helpful when people are in the bottom-right quadrant and have passed through the initial phases of the change curve.

Reframing[15] is a metaphor borrowed from photography where the skilled photographer deliberately chooses certain angles to emphasize a particular point of view. Reframing as a leadership act means paying attention to the words you use and the stories you tell, noticing their emotional impact on others. It means deciding what to emphasize and what interpretation to offer about what is going on, from a process of trial and error. Experiment to see what seems to resonate with others and feels right for you. This is about signalling a sense of direction and purpose and indicates your intentions. It is not so much about managing meaning as you cannot control the meaning others will make of your gestures. However, it is sensegiving that is inviting others to see the situation differently and imagine new possibilities.

The impact of changing words is brilliantly illustrated in a YouTube video. A man sits on a street with his collecting tin.

The notice beside him says. 'I'm blind. Please give generously'. A few coins clatter into his collecting tin. A woman comes by and rewrites his sign. Suddenly the coins are showering in. When she comes back later in the day, he realizes it is her by touching her shoes. He asks her what she wrote on his sign. The camera pans to the sign: 'It's a beautiful day and I can't see it.'[16]

So as a leader, to help people move from the bottom-left quadrant along the curve, you may need to raise the mood rather than just reflect it; you may need to honestly and authentically acknowledge difficult or disturbing news, but at the same time you will need to remind people of some of the strengths or legacies of the past; you may need to amplify what is helpful and progressive and to acknowledge, but not give too much airtime to, voices of criticism and anger. This is a balancing act based on experience and experimentation. In highly emotional situations, it is important to remind yourself that you can never say anything that will get it right for absolutely everyone. We are in the realms of the good enough.

Working with transitions

Another useful framework for working with emotions during change is that of William Bridges.[17] The term 'transitions' was used by Bridges to refer to the emotional and psychological experience of change. While there are many links with the change curve, Bridges helpfully challenges the dominant orthodoxy of starting with the beginning. He argues that, paradoxically, what is needed first is to pay attention to helping people end well. This involves creating a process that helps people let go of old ways of doing things and their attachments to former colleagues, relationships and identities and to acknowledge the loss that this represents to them. This then allows them to move on psychologically. This is followed by a period of uncertainty, of being in limbo, which Bridges refers to as the neutral zone where there is often uncertainty about what next, individually and collectively. It is only from here that, psychologically and emotionally, people are able to start afresh with new beginnings. Bridges suggests that these three

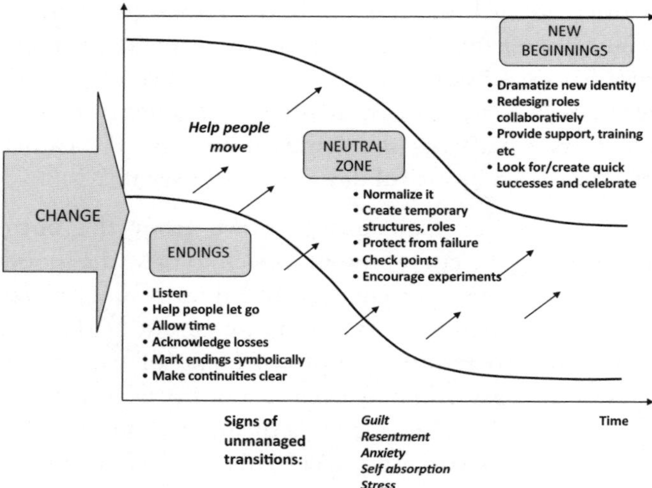

Figure 6.3 Transitions. Adapted from Bridges with input from Ashridge colleagues.

stages are not separated with clear boundaries. Rather one morphs into another so that they overlap, with movement through transition characterized by dominance rather than clearly differentiated boundaries, as can be seen in Figure 6.3 above.

Your role as a leader during endings

There are a number of gestures you can make to help yourself and others end well. Some suggestions are given below.

- Listen well and accept the reality of what others perceive as losses (even if you don't see them that way and think they are over exaggerating). It can be tempting to try and reframe the losses positively but at this point people are not ready to hear this. They just need to you listen and acknowledge that you have heard what they are saying. (There is more on listening in Chapter 8.)
- Try and avoid re-stating the official benefits of the change or offering well-meant but well-worn clichés such as ' never mind', 'always look on the bright side', 'tomorrow is another day'. None of this is what is needed at this point.

- Don't be surprised at 'over-reaction' or people projecting their anger or sadness onto you. We talk more about the psychodynamics of projection and transference in Chapter 8. The key thing is to try not to become defensive - this is their stuff not your stuff. Instead, what can be helpful is to acknowledge that you can hear how emotive this is, and to acknowledge the losses openly and sympathetically.
- Define what is over and what is not, in your view, but at the same time help others identify what is staying the same. This can create some sense of continuity of what really matters, despite the endings.
- Mark the endings and let people take a piece of the old way with them. This can be literally taking a physical thing, like a photo of a team that is disbanding, or it could be more metaphorical talking about what they wish to hold onto in their memory.
- Celebrate what was.

In Chapter 5, we mentioned the power of symbolic acts. As a leader, it can be really helpful to create a process that allows people to collectively grieve the loss of what is no longer there, with some ceremony and ritual. When the Ford assembly plant in Dagenham, Essex, closed in 2002, all employees were invited to be present when the last car came off the line. Everyone was given a chance to sign it and a party was then held to celebrate the past. The car now resides in the Henry Ford museum in Dagenham.[18] Events such as this are hugely significant in marking endings, unambiguously and respectfully.

As a leader, publicly acknowledging your own emotional response can be helpful, making it legitimate for others to show their feelings, too. The CEO of a bank that had been acquired invited all staff to a meeting in the atrium of the London office. It was six months into the merger. There was an expectation he would announce his departure. Some hoped he might 'dish the dirt on the new masters', others that he would try and sell the benefits of the merger and talk up the future. He spoke without slides, remembering key moments in his twenty-year history with the organization. He spoke of his pride in what they had achieved together and he thanked people. And at that point he paused and his voice faltered. It was one of those 'and you could hear a pin drop' moments. The pause seemed to last for an agony of seconds before he resumed with a wobbly voice naming his sadness at this ending, an ending he wouldn't have chosen. The response was audible in sniffing and quiet sobs and visible in a flurry of handkerchiefs and dabbing of eyes in a place where emotion never normally emerged. His voice got stronger and he made a joke, but something had shifted. A powerful gesture. A relational change moment that allowed people to transition psychologically and emotionally and recognize at a very deep level that something had ended.

Afterwards, he told a few of us that he was quite shocked at the palpable impact of his gesture. He hadn't planned to say what he did in quite the way it happened, but it was totally authentic and an example of him being in touch with his own experience and what was going on below the waterline for others. It allowed everyone, himself included, to end well and transition to the next stage.

Your role as a leader during the neutral zone

- Sharing Bridges' transition model can be particularly helpful when people are in the neutral zone, as people rarely understand why they feel so uncertain and uncomfortable. The model can help them recognize that what they are feeling is a 'normal' reaction which can in itself be reassuring.
- Encourage people to keep talking to each other, and to you, so that they do not become isolated. Scheduling some kind of regular meetings or calls can be helpful as it gives a light structure to the immediate future. In those calls, you may want to allow some time for people to share how they are feeling. There may be some desire to go over the past and that too can be fine. However, you will also need to judge how and when you make a gesture that encourages looking forward. Appreciative Inquiry can be a helpful way to do this because it focuses on the strengths of a situation (see later in this chapter).
- Recognize that it takes time to move from the neutral zone into new beginnings, and not everyone will do so at the same time. For some people, reminding them of what is staying the same can be helpful.
- Avoid premature closure. This is a real temptation for both you as a leader and for others. Being in the neutral zone can feel very uncomfortable so there can be a temptation to rush at anything that looks like it might be a way forward. In another model, that represents change as a house, this is acknowledged using the notion of 'the wrong direction door.'[19] So what is needed is to not hold onto

any option as *the* one. The language of experimentation and exploration is important here. More on this and creating Trojan mice in Chapter 9.

- Encourage exploration and activity about the possible futures. In the same Change House model, there is a basement called the 'pit of despair'. One of the other risks when people are in the neutral zone is that they do nothing and start to label themselves a victim of circumstances. This can trigger a particular unhealthy psychodynamic pattern called the drama triangle – more on this in Chapter 8.

Your role as a leader during new beginnings

- Design sessions that enable others to participate in creating the future. See Chapter 7 and read Emma's story in Chapter 13.
- Set out your intentions so that people can understand the rationale and the logic.
- Paint a picture of how it might look and feel so people can start to engage imaginatively and emotionally with what might be on offer.
- Give enough of a forward process so that people can see what the next steps are, but also ensure that they can see how they can help shape that future outcome.

Recognizing how you might feel as the leader of change

All of the above activities can help you as a leader work with the emotional responses of others. And what about your own feelings? There can be no getting away from the fact that sometimes leading change can be tough emotionally. In two recent pieces of research,[20] those responsible for downsizing programmes talked about the following emotional challenges. Here are some quotes:

Deceiving others

One woman came in and said, 'I know I'm going to lose my job'. She was an Office Support Manager. It was a position we could easily do without and she knew that, and I couldn't say anything, and she was a good friend of mine, too.

Making tough, uncertain decisions

Very difficult ... when you're making decisions that are as serious as those ... not having a lot of time to evaluate people ... a lot of anxiety on my part and the other manager's part because it was not as clean a decision as you probably would have liked to have.

Dealing with others' emotional pain

People – they get upset, they get defensive, they get angry, they cry – it's just very difficult to sit here, at this table, with somebody across from me and tell them the bad news and have them go through all those feelings.

Empathy for victims

I sort of put myself in their shoes. And you know, felt 'Jeez, how would I feel if the same thing happened to me' is really what I kept dwelling on.

Being stigmatized

People stare at you funny, they won't even say 'Hello' to you. You know, they think you made the personal decision yourself ... What was my name for it? A grim reaper ...[21]

The purpose of sharing this is to acknowledge that working with emotions – your own and others' – can be one of the more challenging aspects of change. In Chapter 10, we look at ways of attending to your own emotional needs and resilience.

Changing the mood – a brief introduction to Appreciative Inquiry

A key premise of a relational approach to change is that how and what we talk about shapes our perceptions of reality. In Western societies, a dominant approach to change or improvement is to start by looking at what went wrong. In this deficit based approach, we begin by identifying problems, critical incidents and near misses, and then analyse what went wrong so that improvements can be instigated. However, think about how you feel when someone comes with a problem – perhaps a sense of heart sink, or annoyance, or frustration, particularly if it is an ongoing problem. The more we focus on what went wrong, the more that problems and difficulties become all that we see. They become our reality.

Appreciative Inquiry[22] is underpinned by the principle that 'to discover and theorize about the life-giving properties of organizations – what is happening when they are operating at their best – is more likely than problem solving to lead to innovation'.[23] In the 1980s, David Cooperrider, Frank Barrett and Suresh Srivasta at Case Western Reserve University, Ohio, were working on a consulting project for the Cleveland Clinic. The hotel attached to the specialist medical centre was beset with problems and there was a culture of blame and recrimination. Cooperrider and his colleagues noticed that the more the problems were discussed, the larger they loomed in everyone's consciousness and the more staff and leaders seemed submerged in a sense of hopelessness. Cooperrider and his team broke the stuck pattern by taking staff to visit a high-quality, high-performing hotel nearby, but with the instruction that employees could ONLY ask about what led to the hotel's success and explore what enabled them to keep performing well. Once the employees had become trained and practised in asking positive, rigorous inquiry questions, they were invited to turn their attention to their own hotel, but again, to only identify what was working well, looking for sources of strength and success. Attempting to solve problems was not allowed.

Through this project, and other work, Coopperrider and his colleagues created an approach to change called Appreciative Inquiry, often abbreviated to AI.

> AI involves, at its root, the art and practice of crafting questions that support a system's capacity to apprehend, anticipate and heighten positive potential. AI is a quest to discover the 'positive core' of a system – the past, present and future capacities to co-operate for the common good.[24]

Two shifts that are important here: one is from advocacy to inquiry, as explored in Chapter 3. The other is to shift from problem solving and deficit talk to an appreciative stance. In deficit-thinking advocacy, people say 'I think the problem with this is', 'We should have done it differently', 'This won't work because ...' or 'We've tried that before'. In deficit-thinking inquiry, people ask, 'What is the main problem?', 'Why is this not working?' and 'What are the barriers?'

The alternative is Appreciative Inquiry:

- How can we develop more of this?
- What do you think made it work on that occasion?
- What are the enablers of this?

Followed by Appreciative Advocacy:

- This is working really well.
- The right way to do this is.
- It will work even better if you do it this way.

Most people, whether asking or answering appreciative questions, are surprised at how energizing it is to have conversations about what works when they or the team are operating at their best. What differentiates Appreciative Inquiry from wishful thinking and general optimism is that it focuses on exploring *real* examples of positive events in the past or present and thoroughly and rigorously understanding what enabled them to go well. Through systematic appreciative story gathering and storytelling come new ideas for possible actions in the present, a confidence to experiment, and a belief and energy to create a change that builds on existing strengths and practice. Difficulties and pain are acknowledged, but are not central to the conversation or amplified. However, this requires everyone, especially leaders, to be open to what emerges rather than trying to control or second guess.[25]

Appreciative Inquiry has been encapsulated into a five-step method known as the 5D-cycle that includes the following phases: definition, discovery, dream, design and destiny. However, we have found Appreciative Inquiry very helpful even if you do not want to follow the full method. Ways of using it include:

- Start meetings by asking people to share something they have done that they are proud of.
- End meetings by exploring what went well in the meeting and what people would like more of next time (keep to the appreciative by *not* asking what went less well!).
- Plan specific times during the life of a change project to regularly explore and inquire into what is working well and what is enabling this to happen.

Appreciative Inquiry thus makes a shift away from problem solving, root cause analysis and the prescriptive action planning which is a hall mark of a directive approach to change. With the appreciative approach there is a focus on examples of excellence, solution orientations into what is possible, with implementation focused on increasing conditions for success and encouragement of experimentation. In our own work with Appreciative Inquiry, one of the most rewarding aspects is seeing the way the approach creates real but grounded energy and enthusiasm that is infections – a positive example of emotional contagion.

Questions for further reflection

- How do your own personal drivers impact the change you are currently working on?
- Track you own reactions to a change in your life using the change curve. How long were you in each phase and what helped you move on?
- What has helped you in the past deal with loss or being in the neutral zone? How might you use that experience in your work with others?
- What opportunity could you give people to talk about how they are feeling about the changes?
- Who are the toxic handlers in your organization and what could you do to recognize what they are doing and support them?
- How might you build an Appreciative Inquiry approach into what you are doing?

Chapter 7

Re-imagining meetings: How to encourage dialogue and thinking together

Organizational life requires us to work with other people. You probably do some of your connecting with others through email and over the phone, but the chances are that much of your time is taken up in meetings of some kind. When we ask leaders to stand in a line to illustrate how much of their time is spent in meetings some say it is 20 per cent, for others it is 80 per cent or 90 per cent. What about yourself? In this chapter, we look at practical ways of re-imagining meetings to enable you and others to have the conversations you need to progress the change effort; sessions which often need to be different from the standard fare. We explore how to set the tone before people even arrive; the basic structure of sessions; ways of starting and ending well; how to create variety and pace, and how to help groups make decisions. Our intent is thus to give you the practical 'know-how' to create the conditions for yourself and others to have a different kind of meeting where you can engage in change and thinking together.

You might you want to create a different type of meeting for all manner of reasons.

- You might have looked at the different stakeholder groups you need to influence and thought that there are no regular meetings where such a group convenes.
- You may be hearing very different views about 'what's going on' in relation to the change and want to surface this rather than hoping it goes away.
- The existing, formal meeting structures may not seem to be giving people the opportunity to explore ways forward.
- There may be too much other business-as-usual to cover in regular meetings.

- Something significant is about to happen, or has happened, and you want to create an opportunity for people to start to come to terms with the situation.
- You want to encourage some creativity and innovation around a thorny problem and therefore want a different cast of characters to normal.
- A decision is needed and you want to involve others so they will understand the challenges and reasons for the decision, rather than sniping from the side.

In the complex responsive processes way of looking at organizations, change happens through conversation, as explored in earlier chapters. Patricia Shaw,[1] for instance, describes conversation as being 'the key process through which forms of organizing are dynamically sustained and changed'. Issacs[2] talks about dialogue being a conversation with no sides. In this chapter, we explore the practicalities and different steps required to create a different kind of meeting or session.

The choices that make the difference

Who needs to be invited?

If you've decided to hold a session that is not part of the standard pattern of meetings, you will have many choices about whom to invite. You might draw on the stakeholder map if you have one. You may also want to consider:

- Who will need to have a say in what happens because it will involve some aspect of their work?
- Who could bring an 'outsider' perspective to help people see the situation through the eyes of customers or other stakeholders?
- Who could be invited because they are influential? They might have positional or expert power or be someone that is popular and well networked.
- Is there enough diversity for there to be creativity and some 'grit', rather than people who will just agree with each other?
- Who is 'on your side'? A trusted colleague with whom you can run through how it went afterwards?

How to encourage people to come?

It can sometimes be hard to get people to attend a meeting or event that is an additional time commitment. People are busy, diaries are full; not everyone may work at the same physical location. However, there are a number of small, practical gestures that can encourage participation. For instance, ensuring the tone is engaging and welcoming is important. So is being clear, although concise, about why you are holding the session and what role you are wanting others to play. This is a vital aspect of ensuring that others' expectations match yours. Are they being asked to come to share their perspectives on a topic? To come up with creative ideas? To shape the next steps? To be part of a decision-making group? To give feedback on a particular proposal? Being clear about your intentions requires some thought but people are more likely to come if you do.

In our experience, relying purely on an email invitation is often a reason for people not attending a session. A more personal approach means people feel greater connection to you and the issue even before they have arrived. You may take the chance to speak to people when you bump into them in the corridor. You may want to deliberately seek out those whom you think might be a bit reluctant to come or whom you really want to attend. Pull rather than push is important here. If people feel there is lots of arm twisting and push from you, they may still come to the session, but may do so with some resentment, depending on the power dynamics between you. Or they may believe that in the session others won't be interested in what they have to say because that is how they have experienced you.

In these back-stage conversations, you are setting the tone for the session itself; you are also 'doing' some change work, because the conversations you are having to encourage people to come are in themselves already shifting the nature of how people think and feel about the change. It will be altering what they know about the change, regardless of whether they attend the session, or not. Feeling you have gone out of your way to invite them to a session, makes people much more likely to come. At the same time, asking individuals what they'd like to get from the event gives you useful information about where people are 'at' in relation to the issues. This allows you to think about how you may wish to adapt the session, given what you are now hearing, or it may give you the opportunity to 'correct' any unrealistic expectations or misunderstandings about the session.

If some people decline, you may want to find out why, and ask them how they'd like to be kept in the loop about what happens at the session. Again, this is a small gesture but it indicates a desire to keep the connection.

What to call it?

Depending on your context, there will already be words to describe the type of event you are designing. How you choose to describe your session will already start creating a certain expectation. So, you might refer to the session as a workshop, a meeting, a gathering, a conversation, an offsite and away day or, indeed, you may have some other term in mind altogether. Each of these labels will have particular connotations both for you personally and culturally for those where you work. Think about what you are wanting to signal with your choice of name.

A one- off or part of a series?

You may see your first meeting as something of a pilot or experiment so you might want to hold off making any commitment to run more. Alternatively, you may already know that this is the first of a series of events. Communicating this up front is helpful as it signals your intent clearly. See Emma's story in Chapter 13.

Where to hold it?

This will depend on what is practically available in your context. We have found it is worth thinking seriously about this rather than just delegating it to someone else. There will also be cultural norms, so you need to consider the extent to which you want the session to challenge these. Do you want to hold the session in the nicer of the two hotels in town, as you want people coming to feel that they and their input are really valued? What would be seen as a treat for some but might be seen as an extravagance by others? While we can never predict or control how everyone will react, it is worth giving some thought to the potential symbolic meaning of the location. Practicalities are really important too: How easy is it to get there? Is there ample parking? If not, people will arrive late and flustered so the session won't start well. Is there natural light? If not people can tire more easily and feel de-energized.

What happens when not everyone can attend?

Once you've decided to hold a different kind of meeting, it can be frustrating when it seems the only time everyone can attend is next year. We have a couple of phrases that serve us well in such situations. One phrase is 'some is better than none', the other is 'the right people are the people who are right here'. Both phrases encourage us to stay focused in the present and attentive to those who have arrived. This is far more helpful than worrying about why others haven't shown up, or getting angry with them for prioritizing other things or indeed chastizing ourselves for having not written a better invite. We have also found that sometimes a different or smaller combination of people than we had anticipated can yield wonderful conversations and insights. And, of course, your session is part of an unfolding situation so the success of the change does not hang solely on this one meeting. If you know in advance that influential decision makers are not able to make the date, it may be worthwhile having a back stage conversation with them before hand to hear their thoughts so they can be included.

The challenge and expense of getting everyone in a room together may lead you to decide that you need to run a session virtually. A book specifically on virtual sessions by Ghislaine Caulat is mentioned in the Further Reading list in Appendix 3 on page 281.

Running the session yourself or using a facilitator?

As with all aspects of relational change, there are no hard and fast rules but there are choices to be made. You may find there is no money to hire an external facilitator, or your organization may not have an organizational development department whose skills you can draw on. You may feel that designing and running the session is a learning experience for you and the very reason that you bought this book.

Alternatively, you may want to use a facilitator because, as a leader, you are so involved practically and emotionally in the change that it would be hard to notice what is going on for others or to hold back from joining in the discussions. Useful questions to help you decide whether to run the session yourself or have a facilitator include:

- Do you feel strongly about the issues that are going to be discussed and want to be part of the conversation?
- Do you have particularly strong relationships with some people in the group, be they positive or negative?
- Do you have a vested interest in a particular outcome that could emerge from the conversation?
- Do you have a hunch that anyone in the group will censor or change what they say if you run the session because of your perceived expert or positional power?
- Do you feel wary about the idea of challenging what's going on in the group during the session?
- Do you feel there is a potential split in the group or several sides to an argument where you are seen as being aligned to one side?

If your answer is 'yes' to any of these questions, it would be worthwhile bringing in someone else to run the session.

A halfway house may be to have a co-facilitator. This can help with pace and add variety to the day. It can also enable you to be involved as a participant in certain parts of the agenda. If there is a need to redesign the session because of what is emerging in the room, having someone else to process what is going on and think through the options can be hugely helpful and supportive (see Joe's story in Chapter 12.)

Getting input into the design of a session

To plan a session, it is helpful to get input from those who will be attending. In the stories in the second section of the book, Joe and Damian (Chapter 12) did this through interviewing everyone on the Board and Emma (Chapter 13) created a project group to plan and organize engagement sessions. What's your equivalent? Speaking to people whom you know hold a different perspective to your own can be helpful, as is noticing your own feelings about the session. Are you excited? Anxious? Both? This, too, is useful data.

Designing the day

It may sound paradoxical, but one of the reasons for thinking about the different elements of the meeting in advance is that this gives you the confidence to flex the structure on the day in response to what emerges in the room. In our experience, the more you have really thought through what you want to achieve, and have planned the session in detail, the more you are able to deviate from the plan in the moment. It's a bit like being a jazz musician; being able to improvise takes a great deal of practice, and the improvisation has a frame around it, a structure within which it occurs.

A helpful framework for planning a session is known very simply as the ABCDE framework.[3] (It is equally useful for planning an important conversation or communicating key messages about change.) The letters stand for the following:

A - Audience.

B - Behaviour

C - Content

D - Design

E - Evaluation

The beauty of this framework is that it encourages you to be iterative as you develop your thinking and planning. Rather than starting with what you want to achieve, it reminds you to start with others, with the 'A' for 'audience'. So what do they know already? What are their feelings likely to be when they turn up to the session? If you have been able to speak to people who are coming to the session you can check out your assumptions about at least some of the audience.

The 'B' stands for 'behaviour'. Imagine how you want people to feel when they leave the session. What do you want them to think, feel and do as a result of their participation? Thinking about this can help you clarify the purpose of the event. It can also help you sense-check your session design when you've completed it. You may also need to consider the culture and norms where you work. If people's natural instinct is for debate and 'move' and 'oppose', to use Kantor's terms,[4] you may need to plan in some exercise to encourage or enhance people's listening skills. (See Chapter 8 for ideas.)

Then you need to begin to articulate the key themes or topics that you think the session needs to cover. This is the 'C' – 'content'. In thinking about the order of presenting ideas the following questions may be helpful:

- What is the current *situation*?
- What is the *complication*?
- Therefore what is the *question*?[5]

As an example, Joe and Damian, in Chapter 12, identify from their preparatory work a chronic and paralyzing lack of connection between Board members. A key aim of their session was thus to give people the opportunity to develop some meaningful connections. Thinking how to do this was part of their content discussions in their design meeting.

Next 'D' for 'design'. A general structure would include connecting with each other, exploring the issues in ways that encourage listening, personal and group reflection, and closing with an opportunity to consider what action will be useful after the session. In creating the design, the metaphor we find helpful is that of planning a special meal. We have already discussed where you might be serving the meal and who is coming. The focus in this section is what hors d'oeuvres and appetisers would get people in the right mood to enjoy the main course – meat and two veg – and what do we want people to go away with – dessert and chocolates! As with a meal, there needs to be variety in pace, flavour, texture:

- Begin by framing the session, reminding people of the context and specific purpose of meeting together.
- Collectively agree to an outline agenda and ground rules, boundaries, 'hygiene' factors such as timing.
- Encourage people to connect, to introduce themselves and to arrive psychologically.
- 'Meat and two veg': ways of exploring the substantive topics and issues as a group.
- Pudding and coffee: finish by bringing the conversations and discussions to some kind of resolution or understanding of where the

group has got to, as well as an agreed understanding about what to do next.

When we use the word 'finish', we are not suggesting that everything will be resolved or solved in one session. We mean 'finish' for that particular meeting and agreeing what next together. This can range from agreeing there's a need to explore things more deeply, through to making a decision to take a particular action, or acknowledging where there is agreement and where there are differences. We make this point because we have worked with leaders who tried to do too much in one session, and we've been guilty of this ourselves sometimes. If you have overly high expectations you can cause yourself unnecessary stress, especially if you have a Hurry Up driver. Equally, it can give those attending a session the feeling that they are being pushed rather than engaged. It is often a case therefore of 'less is more'.

A session design may look something like Figure 7.1

We now look at some of the choices you have in creating your own design at each stage of the session, along with some practical tips from our own experiences.

Welcome and outline of the session	10mins
Check in and agreeing ground rules for the session	10–30mins depending on group size
Getting to know who is in the room (especially important in situations where groups don't know one another well)	10–30mins depending on group size
Clarifying and agreeing purpose, outcomes, key timings. Understanding the different perspectives in the room	15–30mins depending on group size
Getting into detail and depth. Exploring multiple perspectives. Small group and larger group discussions	30mins–1hr depending per topic(s)
Reflecting together on where the conversation has taken us to	20–30mins
What next: • Taking a decision • Agreeing next steps	30mins–1hr depending on topic(s)
Check out	10mins
Thank you, and next steps	5-10mins

Figure 7.1 An example of a session design.

Beginning: Setting the frame for the session

The first part of your session should:

- Give people a clear understanding of the purpose of the session and an overview of how it will run. This enables people to concentrate on taking part rather than wondering why they are there and what is going to happen.
- Create an atmosphere that is going to help people engage in the conversation that is needed.

Begin by thanking people for coming, reiterating the purpose of the session and broadly outlining how the meeting will run. We've seen leaders sometimes so keen to get going that they forget this step. In outlining the session, confirm end time and any breaks for tea/coffee. There's no need to go into the detail about each section of the session; it is enough to explain what you are hoping to cover during each part (think here of safe uncertainty). We tend to avoid committing publicly to precise timings for each section, even though we may have them in our plan. This is because you can then respond flexibly to the energy and interest in the room and you avoid having to apologize for not sticking to the agenda. It can also be very helpful to remind people that this session is part of an unfolding journey and that you are not expecting everything to be resolved in one meeting - this too can take the pressure off.

Introductions

In some respects, this may seem such an obvious thing to do it shouldn't need stating. However, it can be easy to overlook the fact that even if *you* know everyone, not everyone will know everyone else. The simple gesture of ensuring everyone knows who is in the room is one that symbolically validates everyone's presence. This may just require checking if everyone does know each other or do a names round the room. With larger groups you may want people to just introduce themselves to people sitting next to them or at their table.

The Mexican Wave is a technique which works well with any size of group but is especially effective with large groups. Individuals are asked to take it in turns round the room to stand up and say their name and organization and then sit down again. This works well when it is done with speed so we recommend not asking people to say too much. Whenever we've done this, it creates a good sense of buzz and energy right from the start. Using a technique called 'constellating' is another way of creating some physical energy or movement at the beginning of a session with quite large groups. As well as creating energy, it simultaneously helps the group to get to know something about each other. More details on constellations are included in the section on exercises at the end of the chapter. The key thing here is to judge what will help you create the right mood. Anything too whacky may alienate some people or may suggest that you are trivializing what are going to be serious discussions. Both your judgement and some experimentation are needed.

Check-in

After welcome and introductions, you may want to include a check-in as a means of helping people begin to concentrate on the here and now, to help them let outside distractions diminish so they have psychologically arrived and are ready to listen to each other. The notion of check-ins developed as part of dialogue theory, as discussed in Chapter 3. Groups that know each other well may need little prompting, but for others, you, as the leader, may want to offer a question.

Questions might be:

- What are your hopes for the session?
- How are you feeling as you arrive into this session?
- How has your week been so far?

Use your judgement about which question to use. If you start with formalities and job roles, people will find it harder to talk from their personal perspective and things may stay in the realm of formal power, roles and responsibilities. It will be harder for people to say what they are really thinking and feeling. You might, therefore, choose something more fun and light hearted. Check-ins are not really about having a group conversation, more about preparing for such a conversation, so ask people to just listen rather than reply to what others say. There is no need to go around the group in turn so you may want to invite people to speak when they want to. This reduces 'creeping death' which also limit people's ability to listen, as they become increasingly focused on what to say as their turn draws nearer.

Getting into the topic and making explicit the different perspectives in the room

To encourage people to talk about the topic at hand you may want to introduce some data or evidence, but if so, think about how this will 'land' and how much time people may need to process it if this is unfamiliar. If you are wanting to ensure that a variety of perspectives are heard it is generally helpful to emphasize this in your introduction to this part of the agenda, so that people know they are exploring and hearing different ideas rather than trying to reach decisions. You might want to give everyone an opportunity to describe where they are in relation to what's going on. You can do this during the check-in by asking people to share their hopes for the session. If you have a bigger group, an alternative approach is to use an exercise that illustrates the breadth of perspective in the room, such as constellations, or by inviting people to stand on an imaginary scale of 0 to 10 depending on their response to an issue or question (see end of chapter for more details).

The middle – getting into the heart of the discussion

The main part of the session is an opportunity for people to have a conversation that enables them to generate some new thinking together. What you need to achieve together as a group will influence how you design this part of the session. It is generally useful to include:

- Sharing of facts among participants.
- A chance to reflect on the current situation together from multiple perspectives (those of people in and outside of the room).
- A chance to explore new ideas and to sense what the future could hold.

Your intention here is to encourage empathetic and generative listening. If there are more than eight to ten people in the group it's useful to break up into smaller groups at this point, to give people an opportunity to have a fairly in-depth conversation together. This also varies the pace and rhythm of a session.

When working out what types of group exercises might help people develop a shared sense of what's going on, we find ourselves asking the question: what kind of discussion will we need to have at this point?

- Is there a real lack of understanding of each other's perspectives, which means we just need some time to begin to understand one another better, and so a conversation is what's needed?
- Is there disagreement about what to do next – do we need to articulate the various options and work out which ones are most feasible?
- Do we need to draw on people's energy and creativity to work out what to do next?

Exercises work best when they bring just enough structure and focus to enable the emergence of a conversation which matters and makes a difference. It's about finding the way to draw on people's energy and imagination in relation to the topic at that moment which is why a particular approach can work wonderfully in one session then not at all in another. Creative methods can work well when people are ready to think imaginatively together about a particular problem. However, if there are tensions related to the social, relational side of change that need surfacing, more creative exercises can feel superficial to participants.

How long you spend on the exploration of the issues will depend on the time you have available and where people are at in relation to the topic being discussed. Try and give people the chance to move between small and large group discussions. This enables them to have some detailed conversations with three or four people and then a large group reflection, giving the opportunity for a collective perspective to develop.

Include some time for personal reflection, too. Not everyone makes sense of what they're thinking solely through talking to others. Introverts would typically rather think things through before talking about them, as opposed to extroverts who like to talk things through with others as a way of developing their thinking. Allow some time for people to sit quietly, to write something down or draw something. Invite people to shut their eyes and notice what they are feeling as well as thinking. This often helps everyone, be they introverted or extroverted, to reflect on and clarify their thinking.

Techniques for feeding back

If you have split the group into trios or pairs, there is always the tricky question of how to manage the feedback process when you reconvene as a larger group. We are sure you have sometimes sat through energy sapping moments when every group laboriously goes through every single thing on their illegible flip charts. The liveliness of the previous discussions in smaller groups can bear no relation to what you now seem to be experiencing. We have found the following ways of managing feedback helpful:

- Ask for just three groups to feedback and then ask the rest to add *if* they have anything different to contribute.
- Invite people to put the key themes or ideas from their discussion onto post-it notes - one idea per post-it (use felt-tips or marker pens to write so that they are visible when you stick them up). Invite people to then put the post-its up on a wall and collectively group them to identify themes. This technique, for those of you interested in such things, is called meta-planning.
- Put up the flip charts the smaller groups have created in the coffee break and ask people to look at the 'gallery' and make comments or questions using post-it notes.
- Ask people to move round to the next flipchart with one person staying to explain/present to the next group.
- If people have been talking in pairs, you can ask them to join with another pair to share their conversation so that they are then talking as a four. You may then invite the groups of four to share back with the whole group, or indeed to first share with another four, depending how many people you have in the room.

The ending – converging the thinking

Towards the end of a session, it may be appropriate to move into some form of collective decision making. Agreeing the decision criteria explicitly up front before making the decision can be helpful. This enables people to voice assumptions they were perhaps otherwise unaware of. It also makes it easier to identify where any differences of opinion lie when moving into decision-making. Sometimes exercises can help this process and some are included at the end of this chapter. Often what is needed though is dialogue.

You may also want to create some time for people to articulate and clarify what they have learnt so far and what they want to do next as individuals. The ease of articulating 'what next' will depend on the nature of the conversation you've just had and where the group have got to. Sometimes it can be difficult to move people to action if the conversation has been rather abstract, or if people have got stuck on a particular issue. Drawing on Action Research approaches (see Chapter 10) encourages people to think about what they have learned personally as well as what they have learned from a group perspective. Helpful questions include:

- What possibilities for action, do I or we see, however small?
- What could I or we do about those possibilities?
- What's next for me or for us?[6]

We encourage you to hold off from trying to get everything neat and tidy with clear decisions. This may be possible, in which case – fantastic. If not, remember, change is complex and if the answer was simple it would have been sorted long ago. Rushing to closure prematurely can close down potential possibilities. Making a distinction between decisions and work in progress can be helpful and more than good enough. It may also be helpful to remind yourself and others that this session is part of an unfolding journey.

Bringing the session to a close

Leave time at the end to:

- Agree next steps.
- Check out.
- Thank everyone.

This can be done as a whole group in a circle, ending physically as you began. Agreeing next steps may be as simple as repeating what's gone before in terms of decision-making or discussions about possibilities for action. You could ask someone other than you to share what they think has been agreed, keeping ownership of action with the group. Beware of sharing what you think next steps are without seeking agreement from people in the group, otherwise the ending will feel less engaging.

You may want to invite everyone to share one or two words that capture how they are feeling as the session ends. This can be a useful way of illustrating that not everyone has had the same experience and reality is usually a mixture of perspectives. (You may also want to do a similar exercise mid-way through the session if you want to check how people are feeling, or are concerned that some people are not participating. This allows you to adapt to what is emerging and needed rather than waiting to find this out at the end.)

Finally, thank everyone for coming and participating.

If only it were that neat ...

In describing how a group session might go, it sounds quite neat, and yet this is not always our experience. We are again in the territory of relational change as art, not science. Sometimes too much is going on for people to be able to make sense of it all in one go. Or people are not yet able to move on from their current view and open themselves up to listening to others, or to using this time to think about the possible emerging future. If, in getting to the end of the session, it feels as if there are unresolved things going on, acknowledge that with the group. Share your perspective and invite others to share theirs. There is always a 'what next', even if this is a decision that the group needs to continue talking and thinking together.

As mentioned earlier, designing a session in detail allows you to go with the flow and adapt it during the session in response to what the group needs. Our encouragement here would be to trust yourself and the group. If, for example, you can sense that the energy is waning, or that doing the next exercise you had planned would disrupt the flow of conversation, go with what feels useful in the moment. This is where working with a co-facilitator is useful, as you can make sense of what is going on together. It can also be important to check this out with the group and involve them in the decision about what to do next so that you are being facilitative rather than directive, doing with rather than doing to.

The gestures and responses you make as the session unfolds will also have an impact on the way you and the participants experience the meeting. For example, there may be times when you need to exert some 'push', when people are going off at tangents for instance. There may be other times where you may to have to 'pull' the conversation where people are not so forthcoming. Adapting your own style can be as important as adapting the design. Chapter 8 explores further adapting your gestures to what is happening 'in the moment'.

More detail on useful group exercises

Constellations

A constellations exercise is a way of getting people standing up and moving into different parts of the room, creating energy, bringing informality and lightness to the atmosphere *and* giving participants the chance to learn more about each other.

To make this work, you need to choose a topic that relates to the reason for meeting and is easy for everyone to answer. If they have only just arrived and do not know each other, it would not be good to constellate around anything contentious. You might want to constellate around where people work geographically, so you point to one end of the room as John O'Groats and the other end as Lands' End. People are asked to stand where they work. This requires them to talk to other people to find a position. When everyone is in place, each person is given the opportunity to speak, saying their name and where they work and anything else that feels relevant in the moment. A variation is getting people to stand in their professional groups if you have a range of people in the room representing the whole system. Creating a circle from most recent joiner to the longest serving can be a good way of also surfacing what changes people have seen and getting the perspectives of different people. A couple of rounds are normally enough to create a good atmosphere and ensure that everyone has had a chance to speak.

Standing on a scale – making visible the variety of views in the room

Pose a question to the group which invites people to think about a particular issue on a scale of 0 to 10. For example 'On a scale of 0 to 10, with 0 being not at all and 10 being absolutely definitely, how likely do you think that the changes we're trying to make together are going to make a positive difference to x?' Ask people to imagine a line on the floor with 0 at one end and 10 at the other end. Invite people to stand up and place themselves on this scale in response to your question.

This is a good way of making visible the range of perspective in the room. Follow this up by asking people at the ends to share why they're standing where they are. Open up the discussion to the people in the middle. When people stand like this together, they are often more willing to share their perspective than when sitting down.

Polarities

See a description of how to create a polarity map in Chapter 2, page 39.

Using an appreciative approach

Appreciative Inquiry, explored in detail in Chapter 6, encourages people to focus on what is working well. Fry and Barrett, two of the main proponents of Appreciative Inquiry write: 'Relationships [...] come alive where there is an appreciative question, when there is a deliberate search for the good and the best in one another.'[7]

Framing questions in an appreciative way tends to encourage groups to talk about what is possible and creates a sense of energy, confidence and optimism. The more specific the questions are, and the more they are connected to people's experience, the more likely they are to result in a generative discussion. You might want to ask people to pair up and take it in turns to interview each other on a topic relevant to the session. For instance, if the theme is collaboration, the question could be something like ...

- Tell me about a time when you collaborated with others from across the organization and this worked well. What happened? What was your part in it? How did you feel about the work? What was the outcome that you achieved?

Once the pairs have interviewed each other and explored the themes, they are invited to share what they noticed and learnt with the wider group. This helps identify important themes in relation to the question.

Using visual or tactile creativity

Not everyone will find words are their natural medium of expression so it can sometimes be helpful to introduce variety into a session by asking people to draw or construct something physically as a prompt to creativity and further insights. In Chapter 2, we gave the example of asking people to draw change. Other examples include being asked to draw your department as a part of the body – this can enable people to access insights and feelings they were previously unaware of. Creating physical models with executive Lego can work well with some groups. The possibilities are endless.

You may find some people are initially reticent about such approaches, claiming that they are not creative or unable to draw. You can reassure people by being confident, relaxed and playful in your manner and being clear that it's not about producing something beautiful, but about using the approach to draw out fresh insights and ideas. Once people get going, they normally become absorbed in the activity. Afterwards, individuals need to be asked to explain their drawings/ models to the whole group with enough opportunity to discuss what strikes people as interesting or intriguing. Taking time to do this is vital and will normally prompt some interesting insights and conversations. Rushing on to the next thing without giving this time will leave people feeling unclear about why they were asked to participate in such an exercise in the first place.

Dividing people into groups

People can obviously self-select into different small groups but the risk here is that they may stay with those they know rather than using the opportunity to make new connections. In addition, people sometimes feel it is impolite to move from those they have just been talking with unless you legitimize this. To ensure movement and maximum mixing you may want to encourage people to work with someone they haven't previously spoken to in the next exercise. You may want to randomly divide people into groups. Quick ways of doing this include going round the room numbering people 1, 2, 3, 4 if you want four groups. Other options we've seen and liked include labelling people 'fish', 'chips', 'peas' or 'eggs', 'bacon', 'sausage'. Use your own creativity.

One to one conversations – walk and talk

Invite people to pair up and go for a walk together, and talk about a particular question or reflect on what's been going on so far. This helps people deepen their own understanding of what's going on. Walking alongside one another creates a more open atmosphere than sitting and maintaining eye contact. Movement also can encourage a better conversation, neurologically stimulating both sides of the brain. A change of scene also introduces a variety of pace and place in a session.

Decision-making exercises

Our experience with decision-making exercises is that they often provoke a discussion and a further round of the exercise, or a group decision about which option is most feasible. The usefulness is in getting people to focus on and discuss the various options.

Poker chip voting

You may want to borrow a whole set of poker chips to do this, but you can equally use other things; chocolate coins work well.

- Write the various options that have to be decided onto separate pieces of flip chart paper. Distribute these around the room, so people need to move from one to the other.
- Give everyone the same sum of money in poker chips.
- Invite people to spend 10–15 minutes considering where they would like to put their money. They can place it all on one choice, or they can distribute it among all or some of the choices on offer.
- Once the time is up, ask some volunteers to count up the total sum placed on each choice.

Dot voting

Similar to the poker chip exercise: give people a number of 'dot votes' (this can be asking them put a mark beside an option, or you can hand out small dot stickers). Again, invite people to put as many or as few beside each option as they wish.

Moving around the room towards or away from an issue

This can be a quick and powerful way of getting a decision made about a particular issue. Ask everyone to stand up. Invite people to move towards or away from you if they agree or disagree with the decision being suggested. For example, ask people to move towards you if they'd like to have another workshop and away from you if they wouldn't. If the majority of people move towards you there is a clear desire to hold another workshop. You could follow it up with 'move towards me if you think we need to hold it in the next month, away from me if you think it needs to be in two months' time'. This exercise often illustrates where alliances exist in the group and where there are one or two people who feel very differently from the majority.

Questions for further reflection

- What do you think you might do differently as a result of reading this chapter?
- What might be a first gesture or some initial experimentation to try and change the dynamics of a regular meeting you hold? For instance, in which meetings could you start with a check in or remove the table to create the conditions for dialogue?
- What important meeting do you have in your diary in the next month which needs to be really different from the standard fare? How could you re-imagine it? Who could support you in this before, on the day and in reflecting on how it went afterwards? How might you gather feedback from those who attended?

Chapter 8

Working well with people 'in the moment'

In this chapter, we explore practical choices 'in the moment' when you want to be responsive to what emerges in conversations with others or to what you are personally noticing or feeling. The bit of ourselves that shows up in any interaction is shaped by our sense of self, our role, our upbringing and personality. It is also shaped by what happened in the meeting we just left, or the email we just read and whether we are feeling hassled, tired, hung over, excited or ... well, the list is endless. Adopting a relational approach to change is about developing the skills that enable you to flex your approach depending on how others show up when you meet, how you yourself feel and what emerges as you talk together. When we interact with others, we may not always monitor consciously what we say and do. However, as a leader of change, there will be certain interactions that are of particular importance where you probably will want to pay close attention to what is going on between yourself and others in the moment. This chapter thus invites you to pay attention to small gestures that can encourage dialogue and create understanding, that shape the rhythm and mood of interactions in a constructive way.

We begin with what may be an opportunity to enhance or refresh some core skills that are key to relational change: the ability to be present, to suspend judgement and to listen. We then look briefly at ideas from Transactional Analysis and research on behavioural styles in conflict situations to broaden your repertoire of response. Lastly, we explore how you might notice and respond to group dynamics as they emerge.

In our relationships and interactions, we can neither know nor predict what meaning others may make of our gesture. The possibility of our intentions being misinterpreted is beautifully expressed by the Liverpool poet Roger McGough. It illustrates the importance of paying attention to the micro gestures that shape the nature and quality of our relationships.

YOU and I

I explain quietly. You
hear me shouting. You
try a new tack. I
feel old wounds reopen.

You see both sides. I
see your blinkers. I
am placatory. You
sense a new selfishness.

I am a dove. You
recognize the hawk. You
offer an olive branch. I
feel the thorns.

You bleed. I
see crocodile tears. I
withdraw. You
reel from the impact.

– Roger McGough[1]

To practise the art of relational change is to try and avoid the tragedy of multiple misunderstandings. Many of the ideas, models and terms covered in earlier chapters can help you think about the gestures you make. Here we concentrate on the skills that will enhance your ability to pay attention to, and work with, the emergent; to engage in more pull than push; to create the conditions for dialogue rather than debate and to pay attention to your own experiences and responses, as well as being alert and alive to those of others.

The core skills of listening, presence and suspending

Being able to listen well is a core relational skill that allows us to authentically connect with others. As explored in Chapter 3, we more often encounter debate than dialogue at work. Ask people what is needed for good listening and most can come up with a list of behavioural do's and don'ts, even if they admit to not always following this in practice. Items include eye contact, looking at the other person rather than at your papers or laptop; open body language, no crossed arms or crossed legs; no physical barriers such as a table or desk or having one chair higher than the other; turning your phone to silent; using non-verbal cues such as nods, 'mms' and 'ahs' to indicate that you are, indeed, listening and encouraging further talk; short affirmative verbal comments like 'really,' 'gosh', 'tell me more'; mirroring similar body posture to the other person; paraphrasing and summarizing what it is you've just heard using some of the other person's words – 'If I can just summarize what I heard there, you are saying that ...'.

These are all helpful gestures. To further develop people's listening skills, we often run an exercise that at the same time also gives people a chance to connect relationally and hear something of each other's experiences. Ask people to form groups of four and number themselves A, B, C and D. A is asked to tell a story for 5 or 10 minutes. You need to think what sort of story might be appropriate given what else is happening in the context. It might be something they are proud of at work if there is a need to create an appreciative mood; it might be a personal experience of great customer satisfaction if that is what your change is all about; a GP asked fellow trainers to talk about a difficult trainee.[2] B, C and D are asked to listen, paying attention to one of three levels:

- Level 1 is listening for facts. This is often the easiest thing to listen out for – dates, numbers, names.
- Level 2 is listening for feelings. Here you are not just listening to the words, you are also paying attention to the tone of voice and body language, to the mood music or what are often called paralinguistics – are they sounding anxious, sad, angry? Are they excited and energized? Are their arms folded tightly or are they sitting upright and smiling? The use of unusual metaphors or phrases may also indicate something about the emotional undertow.
- Level 3 is listening for intentions, lightly holding a hypothesis about why the person is telling you this story or anecdote in this particular way, and what they might be hoping to achieve. If they are giving lots of figures and data is this because they are wanting to impress you?

or are they anxious and trying to reassure themselves? This can be the hardest level in terms of listening, but is often the richest source of insight for the other person. In Heron's terms, sharing it can be a challenging intervention. Their unconscious intention may not be quite as you hypothesised but your listening may prompt them to reflect more deeply on their actual intentions.

After ten minutes of A telling their story, B, C and D take five minutes to feed back what they heard to A. This in itself often generates interesting reflections for A. Those in the listening roles are often amazed at just how much is going on when you actually start paying attention to the different levels. To complete the exercise, there are three more rounds with each person having the chance to tell their story and to listen at one of the different levels. In our experience, people love this exercise – not only do they enhance their listening skills, they also feel more connected with others through the act of listening and hearing their experiences, freed from the need to jump in with their own views.

For the purposes of learning, we have deliberately atomized or dissected the act of listening, but in practice what is important is also paying attention to the whole. This is what Peter Senge and Otto Scharmer call developing 'presence' and 'suspending' our assumptions and judgements. Their ideas are rooted in the tradition of seeing organizations as living organisms, where change comes from learning new ways of being in relationship with each other. They emphasize the importance of not being governed by habitual ways of thinking about a situation or other people. Listening deeply means going below surface comments and 'turning our attention to the source rather than the object',[3] redirecting our attention to seeing the whole situation. This means being open to and tolerating ambiguity and uncertainty.

Presence and suspending are key to creating dialogue. It can be helpful to remind yourself that in dialogue, the purpose is to listen and learn rather than to try and win the point. This means not staking your position as an immovable fact. If we do so, we tend very quickly to identify what we say with who we are. If someone attacks our idea we feel as though they are attacking us. Isaacs says:

> Non-negotiable positions are like rocks in the stream of dialogue: they dam it up. One of the central processes for enabling us to enter

> into dialogue is the practice of suspension, the art of loosening our grip and gaining perspective [...] Suspension means that we neither suppress what we think nor advocate it with unilateral conviction. Rather, we display our thinking in a way that lets us and others see and understand it. We simply acknowledge and observe our thoughts and feelings as they arise without being compelled to act on them. This can release tremendous amount of creative energy.[4]

Instead of letting go it becomes about letting come. Dialogue with deep listening is how opportunities for change can be created through conversations. For leaders what is needed is not to control what is happening but to create an area of safe uncertainty, as discussed in Chapter 3. This means creating just enough structure that others can participate in creating something new together.

One of the things that can get in the way of presence and suspending is the voice in our head, the chattering of our mental to do list, our memories of past annoyances with someone in the room, our inner voice. If this voice is too loud, we cannot hear other people and we certainly cannot be present. This is because it is humanly impossible to listen to two voices at the same time. To illustrate this we often ask two people in a group to read aloud from different pages of text and ask everyone else to listen. Some people try and just focus on one voice and ignore the other; some try and do some form of auditory ping pong. Neither works. It really is impossible to listen to two voices and understand what is being said.

If your inner voice is too loud you will be paying more attention to that than to the person or people in front of you. Trying to ignore it or turn it down rarely works. The best thing is to turn it up – become aware of what is bothering you and be curious about what this is telling you. You may then need to write something on your notepad; more often though, the most helpful thing is to voice aloud your concern so that you share with others what you are noticing. Voicing aloud is what often allows your inner voice to subside so you can then be present, suspend and listen well. (For detail on the inner critic, see Chapter 10).

Understanding more about own default settings

Self-awareness can help us 'catch ourselves' so that 'in the moment' we are able to be present and to recognize our own responses to other people's gestures. It forms a key element of being a reflexive leader and is what Stacey refers to as practical judgement.[5] Understanding ourselves can help us recognize what is 'our stuff' and what belongs to others and is especially important when their gestures evoke a strong emotional response in us. You are probably familiar with the Johari window in Figure 8.1.

This is a reminder that for each of us there are aspects of ourselves that are public knowledge; aspects that are private to us and hidden to others and aspects that may be seen by others but to which are blind. The latter will remain hidden to us unless we receive feedback from others, through challenging gestures, to use Heron's term which we introduced in Chapter 2.

As we get to know and understand those hidden aspects of ourselves, we expand our self-awareness. We learn why we respond to particular

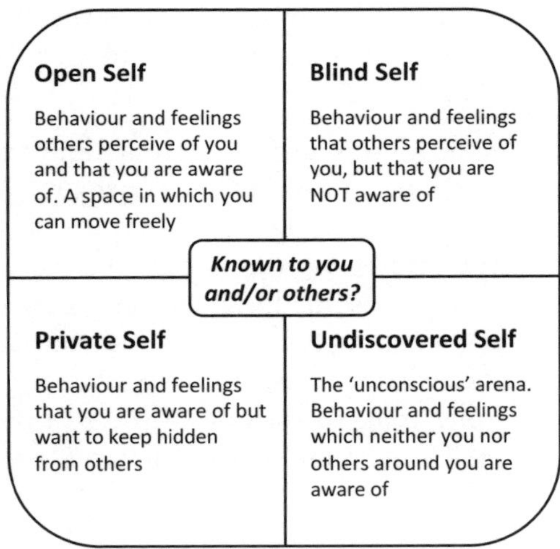

Figure 8.1 The Johari window. Adapted from Luft and Ingham.

gestures in habitual ways. Models such as that of Heron and Personal Drivers give a vocabulary to understand and label our own behaviour, as well as showing alternative ways of responding. Rather than operating on automatic pilot, self-knowledge also enables you to respond more thoughtfully, having considered the different choices open to you. It can prevent you feeling overwhelmed by other people's stuff and falling into the trap of the heroic leader, feeling that you are responsible for their emotions and responses. As a leader of relational change, this is vital given change generally evokes strong emotions, as discussed in Chapter 6.

Many of our responses have their origin in our early experience with authority figures such as parents and teachers, and in the school playground – the first place where we are truly on our own. However, unless we take time to understand ourselves and our patterns, we remain enslaved to the old patterns without considering whether they serve us well in the present. As David Runcorn says:

> When we buy a computer, it comes with programmes installed. We switch it on and templates and control bars appear on the screen, ready to use. These are the default settings, installed at the factory – but we may be unaware that all these setting are negotiable. They can be changed, and they need to be changed if the machine is to become my equipment, doing tasks the way I need them to be done.[6]

A theory that many people find useful as a means of exploring their personal default settings is that of Transactional Analysis, discussed in the following section.

Transactional Analysis (TA)

Transactional Analysis is a wonderfully rich theory that embraces ideas from psychoanalysis, behavioural psychology and humanistic philosophy. 'TA is a way of inquiring into what goes on between people and inside people in order to help them make changes. The transactional aspect is exactly what it says: a two way communication, and exchange, a transaction,' writes Charlotte Sills.[7] A transaction can take place internally when we talk to ourselves, or between two people, and it does not have to be verbal. It might be a raised eyebrow to someone else's smile or silence at some unexpected news. In this respect it is similar to Stacey's ideas of gesture and response.

TA offers a substantial theory of personality and relationship and locates the source of our responses in what the originator of the theory, Eric Berne, called three ego states: Adult, Parent and Child. These are 'coherent systems of thought and feeling manifested by corresponding patterns of behaviour'.[8] According to the theory, we are in an Adult ego state when we are thinking, feeling and behaving in the moment and are, therefore, really 'present', alive to the here and now and what is going on. There is no interference from the past. There are two unconscious reservoirs of past experience, known in TA as the Child ego state and the Parent ego state. These are generalizations of past experiences which become habitual and stylized ways of responding to similar stimuli. What makes a pattern become fixed is the level of stress or emotion that was aroused in the original experience. Other people's behaviour, or emotional situations, can trigger us to respond from the Child or Parent ego state, rather than the Adult. When this happens we are responding in the same way we did in the past.

In the Parent ego state, we have unconsciously taken inside ourselves messages and experiences from others, generally our own parents, carers and teachers. So we have 'introjected' key messages that gradually, through reinforcement, become part of our script, our way of understanding and experiencing the world. There are two aspects of the Parent ego state – the Critical Parent and the Nurturing Parent. When we are in the Child ego state, we are reliving ways we behaved as a child. Here, too, there are two aspects – the Free Child and the Adaptive Child. The relevance of this to leading change is that many of the behaviours or gestures we encounter in others, or indeed may experience ourselves, are quite likely to derive from the Parent or Child ego states, given that change evokes strong emotions. If someone speaks to us from their Parent ego state it can easily trigger us to respond from our Child ego state. Conversely if someone is in a Child ego state we can find ourselves almost automatically responding from our Parent ego state.

What would be the signs of yourself or others being in particular ego states? As a brief guide you might notice the following if someone was in each of the different ego states.

- Critical or Negative Controlling Parent – tells other people what to do; uses many 'push' gestures; uses the words 'should' and 'ought' a great deal; tendency to use quite extreme adverbs such as 'you *always* mess up'; 'you *never* do as you are told'. Other signs of someone being in this ego state would be if they have their hands on their hips and talk at, rather than to, someone else; if they point their finger while shouting at another or if they use belittling words such as 'ridiculous' or 'stupid' to describe their own or others' behaviour.
- Nurturing or Positive Controlling Parent – shows concern for the other person's feelings and well-being; smiles at another's success; leans caringly towards another; greets someone with open arms if they look distressed; has a gentle tone of voice; wants to make things better for the other person even if it fosters dependency.
- Free or Natural Child – expresses feelings of joy, fear, sorrow, separation distress in a very uninhibited way; in this ego state the behaviour tends to be natural, spontaneous and creative. Often takes risks without seeing them as such.
- Adaptive Child – in this mode, there are behaviours that are adaptions to others. When in the Adaptive Child ego state, an individual may be *rebellious*, dig their heels in, question and challenge the authority of another, or express anger when sadness would be more appropriate. Alternatively, when in the Adaptive Child ego state, an individual may be *compliant*, cowering with head down as they ask something from someone else, trying to guess what might please or placate the other. Their voice tone in this ego state is likely to be whingey or placatory and they express fear where anger would be more appropriate.
- Adult – when an individual is in this ego state we would describe them as being observant, practical, able to evaluate, clarifying, constructively questioning, and resourceful. The behaviours you would see when someone was in this mode would be talking in an even voice with precise choice of vocabulary; hypothesizing and processing information; sitting upright with open posture, alert and thoughtful about the problems they are facing.

If we are aware of our own responses and can sense which ego state others are coming from, we can consciously choose to respond from a different ego state. Indeed, the very act of noticing and choosing is a mark of being in the Adult Ego state. For genuine dialogue, being in Adult is important and if you can stay in Adult, you can often help the other person to get back in touch with their Adult Ego state, too. For those times when you want innovation and creativity, the ideal ego state would be that of Free Child for at least part of the time.

The following story about two management consultants working with a group of people in healthcare illustrates how this plays out in a work context.

A clinical commissioning group appointed a prestigious strategy company to help them decide how to reconfigure their local health system. About thirty people from a variety of different GP practices and other organizations attended these meetings which were called 'local engagement sessions' and run by two management consultants. They emphasized verbally the importance of involving everyone in the room and stressed the urgency of making decisions and prioritizing together. So, the intent to engage in an Adult ego state was seemingly there, supported by the right words. However, each meeting followed a similar pattern – a large PowerPoint deck of slides to remind people of the reasons for change, to describe the desired end state and to impress with some cleverly drawn diagrams that showed the financial gap between current and required future state. There was little conversation. This was a one way down load of information, using expert power. People were split into two groups to complete large poster-sized templates with the consultants taking the pen and trying to extract the relevant information from those there. It was hard going. People were disengaged, on their phones, leaving the room for a bit; there were side conversations.

At the end of one such session, one of the management consultants vented her frustration. 'They are *such* hard work. I was completing all the information for them till two a.m. but in the meeting there are those with fixed smiles, nodding politely, but you have no idea if they are really supporting you (in other words people in the ego state of Compliant Adaptive Child); we have people who are grumpy (in the ego state of Rebellious Adaptive Child), and then really awkward ones who mouth off at every moment, challenging the assumptions the data is based on, challenging the process, always finding something to disagree with' (people in the ego state of Critical Parent).

What neither management consultant had realized was that their own gestures had contributed to this dynamic. In acting from the ego state of Nurturing Parents, fostering dependency, they cast the others into the Child ego state. Outside of the meeting, unconstrained by the client relationship, they spoke from the ego state of Critical Parent, furious with the behaviour of people in the room. (This story also illustrates the drama triangle when nobody is in Adult – see end of this chapter.)

Responses to conflict

We are also likely to have default settings in response to conflict. After the Second World War, there was significant interest in understanding how aspects of human behaviour had contributed to the outbreak of war. Two researchers, Thomas and Kilmann,[9] define conflict as a difference of opinion. They suggest that a person's behaviour in conflict situations can be described along two basic dimensions. One they label 'assertiveness', by which they mean how much you try to satisfy your own concerns and meet your own agenda. The other is 'co-operativeness', the degree to which you endeavour to satisfy the other person's concerns and agenda. See Figure 8.2.

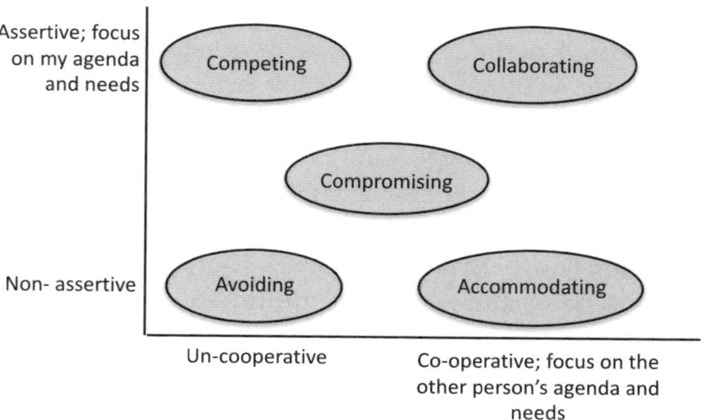

Figure 8.2 Conflict handling styles. Adapted from Thomas and Kilmann.

From this, they identify five different ways of handling differences.

Competing: High on asserting your own agenda and low on co-operation.

Competing is a conflict handling style that often draws on expert or positional sources of power. In change situations, it may be a useful style when an unpopular course of action needs implementing, when there is an emergency and quick, decisive action is vital, or when there are legal or health and safety considerations that mean only one course of action is possible. Some people find it easier to adopt a competing style when they are standing up for what they perceive as the rights or needs of others, but find it harder to do so for themselves. To use this style well, it is helpful to explain why you have made a decision or taken a certain course of action. Others can then understand the reasoning, even if they do not like the outcome. Used too quickly this style can lead to debate or withdrawal rather than dialogue as it can encourage others to believe their views won't be listened to; it can also set you up, unintentionally perhaps, as a heroic leader; you can be seen as insensitive to others and someone who damages good will and relationships. In extreme cases, overuse of this style can be interpreted as bullying.

Accommodating: Low assertiveness; high co-operativeness, giving attention to others' points of view

If preserving harmony and avoiding disruption is important, accommodating would be the style of choice. It is helpful when you realize you are wrong or have made a mistake; when a particular issue is more important to the other person than to you, or when continued competition would damage your cause - you are outmatched and losing. However, there are some traps, especially for those with a strong Please People driver. You can neglect your own concerns in trying to satisfy others and 'disappear' yourself so that your own contribution, ideas and needs go unheard and unmet. You may be seen as soft, too nice and over protective of others if you use this as your default response.

Compromising: Medium on asserting your own agenda and medium on co-operation

Using this style, as the name suggests, is about seeking the middle ground. The end point will not entirely meet your needs and concerns, nor indeed those of others. This style can help you achieve temporary settlements to complex issues or arrive at expedient solutions under time pressure. It can also be used as a backup mode when collaborating or competing aren't successful, or when your goals were moderately important but not worth the effort or potential disruption of using more assertive styles. Managers working with technical or professional experts, be they doctors, lawyers or accountants, often resort to this style, glad to gain some movement, willing to tolerate what is 'good enough' for now. As with the other styles, there are some traps to avoid. In the case of compromising these include compromising too soon or giving away too much; compromising when actually firmness is needed; and seeing compromise as a sacrifice and therefore sounding resentful or in victim mode. If this is your dominant conflict handling style, you can develop a reputation for being always ready to trade, without principles or opinions you will stick to.

Collaborating: High on assertiveness and high on co-operation

With this approach to dealing with differences, both your own agenda and that of the other person are taken fully into account. It is an appropriate style when both sets of concerns are too important to be compromised, when full commitment and engagement is required, and when there is time for real dialogue and understanding to be developed. This would be an example of dialogue which is often the only way of achieving innovative solutions and resolving highly complex issues in a sustainable rather than a quick fix way. However, it requires time and strong relational skills.

Avoiding: Low on asserting your own agenda and low on co-operation

In this style, rather than privileging the other person's agenda or asserting your own, the behaviour is to withdraw. There are times when this is a very sensible way of dealing with difference. For instance, if you or the other person is too tired or emotional, avoiding, in that moment, may be absolutely the right thing to do. Avoiding may also be prudent if the other person cares deeply about something and it really doesn't matter to you. However, over used it too means you are disappearing yourself from situations and conversations that may be difficult. Others may see you as not caring about the issue or not interested in others.

Our own individual preferred styles when dealing with difference are also partly the result of childhood messages. If 'not rocking the boat' was valued in your family, you are more likely to accommodate or avoid. If 'standing up for yourself' was seen as important, competing may feel the most natural mode for you. If everything was contingent on rewards then compromise may feel second nature. These patterns get reinforced through habit and later through the pressures and norms around certain job roles and organizational cultures.

It is helpful to understand the strengths and limitations of your preferred style and to experiment with others so you expand your range of conflict handling styles. You may also have a pattern of starting with one style and then routinely adopting a second if that doesn't seem to be working. An individual may start with competing and then switch to use their second preferred style, compromise. Others may adapt a more 'my way or the highway' approach so if competing doesn't work they will withdraw, taking the avoidance style. It becomes almost like an un-choreographed, unscripted dance until you pause and notice the pattern you've got yourself into. There will of course be an unpredictably about how others will respond, but if you start with a gesture that is competing, the other person may adopt a competing style too - hence, deadlock and breakdown of talks. If you always back down and accommodate when someone you deem to be powerful adopts a competing style, the pattern will stay stuck and you will probably become cross with yourself and the other person and resentful of the whole situation.

From difficult conversations to honest conversations

Many of us anticipate conflict when faced with what we label 'a difficult conversation'. How might the principles of dialogue be helpful? What gestures might you want to make? Clearly every situation is going to be different and dependent on the particularities of your context, but in general there are many stories we can tell ourselves to avoid having a difficult conversation. Options include:

- Blaming others: 'They never consulted us ...'.
- Taking entrenched positions: 'There's no point in talking to them ...'.
- Denying the problem: 'That's got nothing to do with us'.
- Finding false remedies: 'We need better job descriptions'.
- Rewriting the rules: 'We need to restructure'.

If you are faced with a difficult conversation, our first suggestion is to change the way you are labelling this to yourself. Reframe it as an honest conversation rather than as a difficult one so that you are not creating a negative self-fulfilling prophecy. The second thing is to consider the location for the conversation, the timing and the nature of the invitation to the other person. Where will give you and the other person the best chance of having a good enough conversation, given the circumstances? You might also want to think about whether this honest conversation is best had one-on-one as a back-stage conversation rather than in the high stakes of a meeting where many people are present. The third thing is to plan for the conversation. You can't predict how the other person will respond and you will need to be flexible, but some thinking beforehand gives you the opportunity to consider options, useful phrases and clarify your own intentions. This is likely to enable you to stay more in the Adult ago state and respond to what emerges. This is another example of the way that having a clear intention and preparing well paradoxically allows you to improvise and work with uncertainty and the paradox of complexity.

Research by a group of researchers from Harvard[10] has revealed the underlying structure of difficult/honest conversations. They suggest there are four areas that tend to need exploration: Facts – what am I right about? Identity – what does this say about me? Blame – whose fault? And Intentions – what do I think is motivating them? These four areas provide a guide rather than a template and they suggest approaching these conversations in the spirit of a little advocacy and much inquiry, with the aim of learning about how the other person or people see the situation.

Looking at facts

The very word 'facts' suggests solidity, rightness and self-evident truths. Yet what count as facts are often a matter of perspective. Sheen, one of the researchers, shares the story of an argument she had with her six-year old, while waiting at traffic lights. She said the lights were red. The child insisted they were green. She maintained no, this was red. The child continued to insists the lights were green. Was her child being silly, colour blind, perverse? She inquired more and found that they were both right. She was looking at the red lights straight ahead of her. Her son in the back seat, couldn't see those but could see the green lights for the pedestrians to cross.

When there are different views of the facts, using what is called the 'Ladder of Inference'[11] can be helpful (see Figure 8.3). This is a structured approach to discover why we believe what we believe. At the same time, through inquiry, we can help the other person unpack the origin of their beliefs too. We normally assert our beliefs and view of the facts very quickly as an automatic unconscious process. The ladder encourages going back down the ladder, as a set of steps, to uncover through questions where these beliefs that are presented as facts actually have their origin.

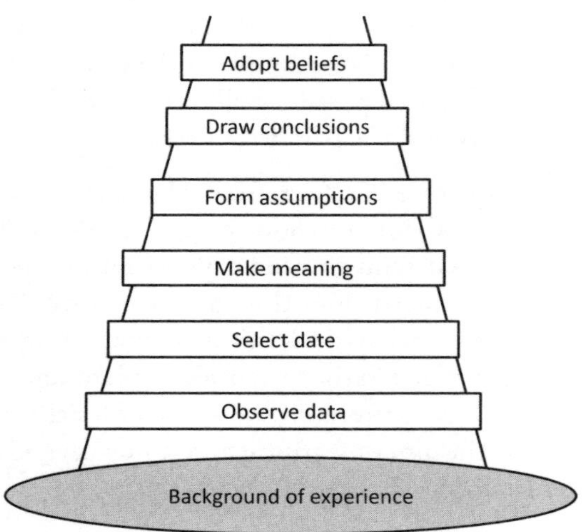

Figure 8.3 The Ladder of Inference. Adapted from Argyris.

Listening well is essential to using the Ladder of Inference; listening out, in particular, for implicit conclusions and opinions. You are checking out assumptions – yours and theirs – not to catch them out but to help you both understand the situation more fully from both your perspectives. You may want to look for more data by asking what information they select and giving them examples of the data you select. In doing this you are making explicit the steps in your reasoning process and you are encouraging others to be explicit in theirs. This requires you slowing things down and suspending judgement, key aspects of dialogue.

Stone[12] gives the following suggestions:

- Assume there is a 'back story' and find ways of eliciting it through internal curiosity:
  a. What's going on?
  b. Help me to understand your thinking ...
  c. Tell me more ...
  d. Can you give me an example ...?
  e. Adopt the 'And And' stance, assuming both stories are correct.
- Hold your views as legitimate, but limited:
  a. Get curious about why you see it differently.
  b. Inquire to understand.
  c. Share to be clear, not to persuade.
- Tell your story with clarity:
  a. Don't present your conclusions as the truth.
  b. Share where your conclusions come from.
  c. Don't exaggerate with 'always' and 'never'.

Looking at identity

When we experience strong negative reactions from someone, it is often because they perceive some slight or attack on their identity. Our sense of identity relates to our fundamental beliefs about who we are as people, in our own eyes as well as those of others. If those beliefs and assumptions about the self are trampled on or discarded, there can be embarrassment, shame and an existential fear of no longer being of value as an individual. Changes to people's status and power relative to others are likely to impact their sense of identity. In an honest conversation, it can be helpful to think: What do I fear the situation says about me? What is true about this? What is not? And then, what might they think the situation says about them?

Looking at blame

When things are going wrong, it is a very human tendency to want to find someone else to blame. This can sometimes lead to a particular dynamic which is called the drama triangle[13] where people unconsciously cycle in an unhealthy dynamic of taking on the role of rescuer, victim or persecutor (see later in this chapter). Helpful things to bear in mind are the following:

- Try not to polarize, assuming it's all your fault or all theirs.
- Map what you have each contributed to the mess.
- Identify what others have contributed to the mess.
- Take responsibility for your contribution ... and not for theirs.

The last point is important. If you take on all the responsibility, you are in effect taking on the mantle of rescuer which will perpetuate the drama triangle of victim–persecutor–rescuer. It also takes away the balance of shared responsibility. Key questions to yourself are therefore: What have I contributed to the current situation? How have they contributed to the current situation?

Ways of exploring Intentions:

Intentions are invisible. We infer intentions from people's actions and the impact on us. Unfortunately, as things deteriorate we tend to assume the worst. This is a personal version of conspiracy theories on the lines of he/she/they are out to get me. It is therefore easy to slip into the roles of victim and persecutor. Some examples:

Jill: 'I feel hurt' (impact) assumes (intent). 'He deliberately wanted to hurt me.'

Jason: 'I felt put down in front of colleagues' (impact) assumes (intent). 'She deliberately wanted to make me feel small.'

The way to raise this with someone in a conversation is to speak about the impact, not the intention. (In Heron terms, this would be making a challenging intervention.) The intention is your assumption that you have inferred from how you felt, but that may not have been their intention, so you are holding that possibility open. Useful phrases might be:

'I don't know if you're aware of this ...' (I'm not saying it is intentional).

'Here's what I see ...' (describe data).

'My concern is that ...' (describe impact).

'What do you think?' (inquire).

In terms of questions to yourself, it might be helpful to consider: What impact has this situation had on me? What were my intentions? Equally, what were their intentions? What impact might this situation have had on them?

In thinking through these different elements, you are allowing yourself to be more present when you actually have the conversation, confident that you have had time to consider the situation from different angles rather than trying to do that in the meeting. The conversation of course won't go exactly as you had planned it in your head beforehand because of the unpredictability of how the other person will respond. However, this preparation allows you to be alert and to respond to what emerges in the conversation from an Adult ego state, which is more likely to lead to a positive outcome.

In the moment in meetings and group situations

In honest conversations there are often just two people involved. In meetings and group situations with more people, it is more complicated. Casey[14] developed a model to train group facilitators, but we find it is equally useful to enable leaders to think about how they lead and work in group settings. Casey identifies three steps which are graphically represented in Figure 8.4.

Step 1 is all about being present and noticing what is going on for yourself and for others. This is partly about taking in what is going on personally for you. For instance, you may notice that you are feeling

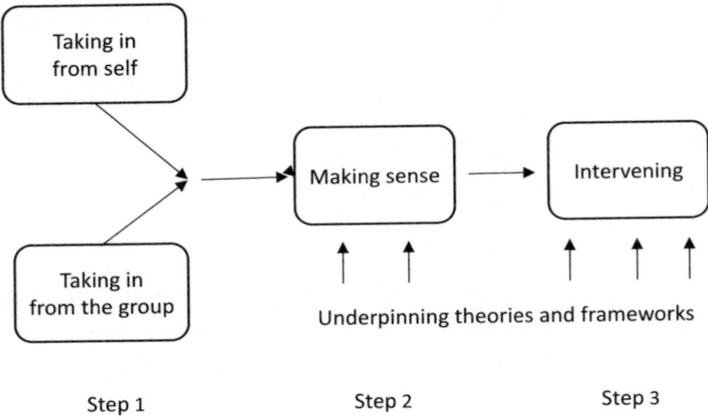

Figure 8.4 Intervening in group situations. Adapted from Casey, Roberts and Salaman.

uncomfortable about the conversation or that your energy is flagging. You may be sitting on the edge of your chair with your muscles tensed, or you may be bit disengaged from the discussion, finding your mind wandering, leaning back in your chair or slouching. What's going on that's causing you to feel this way? Is it something going on in the group? Is it the direction the discussion is going in? Step 1 is also about noticing what is going on in the group in terms of the dynamics and the emotional tone, so paying particular attention to how the group seem to be working together, what is being left unsaid, how they are dealing with feelings that are being evoked. All of this is useful information.

Step 2 is making sense of what is going on using any theories, models and frameworks that you know. So you might want to draw on any of the models introduced in this book to give you insight into what might be going on. It may be that you recognize that one of your own personal drivers has been hooked. You might notice that there is a great deal of advocacy and very little inquiry in the group. You may also make sense of what is going on based on your past experiences of being in groups and your knowledge of yourself. Charlotte Sills[15] recommends holding your sensemaking lightly, given the unpredictability of others responses. 'There is value in musing on a range of possible interpretations,' says Casey.[16]

Step 3 is intervening, again drawing on your own knowledge of different theories and models. Intervening is about choosing how to act, in other words making some kind of gesture to the group. It may be a comment or a question. It may be you changing the dynamic by moving physically to stand up or sit down. Sometimes, just sharing what you have noticed can be an effective way of intervening, trusting others in the group to pick up on this as an invitation to inquire into what's going on. It may be helpful to name what you are personally experiencing rather than suggesting or assuming that the group will share this feeling. For example, 'I notice that my energy is flagging and I'm wondering what that's about. Is it just me, or is anyone else feeling the same?', or 'May I just check – what do people have interest and energy for discussing?' In inviting the group to comment, you are encouraging joint sensemaking and group learning, rather than you taking responsibility and doing this for the group, creating dependence. You are 'doing with' rather that 'doing to' which encourages people to stay in an Adult ego state.

In practice, as with all models, real life is more blended, haphazard and cyclical. At any moment you may be intervening, taking in and sensemaking. This model helpfully reminds us that we, as leaders or facilitators, are part of groups and organizations. We cannot try and be objective. As one of the complexity theorists, Douglas Griffin reminds us,

> There is no detached way of understanding organizations from the position of the objective observer. Instead, organisations (and groups) have to be understood in terms of one's own personal experience of participating with others in the co-creation of the patterns of interaction that are the organisation.[17]

Interventions in the moment

In addition to sharing your own feelings and commenting on what you see within the group, there are multiple gestures you may choose to make to intervene in the moment. We include a small range to stimulate your thinking for particular situations you may encounter, but the list is by no means exhaustive.

- *Drop in energy.* Stop for a break so people can get some fresh air, get up, move around. Consider dividing people into smaller groups, asking people to have a quick discussion in twos or threes and to then come back together as a group to share what came from these discussions. This can change the energy levels in a group and ensure that quieter people who are more introverted can contribute.

- *Conversation going round in circles.* Take some time for individual reflection. Ask people to take a couple of minutes to think in silence and to write down what comes to mind. Invite everyone to share their thoughts one by one with no comment from anyone until everyone has had a chance to speak. This can be a great way of getting some new insight into a discussion.
- *Quietening dominant voices.* Some people don't recognize when they are dominating a conversation. Drawing their attention to this can help. Doing so in a break can be helpful so they are not shamed in front of others. In Heron's terminology, this would be a push/challenging intervention. Gestures may need to be quite direct in front of the group: 'Thank you Mark, I wonder if anyone else would like to share their perspective?' Making eye contact with others while turning away from the dominant speaker can also help.
- *Soliciting quieter perspectives.* Just as some people find it hard not to think out loud, others will be naturally quieter, more reflective and less likely to say a lot. Putting such individuals on the spot by asking them directly to contribute, can make them uncomfortable. Instead, useful questions are:
  - 'Has anyone who hasn't yet contributed got anything they would like to add to the discussion?'
  - 'We've heard the perspective of x and y, does anyone else have anything they'd like to add?'
- *Interrupting a conversation.* This can be difficult and seem impolite, but is often a very important intervention when, for instance, someone has been talking for several minutes and others are looking bored; when you don't understand what someone's saying; when the point has already been made by the person speaking and when it feels like the group is going round in circles. There are some straightforward ways to go about this; lean forward sharply and speak as soon as the person speaking takes a breath; if this is ignored, lift your hand up palm out and start by saying something like,
  - 'I'm just going to interrupt you there because ...'.
  - 'Can I interrupt you?'

- Can I press the pause button?
- 'I'm interrupting you there, Joan, as we seem to be going round in circles at the moment; what do others think?'
- Whenever you interrupt, explain what's behind your interruption to the group, what assumptions you're making and what's on your mind.[18]
- *Allowing and using silence.* Silence can be really valuable in a group discussion as it can indicate that people are reflecting on what they are hearing and thinking about what it means for them. There may be something difficult going on that people are having trouble talking about together, or the conversation may have come to a natural end and there's nothing more to say on the subject. You may feel an overwhelming desire to fill the silence, but it is often from these silences that people are able to get into the conversation they want to have. Useful prompts during silence include:
  - 'Is there anything anyone wants to say that they feel hasn't been said?'
  - 'It feels as if we have reached the end of the conversation; does that feel right to everyone?'

What's going on with the group? A beginner's guide to group dynamics

Much has been written about how we interact with one another in groups so here we include only the briefest of summaries.[19] From a psychodynamic perspective, people in groups behave in ways that are deeply rooted in their unconscious and primitive responses. This is very much taking place below the waterline, to use our earlier image. If you're working with a group, it's useful to have some understanding of these ideas, as it can help you make sense of what might be going on and give you some insight into why you and the participants might be behaving in certain ways.

Wilfred Bion,[20] an influential psychoanalyst, believed that people in groups operate in one of three basic assumption modes: dependence, flight/fight and pairing. He believed that all groups enact one or more of these modes to some extent and that these modes tend to occur when people are experiencing strong emotions. Everyone in the group fantasizes about the motives and characters of the other group members and projects their own emotions onto each other. The majority of this goes on at an unspoken level.

Dependence

The group want to be dependent on a leader and to be looked after by that leader. They have a desire for the leader to magically solve all their problems, to take responsibility for decisions. At the same time, this relinquishing of power leaves people feeling constrained, and they become unhappy at feeling unable to contribute fully and being held back. They look to get rid of the leader and to replace them with someone 'better'. The process repeats itself, as no one can realistically satisfy the needs of the group in this leadership role.

Fight/flight

In this mode, the group avoids the work at hand either by running away from it or looking for 'enemies' whom they believe wish to subvert them from their efforts. If the group choose flight, they will do anything to avoid the work. This often shows up as talking about everything and anything other than the work, laughing and joking a lot together, or finding excuses to break or not meet. If the group choose to fight, they look for scapegoats, either from within or without the group. All their energy goes on blaming these people for the lack of progress. Believing in these 'enemies' may be psychologically easier than examining their own behaviour.

Pairing

In this mode, the group place all their hopes in one or more pairs within the group who are seen as doing brilliant work together. People will use phrases such as 'Phyllis and John are amazing. I'm sure if we leave them to tackle the project we'll get a great outcome.' However, as Phyllis and John are, after all, only human, it's inevitable that they will eventually disappoint the group. Again, this mode is another way for the group to avoid taking responsibility.

In addition to Bion's three basic assumption modes, other psychodynamic patterns to be aware of are:

Projection

Projection is when we criticize other people but, in fact, what we criticize is the very thing that we most fear could be true about ourselves. Projection can happen in all relationships and in groups can occur between group members or between the group leader and the group. You may find yourself projecting your own emotions onto group members, and vice versa. We worked recently with a group of leaders who had come together to form a change team to run a significant integration project. One of them said to us, 'I'm usually very popular but I sense in this group that I am too threatening.' He projected onto them his own fears that they were threatening.

Transference and counter transference

Transference occurs in one-on-one one relationships, and within groups when someone unconsciously projects onto you, or each other, patterns and assumptions from earlier relationships in their lives. For instance, you may unconsciously remind someone of a much loved friend, or a difficult family member and they then start responding to you as if you were that person. Counter transference is how you respond to their transference.

The drama triangle

Developed by Karpman in 1968,[21] the drama triangle describes three characteristic positions that people may take up in interactions with others: victim, rescuer and persecutor. In each position, people replay ineffective patterns of thoughts and behaviour, getting hooked by other people's responses and in turn hooking them so that everyone becomes locked in a vicious dance. The drama triangle can also take place in the conversation we have with ourselves in our head. We will each have a predisposition to one position but can unconsciously get hooked into any of them, depending on other people's responses. We, and they, can also move around the positions. Getting out of the pattern requires one or more people being able to spot the pattern and notice what is happening, i.e. being in an Adult ego state. The different positions can be described in the following way:[22]

Victim. In the position of victim, people tend to feel fearful, singled out and self- pitying. The type of phrases characteristic of someone occupying this position are 'It's all too much for me', 'Why does this always happen to me?' 'I've got so much going on for me you can't expect me to ...', 'He's always picking on me ...', 'It's the fault of the system.'

Persecutor. In the position of persecutor, people tend to feel threatened, pressured and right. The type of phrases characteristic here are: 'She's always making excuses ...', 'We'd be ok if it weren't for...', 'It doesn't matter what you feel, just get on with it ...'.

Rescuer. In the position of rescuer,people tend to feel capable, overburdened and righteous. The phrases here are: 'I'm carrying everyone', 'I'll sort it out', 'They can't manage so I'll do it', 'Don't worry about me'.[23]

In summary

As relational change is an art, there will be many judgement calls to make and there is no certainty about how others will react. Sometimes others' responses may surprise you with their creativity, insights, generosity. At other times, as we explore in Chapter 9, conversation can get stuck. However, the chances are that by having a greater awareness of what is going on in the moment you will help yourself and others to engage in conversations that are honest, acknowledge differences and allow people to say what they care about and why.

Questions for further reflection

- Think about a recent conversation that you were apprehensive about; what helped it go well? What ego states were you in? What helped you to listen to the other person? What can you learn from this to take into other conversations?
- Which are your preferred conflict styles? What limitations might there sometimes be with this style, and which other style would you like to become better at using and why?
- What elements of working with a group do you enjoy and which aspects do you find more challenging? How might you experiment with some different techniques?
- When have you noticed yourself or others experiencing some group dynamics occurring?

Chapter 9

Working with stuckness and reframing resistance

When progress is not forthcoming and you feel like you are wading through treacle; when the naysayers continue to sound loud and declamatory; when there seems little to show for all the effort you've put in, there can be a point in a change programme when as the leader you may think – 'Is this really worth it? Will this ever end? I'm exhausted'. In this chapter, we explore further the idea of stuckness and the way our own thinking can trap us into fixed ways of seeing and responding to problems. We examine how relationships within systems and organizations can get fixed in negative and unproductive patterns because of how people see each other and talk about each other. We then look at ways of breaking out of stuckness, emphasizing the importance of small gestures, experimentation and Trojan mice to develop energy, belief and confidence in the change.

When people disagree with our own ideas or proposals, it can be tempting to dismiss them as being 'resistant to change'. This is a frequent and understandable response. However, by reducing people to stereotypes rather than seeing them as fellow complex human beings, we miss the possibility of understanding different and possibly valid perspectives. We also increase the likelihood of them staying where they are and us staying where we are – stuck. In this chapter, we thus conclude with the latest ideas on reframing resistance as ambivalence.

There are moments when you are leading a change that can feel *really* hard going and you may start to think this isn't going to work. Feeling stuck can impede motivation and sap energy. You probably don't share such thoughts or feelings with many others for fear of them agreeing with you, and thus confirming your worst fears. Or you might be worried that by confiding in a few colleagues they will lose their own confidence in the change or in your ability as a leader.

The notion of 'stuckness' comes from the world of family therapy and psychotherapy. It has been described as when 'a person, a family or a wider social system is enmeshed in a problem in a persistent and repetitive way, despite desire and effort to alter the situation'.[1] In fact, the feeling of being stuck often encourages people to try harder at whatever it is they have been doing. Sadly, in putting in more effort doing the same thing, the situation stays stuck or even deteriorates. A classic example of this at an individual level would be the insomniac – the harder you try to get to sleep, the more sleep evades you.

Stuckness through staying wedded to the search for certainty

As explored in earlier chapters, the mechanistic metaphor for understanding organizations and directive approaches to change can work well in conditions of relative stability and for small incremental improvements. When more innovative or radical change is required and your context is beset with uncertainties, a different way of seeing organizations and working with change is needed. It could be that you are feeling stuck because your assumptions about the nature of organizations are no longer helpful and the way you are going about change is no longer appropriate. As Zohar writes, many organizations,

> thrive on certainty and predictability. They are hierarchical; power emanates from the top, and control is vital at every level. So, often, is fear. They are heavily bureaucratic and rule-bound, and hence inflexible. They stress the single point of view, the one best way forward. They are managed as though the part organizes the whole.... . Human beings work and live in such organizations, but we often feel like passive units of production. Our lives serve the organizations, but the organizations only serve our utilitarian needs, and then only as long as we conform ... .The emphasis on control isolates these organizations from their environments. They don't interact with or respect those environments, including the people who work with them.'[2]

The relational approach to change, in drawing on ideas from seeing organizations as complex responsive processes, encourages leaders to connect with others as fellow human beings, so that there is collective effort and energy in exploring multiple possible ways forward. In liberating yourself from the search for certainty and the silver bullets that solve everything, there is the possibility of seeing people, ideas and opportunities differently.

Stuckness through treating a problem as tame when it is wicked

Stuckness can also originate from misunderstanding the nature of the problem you are facing. Keith Grint[3] introduces a helpful categorization. Tame problems are those which have often been encountered before, and for which a solution or process is already in existence. The action here is to identify the appropriate solution to the puzzle and to find the correct process to answer the issue. Tameness does not necessarily mean simplicity – tame problems can be very complicated, and

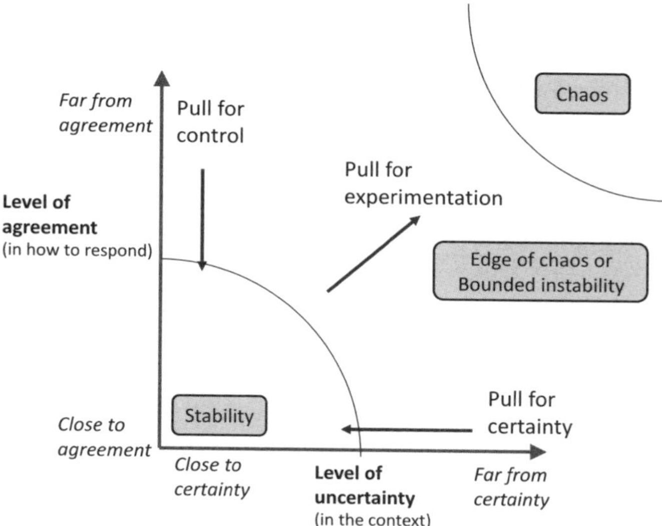

Figure 9.1 Zones of stability and instability. Adapted by Vanstone, Critchley and Ashridge colleagues from original ideas by Stacey.

thus the solution may also be very complicated, such as heart surgery, relocation, and new product launches. Wicked problems, on the other hand, are novel, encompass many uncertainties and unknowns and stubbornly resist any attempts at resolution. Such problems tend not to have an end point or a solution, but rather to be characterized by developments that make things better or worse, and where unintended consequences are to be expected and explored.

It can be helpful to map Grint's ideas onto what we refer to as Stacey's[4] grid, (recognizing that Stacey himself disowns the idea of a grid as suggesting assumptions about planning and predictability that he challenges). Tame problems could be said to be towards the bottom left where there is a relatively high degree of certainty and agreement, while wicked problems are more likely to be towards the top right where there is high uncertainty and little agreement. If your change is feeling stuck, might it be because it is more of a wicked problem than a tame one? Are you leading in a mechanistic way which, while appropriate for some organizational issues, is less appropriate for the change in hand? A response to such stuckness may be to embrace a more facilitative approach, creating the conditions for conversation, innovation and emergence.

In this chapter, we explore in more detail the different gestures that can be required when a change situation has become stuck. Critical to this are:

- Being able to see and think about the situation and people differently.
- Being able to act differently, i.e. make new and different gestures.
- Avoiding familiar cycles and exiting from well-trodden paths.

Difference is key.

To paraphrase a well-known phrase, if you keep doing what you have always done, you will keep getting what you have always got. In other words, you and the situation will remain stuck. Reassuringly, even small differences which are new gestures can create movement. Movement is important motivationally. It doesn't mean that everything is now sorted, but by starting to shift the dynamic, you and others are no longer in 'stuckness'.

Stuckness at the system level

You might also feel stuck because of where you are within your system, whether you see the system as your own organization or more broadly as including customers, suppliers, competitors and regulators. Barry Oshry[5] has been researching the dynamics of systems for over thirty years and argues that we are often blind to the set dances or patterns that take place. When we are blind to these patterns, we continue to act in unproductive ways that reinforce the problems and maintain stuckness. Part of the answer is to 'see the system'. This means changing our mental model of how and where we see ourselves in relation to others. This also gives us the chance to empathize with them, to see things from their perspective.

Oshry identifies four roles which we may occupy in different situations at various points in time. They are Tops, Bottoms, Middles and Customers and the positions are fluid. A Market Research Director may be a Top in relation to his team, as he is their boss and has overall responsibility for the action, but he may be a Middle in relation to the Chief Executive. He may feel like a Bottom when most people around him are familiar with the new IT system but he is not. Chief Executives may be a Top to the majority of people in their organization, but when change is imposed by new legislation, the industry regulator or the holding company board, they, too, can feel like a Middle.

Oshry describes, in what is almost a poem, what it feels like when we occupy these various positions:

> Tops are burdened by what feels like unmanageable complexity;
> Bottoms are oppressed by what they see as distant and uncaring Tops;
> Middles are torn and confused between the conflicting demands and priorities coming at them from Tops and Bottoms;
> Customers feel done-to by non-responsive delivery systems [...]
>
> Tops are fighting fires when they should be shaping the system's future;
> Middles are isolated from one another when they should be working together to coordinate system processes;
> Bottoms' negative feelings toward Tops and Middles distracts them

from putting their creative energies into the delivery of products and services;
Customers' disgruntlement with the system keeps them from being active partners in helping the system produce the products and services they need.

Throughout the system there is personal stress, relationship breakdowns and severe limitations in the system's capacity to do what it intends to do.[6]

Stuckness comes from being blind to various patterns in the system. Spatial blindness is when we only see our part of the system but not the whole. Oshry describes this in the following way:

We see what's happening with us

but not what is happening elsewhere;

we don't see what others' worlds are like [...]

we develop stereotypes of one another,

we take personally much that is not personal.[7]

We can also suffer from temporal blindness when we only see the present and fail to inquire into or appreciate the way the past may cast long shadows over the present for some. The impact of this is illustrated in Joe's story in Chapter 12.

This model allows you to see the system you inhabit, and your place in it, from different perspectives. The language of Tops, Middles and Bottoms, as well as the different types of blindness, can be a useful starting place to help you and others become unstuck. However, this requires going and talking to others in your own context to really understand how this applies, inquiring into their positions as well as sharing yours. This relational approach through dialogue helps unstick the system by creating the possibility of mutual understanding. We've also noticed that it can help develop empathy for the challenges and tribulations that accompany other people's positions. When we feel frustrated or angry, we often assume that negative behaviour from others towards us is personally motivated. However, it is useful to remember that while we may *feel* the attack is personal, it may be driven by the roles people, including ourselves, are playing in the system. Taking it less personally can allow us to see things from an Adult, rather than a Child or Parent mode, to use TA terms (see Chapter 8).

When you are occupying these different positions or roles, what are the implications in terms of leading change? When you are feeling like a Top, responsible for the action, change can feel both burdensome and lonely. Connecting with others and reminding yourself that you do not have to be the heroic leader is important. One way to mitigate this is to work with someone else in a pair (see Chapters 7 and 10). Alternatively, you may want to talk regularly with a colleague, a coach or an external consultant to help you reflect on what is going on for you, help you see how you may be contributing to the patterns around you, and where you need to make a different gesture. (More on this in Chapter 10.)

The chances are that sometimes in relation to a change you will be a Middle, too. A significant role here is helping Bottoms deal with the emotions associated with change. Unlike Tops, you will know personally the individuals in your team. You may also find you are far closer than Tops to the detail of work, so are better placed to fine tune or adapt existing processes and procedures. Tops and Middles also play a key sensemaking role for themselves and others around them. Yet Middles are only able to perform this role if they themselves are involved in the right meetings and therefore have information power. This can help explain the strong feelings aroused if your Top decides to exclude you from meetings. Not only do you suffer a sense of demotion, you also lose the source of information that enabled you to carry out your interpretive, sensegiving role for those people who are, in Oshry's terms, Bottoms.

Middles often feel pressure to tell stories about how or why the organization is changing that make sense to three different audiences: (1) your superiors or Tops, who often demand a coherent account of what you are doing that is neater and tidier than the reality; (2) your subordinates or Bottoms, who need to understand how what they are being asked to do fits in with the bigger picture, to avoid a sense of meaninglessness; and (3) yourself.

Oshry graphically describes this as 'tearing': Middles are torn by demands and needs from those above them *and* below them. Juniors may view Middle's stories with suspicion or hostility while Tops often publicly trample on and unwittingly destroy the carefully constructed stories of Middles. One researcher, Sims,[8] recounted the experience of Andy, who had been enthusing his team about their change project for two years, only to have it scrapped because of a political need to demonstrate to head office that costs were being got under control. 'What story can he tell now?' asks Sims.

Stuckness through stereotyping and over generalizing

Stereotypes work for us some of the time, as they categorize and simplify the world, making it more manageable. They are a cognitive shorthand for making sense of what to expect and how we might respond to the constant stream of data that is coming at us. Over time and through experience, we gradually build up our own personal picture of how certain people and groups are likely to behave.

When we join a new team, department or organization, we become exposed to individual stereotyping as we are given brief synopses: 'Jane – she's a tricky character so don't cross her', 'John – very laid back but a good guy who will support you if you make it easy'. We are also exposed to organizational stereotypes through the process of socialization and acculturation. Other departments, competitors, or certain groups of customers may be labelled as helpful, suspicious, stupid, etc. That labelling can fix a meaning, an interpretation or a reputation to a person or group. The risk, in terms of organizational change, is that sometimes the label sticks too firmly so that those leading change can't see that group or those individuals in any other way. Indeed, a well proven psychological pattern is that of the confirmation bias[9], which means we unconsciously seek out, notice and remember data that reinforces our existing views. This can be a significant issue during mergers and takeovers when both sides can easily stereotype the characteristics of the other. In terms of Stacey's core ideas about gesture and response, we are therefore likely to behave towards the others in ways which reinforce our view of them, which in turn reinforces their view of us. In other words, stuckness.

A related risk that can contribute to stuckness is generalization. People sometimes say with great confidence, 'Doctors think x', 'Customers want y', 'The management team believe z'. The underlying assumption is that everyone in that group thinks, believes or wants the same thing. Such phrases could be true but are often a convenient shorthand. For instance, when creating a stakeholder map it is impossible to consider every single individual impacted by a change. We have to generalize. Yet in generalizing, and holding onto generalizations too firmly, certain groups can take on a more solid, overpowering and impenetrable persona as we construct in our heads an image of what psychologists call 'the generalized other'[10]. Thus the way we talk about certain phenomena, the very language we use, can restrict and constrain our options. The risk of talking and thinking about the solid mass of 'the generalized other', is that 'the other' becomes too abstract, too big, too hard to get a meaningful handle on. Such categorizing may meet our desire for order, simplicity and predictability, but the shadow side is that you cannot relate to or have a conversation with the generalized other. Trying to engage 'all the doctors' or 'all the managers' can sound daunting and be practically impossible. It is easy to feel stuck when we forget that there will be individuals in that group who will think differently.

A relational approach to change has, at its heart, a belief that change happens through conversation and genuinely seeking to relate to others as people. The encouragement is therefore to go and talk to some individuals so as to disaggregate the amorphous mass of 'the generalized other'. Those conversations clearly need to be done with an open mind and an attitude of inquiry, ready to be surprised. If you enter into them with advocacy rather than inquiry and push rather than pull, the chances are you and they will stay stuck and you will mutually reinforce the old patterns. However, being in a conversation can create understanding, movement, and therefore hope. In our experience, there will be far more nuance and difference of opinion than talk of the generalized other would suggest. This is why, for instance, Joe and Damian in their story talk about the conversations they had with each of the Executive team (see Chapter 12).

To illustrate this, a Deputy Medical Director in a large teaching hospital noticed that a certain group of consultants never attended any of the quality improvement meetings. The general view was that they were 'dinosaurs', resistant to change and they were thus written off in most people's minds. They had become a 'generalized other'. However, the man decided to go and talk to the consultants individually and, in doing so, found that while their individual stories were different, there was a commonality of feeling outsiders and excluded, that no one was interested in their ideas. Over time, they had all retreated into their shells, doing what was required to do the job but no more than that. They never volunteered for anything extra or bothered to put their heads above the parapet as they never expected their ideas to be welcomed. This behaviour unwittingly reinforced everyone else's prejudice about them as people who were not engaged and who were resistant to change. So they continued to be ignored, which, in turn, perpetuated their feelings and beliefs about themselves as outsiders. A stuck, mutually reinforcing pattern had been created which became a self-fulfilling prophecy. And it would have stayed like that if the Deputy Medical Director hadn't made a different gesture by challenging the dominant stereotype and seeking them out and listening to their views. His conversation with them started to shift the way they saw themselves and created ways for them to see how they could contribute to the change. It didn't all happen through one conversation, but the initial discussions were a gesture that created a new and different dynamic, that started to thaw the ice. And let's also be realistic here. There were a couple of people who did not respond to his initial gesture. As tends to be the case when engaging others in change, there was a shift with some people and a change in momentum. That was good enough.

There are a number of conclusions to draw here. Labelling a whole group of people as resistant to change impacts how you and others will see them and often how they see themselves too. Try instead to hold the label 'resistant to change' lightly, allowing for the possibility that there is some other dynamic at play. Inquiry, finding out what people really think and feel, is vital. There is also a risk in assuming that everyone in a group will think and feel the same. Finding some traction with a few already changes the dynamic with others and will impact the way you feel. There will be less stuckness, less amorphousness and more sense of movement and hope. Leaders often ask us 'How many people do we need to have in support of a change?' It all depends, of course, but it is certainly not necessary to spend significant energy trying to convert everyone. It is about creating critical mass, or to use Malcom Gladwell's term, a 'tipping point'.[11]

Reframing resistance

One of the most frustrating aspects of leading change is when other people are not up for it. They don't agree with our views; they are apathetic or indeed may actively attempt to sabotage our efforts. We are then tempted to label such individuals or groups using disparaging terms. As explored in the last section, we may well stereotype them as being 'resistant to change'. However, resistance is a topic that merits some exploration. Acts of resistance may be people doing something they should not, or indeed deliberately not doing something they should. In terms of seriousness, resistance can vary from gossip, to in some way 'getting your own back', non-co-operation, active confrontation, sabotage and strikes. It can sometimes come with a high moral tone, cloaked with noble ideals such as justice and dignity and talk of 'objection in principle', 'moral outrage', 'upholding standards' and 'righteous indignation'. And the chances are that there will have been times when you yourself have opposed particular changes, in which case, other people may well have seen you as a resistor (see Moira's story in Chapter 11).

The term 'resistance' literally means a restraining force that attempts to maintain the status quo. The notion of resistance implies opposition against something, usually the exercise of power – i.e. an attempt to influence or control the resistor. Leaders often perceive resistance negatively as it can get in the way of them achieving their goals. This can encourage a view of resistors as obstacles, ostriches, short-sighted, insubordinate and disobedient – the creation of a negatively perceived generalized other. The label of resistance can also encourage a dismissive attitude to potentially valid reasons for opposing a change. Yet, it is somewhat arbitrary to label behaviour from formal leaders, or Tops, as acts of control and power while behaviour from Middles or Bottoms is seen as acts of resistance. As Knights and Vurdubakis argue, 'acts of resistance are also act of power',[12] and indeed we can talk of resistance leaders. Whether resistance is seen as positive or negative is largely a matter of perspective. The reasons for resistance may seem illogical or irrational to some but will have meaning for those resisting. The civil rights movement in the United States, the anti-apartheid movement in South Africa and the French Resistance in the Second World War are all examples of resistance movements that we would now see as morally right, but, at the time, those in power, for the most part, saw as anti-establishment, dangerous and wrong. This is why resistance is a tricky area, whichever 'side' you are on.

A relational approach to resistance emphasizes two things:

- Understanding why it might be happening rather than seeing resistance as a problem to be managed.
- Reframing resistance as ambivalence, so that it is less binary than being 'for' or 'against' change. Ambivalence allows for a more nuanced understanding of what is going on with greater possibilities for conversation and action.

Reframing resistance as ambivalence

A growing number of authors suggest retiring the phrase 'resistance to change', which sees resistance in very binary, black and white terms. Piderit,[13] instead, introduces the term 'ambivalence to change'. She suggests categorizing employees' attitudes to change along three dimensions:

- Emotional – how they feel in response to it.
- Cognitive – what they think and believe about it.
- Intentional – what actions they might be intending to take.

An employee's response to an organizational change along the cognitive dimension may range from strong positive beliefs (e.g. 'This change is absolutely what the organization needs') to strong negative beliefs (e.g. 'This change will sink the organization'). On the emotional dimension, responses may range from anger to anxiety and despair to excitement. On the intentional dimension, an employee's response may be to support the change or oppose it (which includes ignoring it).

You might label someone resistant to change when there are negative responses along all three dimensions, and supportive of the change when there are positive responses in all three dimensions. However, the likelihood is that there will be many who have a mix of reactions. These are the people Piderit would label ambivalent. The subtly of this approach is that it recognizes that initial responses to change may not be consistently negative or consistently positive but can be a mixture of the two. Hence the importance of not labelling and fixing people with a label of resistance.

To illustrate the subtleties and shifts of this approach, let us take the story of Kallur, who is angry and upset at the proposed discontinuation of a particular product range. His boss could label him as resistant to change. However, Kallur's emotional response may be because he has been working on this product for five years and, therefore, has a great deal of personal investment and pride in it. He may also be angry that management didn't invest in the range several years ago. However, when he has seen the market share data, the profitability reports and the new pipeline of products, he knows rationally that there isn't much hope of the range surviving (cognitive response). His behaviour (intentional response) may depend on where he is in the change cycle and what career options he is considering. If he thinks he is going to lose his job anyway with the discontinuation of the product range and his predominant emotion is anger, he may well be, in political terms, a bit of a donkey and continue to ask awkward questions in meetings and bad-mouth management. If he thinks that he wants a good pay off or that there may be other job opportunities, he may be more circumspect, waiting to see what happens, not yet decided.

This illustrates the complexity of possible responses. Simply labelling Kallur as resistant to change fails to do justice to what is going on. It also fails to give you as a leader many options for action, whereas recognizing the three dimensions does. In terms of the emotional component, listening to Kallur, giving him an opportunity to express his anger and sadness, acknowledging his feelings, sharing the change curve or Bridges transition model[14] (Chapter 6) could all be helpful actions and gestures. Communicating the business rationale for the decision and sharing the facts and figures in a clear way can help individuals cognitively accept the situation. In terms of intentions, this will undoubtedly shift over time, in part as result of the emotional and cognitive responses, but also depending on the gestures you and others make and what job opportunities exist.

The benefit of this more subtle understanding of ambivalence is that it gives you the opportunity to work at emotional, cognitive and behavioural levels with people. It doesn't mean that all conflict will go away or that everyone can be persuaded to shift from ambivalence to positive enthusiasm, but it does allow you more possibilities for conversation, engagement and subsequent movement.

So what tend to be the emotional and cognitive reasons for being against change?

Emotional reasons for being against change

- *Loss and Self-interest.* People may resist change because they believe they will lose something they value from the change, and so focus purely on their own best interests rather than the whole organization.
- *Fear about own ability to change.* Sometimes people resist change because they worry they will not be able to develop the new skills or behaviours required.
- *Search for someone or something to blame.* People tend to believe that bad things do not happen accidentally and that they require a causal agent. The stronger the threat to an individual's personal identity, the more likely they are to believe that the threat was deliberate and to blame the organization or management.[15] The need to find something to blame may be part of a phase depending where people are on the change cycle, which can be exacerbated by not feeling heard (see Chapter 6). It may also be part of the drama cycle if that is a familiar pattern of behaving for that particular individual.
- *Shared sense of fate or identity with others.* If a change impacts many people, official or unofficial coalitions of like-minded people can form. When individuals join a coalition they may go from being passive to more actively negative, since belonging to the group gives them a new identity and enables them to hold onto an attitude which may have been harder to sustain as an individual. As these groupings recur and are repeated over time, they can become more entrenched and the source of overt organizationally situated political identities, such as 'head office', 'the regions', 'the old guard', with reputations

for, or against, change. In other words, they can become examples of stereotyping and 'the generalized other'.

Cognitive reasons for being against change

- *Misunderstanding.* People resist change when they do not understand its implications and assume, sometimes incorrectly, that they will lose far more than they will gain.
- *Different information.* People may also have access to different information. They may therefore conclude that there are more costs and fewer benefits to themselves and/or the organization itself than those presented. This is an example of where listening to those perceived as resistors may give those leading the change important new insights and information. In addition, it may suggest the importance of sharing, say, customer or patient stories to provide new information to challenge the 'professional' or received view.
- *Different assessments of benefits and risks.* Sometimes individuals or groups interpret the facts or data differently from those initiating or explaining the change.

What then to do as a leader when you're faced with ambivalence?

Many of the ideas covered in Chapter 6 about emotions support working with the emotional component of ambivalence to change. Communicating, listening and empathizing are key. Listening hard may help you identify where the area of disagreement is and you may learn some important facts or insights that you might have otherwise overlooked. When the Space Shuttle Challenger crashed, workers had tried to flag their concerns about the lack of safety features for re-entry into the earth's atmosphere, but leaders hadn't heard. A disastrous example of the phenomenon of only paying attention to confirmatory data rather than being really open to others. Actively listening involves suspending your judgement about right and wrong, as explored in Chapter 7.

In terms of the more cognitive aspects of ambivalence to change, it may be helpful to locate exactly where the difference of opinion lies. This means engaging others in dialogue to understand what their concerns are. This deeper understanding will help you move from stuckness to a more fine-grained appreciation of where the differences in perspective may lie.

- It may be that there are fundamental differences about the nature of the problem and/or the ownership of it. Listen first to really understand their perspective rather than trying to keep selling yours. Stay curious and keep asking why, but do so gently so it doesn't feel like an interrogation which would be likely to lead to a defensive response. (See Chapter 8 for more on listening.)
- You may agree on the problem but not how to solve it. Explore your own solution as a starter for ten, looking at its strengths and weaknesses, and then do the same for their solution. In terms of the conflict styles in Chapter 8, this would be using collaboration, and then perhaps compromise.
- You agree on the problem and the solution but they have concerns about implementation. Remember that they are agreeing with you and are trying to help get things right, so don't see this as negative whinging. Explore their concerns and identify what actions could be taken to protect against these potential challenges.
- They are positive about the change but are worried that others aren't, and that they will be left exposed if they stick their necks out. Start small without a big fanfare so it is easier and less public to take risks.

In praise of small gestures

The impact of changing even small things is supported in early research that took place at the Hawthorne Works, a large factory complex in Illinois, where the intention was to investigate how changing the lighting levels and the scheduling of break times impacted productivity.[16] The workers' productivity seemed to improve when *any* changes were made, however small. There have been various interpretations of these studies, but two seem most pertinent here. First, that the productivity gain occurred as a result of the motivational effect on the workers of the interest being shown in them. Then more recently, Clark and Sugrue,[17] re-analysing the data, suggest that uncontrolled novelty effects, anything new, caused on average 50–63 per cent of the rise in productivity, even though this then tailed off after eight weeks. In terms of working with stuckness, these studies reinforce the positive impact that comes from taking an interest in people and the importance of introducing something new that breaks the pattern of the old. In the complexity sciences too small effects count. A key principle is that as what appear to be stable states consist of patterned dynamic movement, they can 'tip' into new states on the basis of small, perhaps un-noticed, variations.[18] As Stacey himself says, 'small differences can escalate into major, completely unpredictable changes.[19]

What small gestures might you wish to make in practice? Chapter 7, on re-imagining meetings, and Chapter 8, on different gestures in the moment, cover many practical suggestions about small gestures that make a big difference. In addition, communication plays a part. Stuckness may occur as a result of people simply being unaware of progress or not believing the corporate communication that is expressed in management soundbites. Initiating sessions where people can come and understand what is going on and share their ideas can create a sense of momentum. Emma's story (Chapter 13) includes examples of this. Drop-in sessions, open doors, walking about and using the opportunity of spontaneously interacting with people are all opportunities to communicate what is happening and allow others to hear, and be part of, the evolving narrative. Ensuring that there is a regular update on progress is also important. Updates that are authentic and balanced are more likely to be believed than a carefully polished power point presentation. And sometimes it may be setbacks rather than progress that have to be communicated, as in Moira's story (Chapter 11).

Kotter[20] was one of the first writers on change to emphasize the importance of communicating quick wins. Stacey[21] too talks about the leader's role in amplifying key themes from what is emerging in conversation. More recently, research by Amabile and Kramer[20] found people are highly motivated by having a sense of progress, even though leaders tend to forget to share news of such progress.

Experimentation is also key to creating movement. This might be thought experiments, such as scenario planning which, in helping people imagine different possible futures, can reduce anxiety about having one 'right' solution. Scenario planning can also sensitize people into noticing what is emerging. Practical experimentation can also help people get unstuck and create energy and confidence that different ways are possible. There are formal processes for this such as the PDSA

(Plan, Do, Study, Act) cycle. What can be termed Trojan Mice[23] can be useful to describe experiments that are small, fast and under the radar. As such, Trojan mice are relatively risk free experiments from which much can be learned without them bearing the weight of expectation that can come with more public experiments.

As a leader, you may need to create the conditions for safe uncertainty that allow and encourage experimentation. This may mean making gestures that recognize that with experimentation failure is inevitable. In the words of jazz musician Miles Davis, 'If you're not making a mistake, it's a mistake'. However, in some cultures there can be significant fear of failure and public shaming from mistakes. You as a leader may need to publicly legitimize failure and reframe it as an opportunity for learning. Chapman introduces the idea of 'fail happy' and encourages people to have 10 per cent more curiosity =10 per cent more bravery = 10 per cent more experimentation = 10 per cent more creative adventure and 10 per cent more happy failures. Say 'yes' to the mess, is one of his mantras:

> While *no* is the language of safety and certainty, *yes* is the language of possibility, creativity and adventure. This practice is about becoming more aware of where our biases lie and, no matter where they are balanced, to tip them further towards yes. It is about realizing that by saying 'yes', we are acknowledging and accepting possibility [...] It is about willingly seeking out the mess and getting good at spotting the creative clues that are lurking in the metaphorical fog.[24]

Questions for further reflection

- What aspects of the change in which you are involved feel stuck?
- How might your own thinking contribute to this stuckness?
- What might help you see the issues differently?
- What experimentation might you try?
- Who are you currently labelling as resistant, and what gestures might you make to inquire into their perspective?
- How might you encourage others to experiment?

Chapter 10

Sustaining yourself, others and change

In what sense does a change begin and end? You may have embarked on a change programme, but the likelihood is that much was already happening before it officially 'started'. The plan may have a particular end point, and by then some aspects may indeed have altered in expected as well as unanticipated ways. Other elements have perhaps stayed much as they were. When we talk about change having a beginning and ending, it is usually because we are drawing attention to particular activities, branding them as the 'change programme'. However, as we know from thinking about organizations as complex responsive processes, below the waterline there is constant flux as people are talking, making decisions, agreeing and falling out, experimenting, making products, selling services, talking to customers and gossiping. So what practices enable yourself and others to keep going, to continue to respond to what is emerging in the ongoing process of change? This is the focus of this last chapter.

According to Stacey, 'The practice [of effective leadership] is that of participating skillfully in interaction with others in reflective and imaginative ways, aware of the potentially destructive processes one may be caught up in. It is in this practice that one is recognized as leader, as one who had the capacity to assist the group to continue to act ethically, creatively and courageously into the unknown.'[1] Certainly, leading change can be intense, exhilarating, exhausting and all consuming. It can be political, emotional and involve you consciously and unconsciously in situations where power play and psychodynamics are at work. We believe that paying attention to your own needs as an individual and connecting with others are essential elements of a relational approach to change.

Binney[2] talks about the importance of connecting with self and connecting with others. In previous chapters, we have explored many different models and ideas that can help you become more self-aware and draw attention to the possibility of making different gestures and responses. We have also looked at different ways of creating the conditions for dialogue, re-imagining meetings, engaging others in conversation and adopting a facilitative approach to change. In this chapter we offer additional insights and ideas by first looking at how you stay connected to yourself through the act of reflection. We then explore ways of connecting with others to seek out additional support and challenge. Lastly, we look at three organizational interventions that can sustain you, others and change. These are Action Research, Action Inquiry and the use of storytelling.

Connecting with yourself

Acknowledge and diminishing your inner critic

It is a common experience of leaders who are in the midst of change to be suddenly wracked by doubts and experience a crisis of confidence. This may well have happened to you. Imposter syndrome was a term first coined by clinical psychologists Pauline Clance and Suzanne Imes[3] in the late 1970s. They noticed a pattern in some high-achieving women (now also recognized in men) who seemed unable to internalize their accomplishments, putting their success down to luck, timing or the fact they had somehow duped others into believing they were better than they themselves believed they really were. Despite being outwardly successful, those who experience this syndrome had a persistent fear of being found out and exposed as a fraud. Cheryl Sandberg, COO of Facebook, acknowledges her experience of this in her book, *Lean In*.[4]

Working with a coach is one way of seeking support should this happen to you. However, leaders have also said that just knowing that this is a recognized syndrome has been a source of relief, as it means they feel less alone or abnormal in having such feelings. Even if you do not ever suffer from full blown imposter syndrome, you may still possess an inner critic, a voice that is quick to give you all the reasons why you should NOT try something new and different. The inner critic is highly skilled at conjuring up images of things going disastrously wrong, of social embarrassment and shame.

Steve Chapman[5] writes about how he visualized his inner critic as a mean old man inside him who, he discovers, 'looks and sounds like a wise sage but has the intellect and temperament of an overtired toddler'. Through paying attention to what his inner critic was saying and by creating a character for him (first in drawings then in actually making a puppet), he discovered that his inner critic's powers had diminished. In a similar vein, another leader we know visualized her inner critic as Gollum from *Lord of the Rings*. Whenever his voice came into her head, undermining what she was about to do, she visualized his small head on the desk in front of her and mentally squashed him with her thumb. At the same time reminding herself of the voice of a supportive friend as a counter weight. You may find it helpful to find ways of silencing your own inner critic.

Connecting with your own experience: The role of reflection

When we talk to leaders about the importance of making time for reflection, some make comments like:

- Only people with too much time on their hands have time for reflection. When would I possibly fit that in?
- I wouldn't know what that really means.
- The only people who talk about reflection are people who never do anything.
- I know what I'm doing; I've had many years of experience in my business so I don't see how reflection would help me.

If we are too busily involved in what Stacey calls mindless action,[6] we are on the human equivalent of the hamster wheel, destined to keep running round in circles without stopping to consider whether there are better or different ways of doing things. In many organizations, the dominant orthodoxy is often to value action over reflection, although the growing popularity of mindfulness may serve to counter this trend. Reflection is a practice that enables you to notice and connect with your own experience of what is going on around you, paying attention to the myriad interactions and conversations in which you participate. It is also fundamental to the way adults learn and change. When we talk about reflection, we are meaning more than sitting down with a glass of wine and thinking, 'Gosh today was awful

– that meeting went really badly and I wish I'd told Bob what I really think about the expansion plans. Oh well, that's me, always miss the moment.' Reflection can be defined as 'the capability to reflect critically and systematically on the work-self interface [...] fostering a personal awareness and resilience'.[7] Stacey defines it as 'the intellectual and emotional exercise of the mind to reason, to give careful consideration to something, make inferences and decisions, and find solutions'.[8] As a leader, there will be times when you want to reflect on what has been happening in the recent past, what Schön[9] calls 'reflection-on-action'. At other times, you may want to reflect on what you notice and respond to, in the moment. Schön calls this 'reflection-*in*-action' and it is a similar idea to Casey's model for working with groups (see Chapter 8). This ability to notice and respond is what Stacey refers to as 'practical judgement' and we refer to as being 'choiceful' in this book.

The process of taking your experience and literally examining it is imaginatively described in one of the Harry Potter stories.

> Harry stared at the stone basin. The contents had returned to their original, silvery white state, swirling and rippling beneath his gaze.
>
> 'What is it?' Harry asked shakily.
>
> 'This? It is called a Penseive,'said Dumbledore. 'I sometimes find, and I'm sure you know the feeling, that I simply have too many thoughts and memories crammed into my mind'.
>
> 'Err,' said Harry who couldn't truthfully say that he had ever felt anything of the sort.
>
> 'At these times,' said Dumbledore, indicating the stone basin,' I use the Penseive. One simply siphons the excess thoughts from one's mind, pours them into a basin, and examines them at one's leisure. It becomes easier to spot patterns and links [...] when they are in this form.'[10]

What are the twenty-first century equivalents to the imagined Penseive? And what sometimes holds people back from engaging in reflection? The greatest barrier to reflective practice is often time pressure, but there can be psychological barriers, too. In some cases social, professional or cultural norms can deride reflection, labelling it as a somehow an odd or self-indulgent practice. Those with Be Perfect or Be Strong drivers may feel they would rather not look at their own behaviour and attitudes for fear of what they might discover. As we mentioned in Chapter 1, exploring your own assumptions, and what Argyris[11] calls your theories in use, can be challenging. Others reframe reflection as investment in their personal learning for the benefit of themselves, others and the change.

How to create time in your day or your week for refection is a matter of personal preference and dependent on the practicalities and constraints of your own work pattern. Cognisant of this, we share some of the practices adopted by leaders we have worked with, as a stimulus to your own ideas and experimentation.

- Take ten minutes at the beginning or end of a day to reflect.
- End meetings at five minutes to the hour so you have time to reflect between meetings.
- Book a 30-minute slot around lunchtime that is your time and write in your journal for ten minutes before looking at emails.
- Use mind maps or sketches. Use the first part of your journey to work to journal (see below) before looking at emails.
- Journal on a regular basis, buying a particularly attractive notebook or using the convenience of your iPad.

What do we mean by journaling?

Journaling is not a form of 'Dear Diary' in which you need to make an entry every day. Instead, it is a means of noticing and writing down experiences which either went particularly well or left you feeling disturbed or confused. These are the ones that are worth capturing for further pondering so that you can learn what might have been going on, how you might have contributed to the situation and how you might want to respond differently in future. A journal is only ever for your use, so there is no need to write as if someone else is going to read it. The kind of questions that you might want to ask yourself include:

- What do I make of this?
- What might have caused me to feel that way?
- How am I feeling about this and why might that be?
- What assumptions am I making about myself and others?

- What theory am I using to make sense of this? Are there other ways of looking at this? Would others agree with my meaning-making?
- Can I spot a pattern here? Is this something I have noticed before?
- Was I reacting in a way that was useful to me?
- What might I want to try differently next time?
- What could I learn from this?
- What could I do which would help me be more conscious in how I respond (rather than just reacting)?
- What situations at work might be similar to this, and therefore give me an opportunity to try out something different?

The very act of writing things down often gives a new perspective or additional clarity. You can also look back through your writing to identify patterns in what has been happening and how you may have been behaving. Reflection is an opportunity to learn about our own gestures and responses in our interactions with others. Many people find it helpful to work with a coach or as part of an action learning set to explore themes or particular situations they have noted in their journal.

Connecting with others

Seeking out support and challenge from others

When you're feeling under pressure, it can be easy to withdraw from others in an attempt to get to grips with the enormity of the inbox and a diary that is back to back with meetings. However, in retreating, it can be easy to fall prey to your own hooks and drivers and adopt, almost by default, the loneliness and isolation of the heroic leader who is trying to fix everything - an impossible task. A relational approach to change emphasizes the importance of connecting with others to make sense of what is emerging and to involve other people in shaping the next part of the change. Talking to others can be a source of energy and affirmation. You might want to consider how best to encourage others to share their reflections and experiences with you. This may be by engaging in planned and impromptu conversations with people in your organization.

Other people can often helpfully see new courses of action that you may be blind to. In Moira's story (Chapter 11), the unexpected announcement that her division were not going to get the beds they had been promised in the new hospital made her so angry she couldn't see any way forward. However, by involving the team around her in what was going on, they found creative ways to adapt to the emerging situation.

You may also choose to seek out specific individuals, depending on your needs and intent. You may choose to co-lead the work with a trusted colleague or to work with an external facilitator on certain aspects of the change. Regular meetings with an executive coach can help support your own developing self-awareness as a leader. A mentor who is an expert in the system or organization may also be able to offer advice on some of the contextual aspects of the change.

Colleagues can also give you insights into your own behaviour. Rather than just asking them for general feedback, it is sometimes helpful to think what questions would elicit maximum learning and support. Heron's discovery questions[12] tend to work well and examples include:

- Tell me what you appreciated about my contribution.
- Tell me one thing that would have made it a better experience for you.
- What could I start, stop and continue?

Greg is Head of Communications in a large multinational corporation. When an organization-wide change programme was outlined by the Executive Team, he was thrilled to be part of it, but a few months in, the overall leadership of the work was being fought over by three senior executives. Greg found himself trying to link up several projects which had become disconnected from each other. There was conflict about what was important and the approach to change. He asked a colleague what she thought of how he had behaved in a particularly frustrating meeting. She looked him in the eye and said: 'You seem to be carrying a huge sense of responsibility for it all.' He suddenly realized he was working on the assumption that if he worked harder to bring people together, he would somehow be able to 'fix' things. He recognized this was a pattern of his, trying to rescue and take personal responsibility for something when actually that wasn't his job. Stopping and reflecting,

Greg recognized he was one person in a complex system and decided to concentrate on spotting opportunities to influence people's perspectives, rather than trying to plan and control what was happening. As a result he felt lighter, more productive and better connected with those around him and to what was emerging in the organization.

Consider Change supervision

Supervision is considered essential to ethical and safe practice in what are often known as the helping professions. So for social workers, executive coaches, organization development practitioners, those engaged in mental health work and palliative care, supervision provides what Erik de Haan[13] calls 'an intermediate space between work and home'. This type of work is emotional and, as is also the case when leading change, you can be subject to many of the psychodynamic processes touched on in Chapter 8. It can be hard sometimes to disentangle what is your own 'stuff' and what belongs to others. De Haan describes supervision as a place where metaphorically speaking, 'we wipe the sweat from our brows and the dirt from our faces ... look ourselves in the mirror and get ready to become an "ordinary" person again, without a "role" or "function"'. The supervisor is someone who is not directly involved in the work and can help you see it differently – literally super-vision – noticing patterns and themes, working with you to facilitate your thinking, giving you a chance to stand back to see from a different angle the dynamics and patterns of what is taking place in your context.

Cathy Reilly and David Birch[14] have pioneered the development of what they call change supervision for those involved in leading change. This is rather like coaching but is offered by those who have expertise in understanding change, are skilled as a supervisor and also bring an outside perspective with no axe to grind or product to sell. Sometimes leaders choose to have change supervision just for themselves; sometimes it is offered for a team of people who are jointly leading a particular change project. They describe the purpose of the supervision as providing a safe space that allows leaders the time and support to:

- Explore their own blind spots, as it is easy to become caught up in unconscious dynamics that are (by definition) happening outside awareness, but which can slow down change.

- Take the time out from their general busyness to 'notice what they are noticing' in the complexity and messiness of what is going on.
- Make sense of this through being on the receiving end of good inquiry questions and attentive listening. Weick,[15] one of the main writers on sensemaking, describes the benefits of talking aloud when he says, 'How do I know what I think until I see what I say'. Through thinking and talking aloud, leaders can thus become clearer about their own intentions.
- Pay attention to their own relationship with the change - how they are feeling about it; where they are in the change curve; personal losses and gains they may be experiencing; areas of risk personally; how they might personally need to change. They have found that leaders who do not take time to reflect on this often project their fears and anxieties about change onto others, or can easily abdicate responsibility for change, blaming others.
- Reflect upon their relationships with others in the change process: with internal and external stakeholders; with others in the organization; are they paying enough attention to others' experiences through use of pull and facilitative approaches? Are they balancing sufficient inquiry with advocacy? What kinds of conversation are missing from this change effort?
- Develop self-awareness and resilience, which are sometimes neglected. Even the most resilient leaders can benefit from monitoring these to have the stamina to keep going.
- Remind themselves of their own strengths and what is going well.

A trio of leaders who had been asked to integrate three different organizations used a change supervisor and found it made a significant difference to the way they were able to lead the merger. They were able to have difficult conversations between themselves and pay attention to their evolving relationships with each other and the three businesses. However, given the nature of the work, their change supervisor insisted she would only work with them if they committed to a two hour meeting once a fortnight. That felt a big ask at the time. Afterwards, all three felt it was absolute the right thing to have done as the regular change supervision session meant they had a forum for discussing some of the more tricky aspects of the change, and were therefore able to move forward with the integration far quicker than their sponsors had expected.

Action Research: Reflecting with others

Personal reflection can lead you to new insights about yourself and about what is going on around you. The same is true of reflection with others. The very act of asking questions about what is going on, being curious and wondering together what to do next, can sustain change by keeping conversations about it in play.[16]

Action Research is a way of doing this with others in a disciplined and deliberate way. It is a research method that challenges the idea of the unbiased researcher conducting research on others through randomized control trails, that may lead to insights of academic relevance but not necessarily to practice. Action Research, however, has dual aims: to know more about the issues being studied (an inquiry aim) *and* to try to change it (an action aim). It is concerned with making a practical difference to what is being studied, while it is being studied, and the researchers are those who have an active interest in wanting the situation to be improved in some way.[17] So those involved in the change, such as yourself or others, might take on the additional role of studying what is happening. This is why it can play a useful role as part of a change process. Unlike mainstream research, it is reflexive in that it acknowledges the research process will affect what is being studied and that researchers will be affected by the process. In other words, it does not separate out the researcher from the research subjects. It is conducted *with* people not *on* people, so is congruent with a relational approach to leading change. It also works with the evolving nature of organizational life, recognizing and embracing emergence rather than trying to ignore or explain it away.

Appreciative Inquiry can be a useful way to frame inquiry questions in a positive way (see Chapter 6). Rather than evaluating a change at the end, with outsiders who are 'unbiased', Action Research encourages those who are part of the change process to inquire into it themselves. This both changes it and allows them to make more informed choices about what to do next as they go, paying attention to what is actually happening and being experienced below the waterline. The iterative nature of Action Research is depicted in Figure 10.1.

Action Research can thus also be seen as a form of personal and collective learning in which participant researchers make sense of and

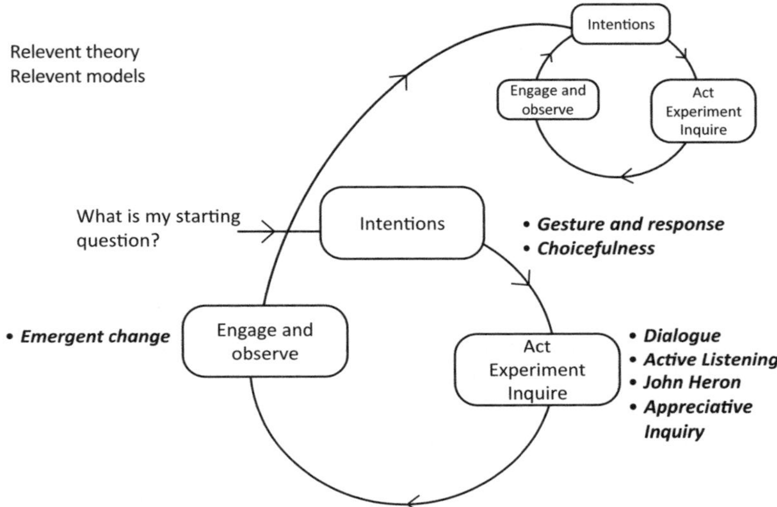

Figure 10.1 The iterative nature of Action Research. Adapted from Coleman, Wiggins, Marshall and Smallwood.

'theorize' about the change they are involved in, using theories and models to help them make sense of what might be happening. On the basis of this learning, they can then choose how to act next to help bring about positive impact, as defined by participants themselves, and do so in iterative cycles. In doing this, people are able to explore the gap between what they thought should be happening and what they discover is actually taking place, and modify and adapt what gestures they make in response in real time. They can notice and start to close the gap between Argyris's[18] espoused theories and theories in use, as discussed in Chapter 1.

Action Research is often done in organizations with the support of external action researchers who train internal people to be co-researchers. We took on this role in work with the Ambulance Service in Qatar.

This organization had invested heavily in new equipment, restructuring and developing standard operating procedures. The approach to change had been directive and deficit based and the leaders had little idea about how staff felt about the changes, what impact they were having or what to do next. They decided to engage some external action researchers to work with their own staff, who were from many different countries, primarily Tunisia, the Philippines, South Africa and India. A group of ten co-researchers were recruited who were all in front line jobs, not managers. They were trained in conducting Appreciative Inquiry interviews, and then interviewed colleagues throughout the service, as well as recruiting and training more co-researchers. They also interviewed senior managers. Joint reflection/sense-making sessions were run between the senior managers and the co-researchers to explore what they were learning. This process changed the nature of the relationships between those at very different levels in the hierarchy; it changed the way the co-researchers saw their role in improving the Ambulance Service and it changed the way they saw fellow staff from other nationalities. A few quotes from the co-researchers illustrate this:

> 'The most incredible part of the process has got to be the sessions we have had with the senior managers and Executive Team. We are able to sit and share ideas and start to work on areas ... it feels like we are the voice of the staff and have created a connection between lower and upper levels, and rather than present managers with problems to fix we are part of the change.'
>
> 'I believe I can make a real change in our work environment and this research gave me the opportunity to do so.'
>
> 'I was actually impressed by the passion that each and every staff member from different cultural backgrounds have expressed during the interviews. I did not expect that they care a lot about their work and about their patients.'
>
> 'I would often stereotype my colleagues ... I have come to realize how many hidden similarities there are between us.'[19]

The above example illustrates the power of Action Research to allow different groups in the system to connect differently and to have different conversations about change and about what to do next. Sometimes though, a lighter touch version of Action Research may be used, without using external research support. This is sometimes called Action Inquiry. The following example illustrates the practical use of Action Inquiry.

Margaret was leading the merger of a communications and a marketing team in a large soft drinks organization. Both teams were seen as very different tribes so Margaret had a hunch that just focusing on structures and job roles wouldn't be enough. She used Action Inquiry to help the newly formed team learn from and sustain the changes that were taking place. In the first team meeting, with Margaret's help, the four team leaders developed some questions which they thought would help them get to the heart of the issues they were encountering as part of the merger:

- What is changing about my work as we bring together our teams?
- What have we done well as separate teams which we would like to bring to the new team, and how might we do that?
- What are we learning about working together as we merge our teams?
- What is changing about the way we promote our products?

The group agreed to reflect on these questions during team meetings and to spend time between meetings talking to colleagues about these questions and journaling what they themselves were noticing. When they next met, they shared their reflections, which helped them notice what was working well and what they wanted to change. At the third meeting, all four shared their frustrations trying to work on the promotion of a new product. People from marketing were using different terms from those in communications, which left people feeling their views were being discounted or ignored, and there were misunderstandings. Talking this through during the Action Inquiry session, it became apparent that the process for developing product promotions was unclear. This mutual understanding, a forum for talking about what was happening and a desire to change things helped them work together differently. The four of them spent time together before the next session to clarify the process. The team continued to meet once a month for eight months with Action Inquiry as their focus. Through this regular time together to talk about their experiences of the day to day, they noticed what was working well and built on it, supporting each other through some difficult changes and coming to a better understanding of each other's ways of thinking and working.

There are two aspects of this approach that are particularly valuable – asking people to identify the questions they have about the change that they are involved in and, secondly, creating an opportunity for them to regularly come back to talk about what they are experiencing in relation to these questions. The joint creation of questions and subsequent discussions helps surface some of the relational aspects of change in a way that merely focusing on a described aim or outcome won't always do. This approach of continually reflecting and reviewing together on what's happening helps everyone notice and work with the emergent and unexpected things that occur during change, and allows leaders to reinforce and amplify what is working well, in addition to taking more deliberate choices about what to do together as things emerge.

Connecting through creating ongoing stories

Another way in which leaders can connect with those around them is through the stories they tell. This is not about having anything as fixed as a vision. Geoff Mead[20] describes how storytelling is essentially a relational activity, a social process which is about making meaning together. As the Booker prize-winning author Ben Okri says: 'A people are as healthy and confident as the stories they tell themselves. Sick storytellers can make nations sick. Without stories we would go mad. Life would lose its moorings or orientation [...] Stories can conquer fear, you know. They can make the heart larger.'[21] Similarly, American writer John Steinbeck also talks of the way that an ancient method of feeling less alone is through stories so that as the listener you feel: 'Yes, that is the way it is, or at least that is the way I feel it, and you are not as alone as you thought.' So as a leader, one of the ways you can give others some confidence and connection is through the stories you tell as you explain and illustrate your views, as well as listening to the experiences of others through inquiry, paying attention to what is going on to both modify your own story and amplify or reframe the stories of others.

To illustrate the power of using stories, we give the example of Sarah who worked for an NHS hospital. She had tried introducing various quality improvement techniques such as Lean into her organization, but somehow nothing had really worked. Six months later, she was asked by James, the CEO, to employ an external facilitator to run a Board session to review progress. Sarah had winced at the idea. She wasn't on the Board herself so she was fully expecting that she would be publicly blamed and shamed. However, at the Board session the facilitator drew their attention to the fact that the organization's identity and story was almost exclusively defined by outsiders, by government bodies such as the CQC and Monitor, who focused on missed targets and low ratings and had put the hospital in 'special measures', the organizational equivalent of the naughty step. The Board already knew that morale was low and staff absence a real problem which made meeting the NHS England targets even harder. The Board hadn't thought about the fact that they had not given staff, nor indeed themselves, any other story to believe in. They could suddenly see why there was no enthusiasm for implementing Lean. People needed something to believe in. In fact, they as a leadership team needed something to believe in. The facilitator then helped the Board talk together to start creating a new story.

A process was developed using Appreciative Inquiry which involved staff. The leadership team were amazed how different they themselves felt, and gradually the mood in the place shifted. So did the performance against the targets, and they came out of special measures. There were still some bumps along the way but by creating their own story, which was an emerging narrative of who they were as an organization and what they were wanting to become, they were no longer victims, defined by others. They were purposeful and had a sense of intent that energized them and others.

There are a number of learnings from this: the value of using a facilitator from outside the organization to draw attention to something that those on the inside were too wrapped up in firefighting to have noticed; the importance of leaders acting with purposeful intent in shaping their own future rather than passively allowing others to do this for them; the importance of staff having a positive enough, while still realistic, story to believe in; the importance of having an internal locus of control rather than an external one, and of acting so that you are no longer in the victim position on the drama triangle.

For Sarah, the other surprise was how those few comments from the external facilitator were noticed and amplified by the CEO so that the Board session turned out to be completely different to what she had expected.

In summary, there are a number of different ways of sustaining yourself, the change and others around you, wherever you are in the process. Some involve reflection and connecting more deeply with whatever is going on for you personally. Others involve connecting with others through coaching, change supervision or introducing processes such as Action Research and storytelling. Whichever approach you adopt, the importance is to recognize that these kind of activities are an integral part of being a relational leader of change.

Questions for further reflection

- How might you ensure you make time for yourself to reflect?
- Who are the specific people that are important for you to connect with regularly?
- What other ways of connecting with others might help sustain you?
- What approaches may help others connect with what is emerging?

Part II

Leaders' stories of change

Introduction

In Chapters 1 to 10, we have brought together theories, research and ideas that we've found to be of practical use for those leading change. Our aim has been to illustrate how to lead change relationally, working with people, rather than doing to them, while acknowledging the inevitable messiness and emotional roller coaster that is the lived experience of change.

In the following three chapters, we share with you three 'warts and all' stories of fellow leaders of change. We did not want to offer polished case studies, in which the protagonists are superheroes who recount tales of the wise choices they have made, where every plan becomes a reality, all objectives are achieved and there are no frustrations or surprising turns. There is little learning in such airbrushed accounts. In our experience, they can just make the rest of us feel inadequate in comparison.

Instead, the stories that follow are ones where we hope you will empathize with the leaders, as well as learn from them. They are the stories of people who were kind enough to share their experiences with us, but we have changed certain details such as their names, the names of their organizations and their locations to protect their anonymity.

In our desire to tell an honest tale, we've discovered that a good story still needs a beginning, a middle, an end and moments of drama to hold your interest. This means that we have adapted the stories a little and taken some literary license to bring them to life on the page. Where we've done this, we've stayed true to the essence of people's experiences and the story owners have read and approved them. To indicate how the theory and practice covered in previous chapters shows up in real life, we have made links to the relevant chapters in the margins of each of the stories that follow.

Chapter 11

The ups and downs of change

Moira's story

When The Ribble Vale Hospital relocated to a new site, different departments were jockeying for position to ensure they got the location and space they wanted. Moira, Deputy Medical Director for obstetrics and gynaecology, experienced the political consequences of her department being relatively small. Despite strong cultural pressure to just accept the changes that were imposed and keep quiet, she involved her team in what was happening and in working out what to do next. This is her story.

Moira's tone was indignant as she vented to her husband.

'They just told us they were taking our beds away, putting us down the end of the corridor and having the labour ward and gynaecology a ten minute sprint apart. No consultation. No apology. No consideration of the safety implications for women. Just an order.

'At the eleventh hour, the big boys of acute medicine and A&E, with their heavily branded "One Front Door" policy, are being allowed a land grab. And to add to the insult, taking over our bit of the ward is never going to give them the capacity they say they now need.'

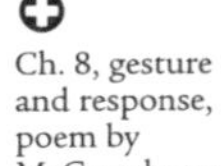

Ch. 8, gesture and response, poem by McGough; see p. 156

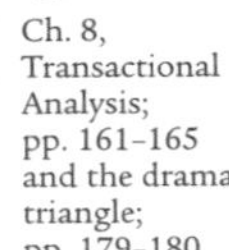

Ch. 8, Transactional Analysis; pp. 161–165 and the drama triangle; pp. 179–180.

She paused, her normally soft voice steely with barely controlled anger. 'The biggest insult was from the Chief Operating Officer. In this big meeting, with all my consultant colleagues present, she looked down her nose at me and said in a patronizing voice, "Well, a small speciality like Obs and Gynae is just a cat flap on the front door."' Moira shook her head. 'My service and everything we've achieved dismissed as nothing.'

Moira had been at the Ribble Vale Hospital in Yorkshire for two years. She had come up with the idea of the 'gynaecology consultant of the week' which meant there was continuity: if somebody needed surgery the next day the same consultant was around to make sure it happened.

A further improvement was around phones. It had become apparent that mobile phones were not going to work in the new hospital. Some parts of the building were very dense, with many internal metal blinds. Discussions with the phone company to install boosters led nowhere as the costs were too high. Instead, IT gave every consultant a WiFi phone when they were on call. In Obs and Gynae, they decided to start using them immediately, rather than waiting until the move. However, as Moira recounts:

Ch. 9, in praise of small gestures, experimentation and trojan mice; see pp. 197–198.

> 'There was a problem. Although the WiFi phones were intended to ensure senior clinical expertise was accessible to GPs, there was quite a lot of inappropriate use and no agreed etiquette ... Consultants got bothered the whole time. I was, too. The phones created additional work and stress.'

In Obs and Gynae, Moira and her consultants decided to pilot a different way of using the new WiFi phones. They trialled giving the 'consultant of the week' the WiFi phone, hoping that this would prevent anxious GPs sending women in to hospital when it wasn't necessary.

> 'We wanted to recognize that this was a proper use of consultants' time and therefore made it part of their job plan. We also found that trying to have one consultant covering both Obs and Gynae didn't work. Gynae was always the poor relation as consultants would always have to prioritize an emergency on the labour ward, and then there wouldn't be anyone to take the GPs' calls.'

Moira continued:

> 'A month later, we'd made this change and sent out an email to all the GPs explaining the new system of "consultant of the week" and giving them the WiFi number. At a meeting of hospital doctors and GPs, I got chatting to a GP. I asked him how he was finding the new WiFi number. "What number?" he said. I was a bit taken aback at that, I have to admit. This friendly GP hadn't heard of the consultant of the week role either. We'd done all this to help the GPs so it was a bit galling.'

When Moira recounted this conversation to one of her consultant colleagues, Brian, he replied: 'It's to be expected. They're busy people.

My wife's a GP and they get bombarded with emails so we need to do something else that is more engaging.'

After the operation, he came up to Moira with the idea of running a session at the next Education meeting when GPs came to the hospital lecture theatre for an update from different specialists. Six weeks later, that's exactly what they did. Unfortunately, they were the last slot on the agenda and other speakers had overrun. Moira had to say a few introductory words and Brian and one of the midwives ran the session and their humour really changed the atmosphere. They had created a quiz that covered the latest guidelines on preventing early deliveries and detecting ovarian cancer, but also included details of the consultant of the week and the WiFi phone number. There were several questions on the latter which got the message home, but also made people laugh. The GPs were asked to do the quiz with the person sitting next to them so there was a buzz of conversation and energy in the room. People loved it, as it was such a change from sitting and listening to a lecture. At the end, everyone was given a pack of information and there was an evaluation form with just three questions to make it more likely they would respond:

Ch. 7, designing and planning sessions; see pp. 139–141.

- What had they liked about the session?
- What could have been different to make this an even better use of their time?
- Was there anything else that would help them manage the needs of their Obs and Gynae patients?

The session received excellent feedback. More importantly they had definitely publicized what mattered. There were also some unexpected consequences. On the evaluation forms, there were suggestions of a couple of easy to implement changes to the hospital website and to referral forms which they never would have thought of. One of the chest consultants was in the audience, as he'd done the earlier slot. He told Moira afterwards that he was going to try out 'consultant of the week' in his department.

Later, Moira reflected on the department's success in making these improvements in those first two years.

> 'The forty per cent target in reduction of beds concentrated our minds but we really all believed we could do it. We had a great

General Manager working with us at the time, Flora Smith, who really understood and supported what we were doing; we were genuinely a team. Part of our success may have also been because we were small compared to the really big specialties, we could experiment more easily and were under the radar. The skill mix is also different from some other departments. We're used to working with midwives who, when you've got women arriving in labour, are highly skilled independent practitioners who can initiate management and prescribe drugs. The expectation, and reality, is that they make a lot of decisions. Gynaecology nurses are also empowered to take decisions, initiate treatment, give telephone advice and discharge patients. However, because our service is small perhaps those at the top didn't pay attention to what we were doing. They were dismissive and missed an opportunity to learn from us, which was a shame.'

Ch. 5, understanding culture in more detail; see pp. 98–103.

Back to the land grab though ... Planning for a forty per cent reduction in beds was one thing, but to be told suddenly that they were losing half of their promised new ward space to A&E was something else. Flora, the General Manager for Obs and Gynae, had left and Bill Spink had taken her place; Moira was already finding him rather unsupportive. He informed her that due process had been followed and the Executive Team had reviewed different options. Moira viewed this differently – it had all been done behind closed doors and presented as a fait accompli. Even worse, they were proposing to have the Obstetrics ward and the Gynae ward on different floors. That would be a nightmare in terms of staffing and more importantly bad for patient safety.

Ch. 4, understanding your own sources of power, pp. 89–93.

'I thought, bloody hell, you so-and-sos! You're taking away the ward area we've been promised before we even get it ... and I did a very angry email to all the people involved in that sham options' appraisal. A very dim view was taken of my behaviour.'

When the Medical Director passed her in the corridor two days later, he said tersely: 'That email was not a very wise move, Moira.'

Later the same morning, Rachel Mountsfort, a small, stocky woman whom Moira had never had much time for turned up at her office. She seemed to enjoy being the mouthpiece of the Executive, especially when she was able to challenge a medic. Moira secretly thought that Rachel was annoyed that Moira got on with making changes to her service without calling on Rachel's professional services as the hospital's official change agent. As she strutted into Moira's room, she said in a very superior tone: 'You're being far too emotional about this, Moira.'

Ch. 3, push vs pull; pp. 49–56.

Ch. 9, stereotyping; pp. 188–191.

'Of course I'm emotional,' Moira almost shouted at her. 'I'm absolutely furious that our ward space is being taken away after all the work we've done to reduce in-patient stays. And the options appraisal thing is a complete sham.'

The words tumbled out of the usually reserved Moira, but this had hit a raw nerve. She wasn't really thinking about what she was saying. 'And my team agree with me. It's outrageous'.

Ch. 8, responses to conflict; pp. 165–168.

Ch. 8, Transactional analysis; pp. 161–165.

Rachel let out a soft hiss of disapproval and shook her head. 'You've told your team? I thought the Exec asked everyone to keep this under wraps until we'd had a chance to manage the communication from the options appraisal exercise.'

'Of course I told my team. I believe in open communication,' Moira fumed. 'Also it's their service as well as mine.'

'Well that's not what was agreed. We don't want people being worried unnecessarily until we know what is happening.'

There was no way Moira would have kept that information to herself. How could she have faced her team? For a moment, she thought about saying so to Rachel but why bother? Looking at her watch, she gave the woman a stony look. 'I'm due in clinic,' she said and left.

Ch. 6, working with transitions; pp. 123–127.

Ch. 9, reframing resistance; pp. 191–196.

As she hurried along the corridor, Moira was aware her pulse was racing. She was relieved when she got to the clinic and had a patient in front of her. She was back to her core role and the sanity and safety of clinical medicine, without all the mess and political stuff of change.

Moira's husband was a Scot and a great lover of Robert Burns. He was also very good at listening but eventually, later that night, he stopped her ranting, saying:

'Do you remember Tam O'Shanter who gets into trouble with "warlocks and witches" after drinking too much and riding out on a stormy Ayrshire night? His wife is waiting at home, furious.'

Ch. 10, seeking out support and challenge from others; pp. 204–206.

Moira did vaguely, but had no idea where he was going with this.

'Well there's a great line in there about Tam O'Shanter's wife, Kate "nursing her wrath to keep it warm".'

He paused. 'It strikes me that you're a bit like Tam O'Shanter's Kate. The more you keep going over this whole thing in your head, the more you are keeping yourself angry. What are you going to do to move things forward?'

Moira shrugged. She wasn't ready to give up her sense of righteous indignation just yet. And her husband had the wisdom not to press his point.

Two days later, it was the Obs and Gynae team meeting. Moira was still in a bad mood.

'I'm just not sure what we should do next,' she admitted to the team.

She looked around at the despondent faces. Luckily Bill, the General Manager, who was always gloom and doom, was away that day. Despite this, the atmosphere was heavy with muted anger, disappointment and despair. Danny, one of the older serving consultants, came in bearing a tin of homemade biscuits.

'You didn't make these yourself, did you?' said Maggie, one of the nurses, incredulity in her voice. Danny didn't normally notice nuances or see the funny side of things, but he managed a laugh and said 'No, that would have been a step too far. I asked the wife.'

Moira smiled as she reached her hand into the tin. 'Thank you Danny and do thank her.' Bringing in cakes occasionally for the team was something that Moira had initiated when she'd arrived. This was the first time Danny had brought anything and she interpreted it as a real gesture of support and solidarity for the team as a whole, as well as for her as their leader.

The biscuits and the banter about Danny's (lack of) culinary skills seemed to break the mood. While some people openly expressed their anger, it was in much more measured tones than the previous week. Another person was all for going to the press, something that had come up the previous week, but Moira spoke out firmly against that.

'That would really place us in opposition to the organization. We need to find some sort of compromise.'

Others voiced their support for Moira; one of the midwives thanking her for sharing what was happening with them, rather than treating them as children who couldn't be trusted.

Ch. 1, leadership styles and being authentic; p. 39.

'Well, that was an obvious decision for me,' she replied. 'I wasn't going to behave counter to my own values and the way we work as a team.'

'But we do need to move this thing forward,' said Danny.

'You're right Danny,' Moira acknowledged. All eyes were on her. A few years ago she would have leapt in there with a solution but she had been deliberately trying to create a more collaborative problem-solving approach in the team.

'So any ideas?'

She let the silence hang, resisting the impulse to fill the space. Then, one of the nurses piped up. 'Why don't a couple of us nurses go and chat with the nurses over there in A&E and Acute. Mary worked over here about five years ago, and Jenny and I were on the same resuscitation training a couple of months ago. We could just look at the plans to see what might be possible.' There was much nodding. One of the consultants volunteered to go and have a chat with a mate of his in finance to see if he could get the story behind the official numbers.

Ch. 8, in the moment in meetings and group situations; pp. 173–177.

Moira decided she would go and see the Chair and the CEO. A year ago, the Chair's niece, who was having private fertility treatment in Glasgow, was holidaying in the Dales and needed an emergency admission. The Chair had been really impressed at the standard of care she'd received. 'It's what we offer all women,' Moira had been keen to emphasize. He'd come down to the ward to thank the staff who'd been on duty. Moira had also had really good feedback from him when she'd applied for the Medical Director role and narrowly missed being appointed. She might as well use these connections. As for the CEO, she was Moira's sponsor on a leadership programme so they had quarterly update meetings, which were often cancelled, but at least Moira had some sort of relationship with her.

Ch. 4, back- and front-stage work; pp. 70–73.

Ch. 4, who you need to influence and how: stakeholder mapping; pp. 75–79.

Two weeks later, however, just before the next team meeting, Moira realized that she still felt hugely angry at what had happened. Even worse, she was being made to feel that she was somehow now the problem or at least a problem. If sticking up for what she believed was needed to run a safe service for women, she was being labelled as troublesome and somehow 'un-corporate' and not playing the game. She'd had separate meetings with both the Chair and the CEO, but both were rather like Pontius Pilate, washing their hands of her and deferring to the 'process', reminding her this was 'an operational issue'. Still, at least they had heard her side of things.

Ch. 9, stuckness at the system level; pp. 185–188.

Bill, her General Manager, far from supporting Moira was continually reminding her of the importance of One Front Door, the financials and the promises that had been made to the public. Moira didn't actually disagree with the strategy. She realized her anger was at the lack of consultation and absence of respect for her personally. She also felt that because they were a small service and serving women, there was no recognition or desire to learn from them about how they had reduced demand and the need for beds. They seemed to be being punished rather than rewarded for having been good corporate citizens. Bill was one of those managers who thought all doctors were the same and were anti-management and never bothered to explore whether this was the case. Moira decided to minimize contact with him for now – he was too much of an energy drain.

Ch. 10, sustaining self; pp. 200–207.

When Moira arrived at the departmental meeting, everyone was already poring over a plan with the two nurses, excitedly building on each other's ideas. They stopped momentarily as she came into the room but she just nodded quietly and said carry on. She caught the eye of one of the consultants who smiled, mouthing, 'It's good'.

Moira reflected on what happened next.

> 'I suppose that we made quite a big noise, talking to the Chief Exec and the Chair, and seeking out some of the other Execs and non-Execs. This led to the Medical Director, the Director of Nursing and the clinical governance lead being tasked with getting this resolved and getting folk together to work out a way forward. I think actually that was the influence that came from above. Interestingly though, while this formal piece was happening, the nurses had

spoken to each other and found a pragmatic way of sharing the ward area. Their work totally defused the whole situation so that we found a compromise that all sides could live with. There were quite a lot of nursing problems because the ward nurses were split between two areas. However, it's interesting, there are often unintended consequences which are beneficial. So in this case, the gynae nurses and the midwives began to do a little bit more together because they were all sharing the same ward area. And then, because we had so few beds it really made us think about laparoscopic surgery to reduce the length of stay. One of the younger consultants led the way on this so we could offer laparoscopic hysterectomy for women with endometrial cancer. This surgical procedure means smaller wounds, less complications and hospital stay reduced from five days to 48 hours. And we did this before the bigger hospitals in the region. There was resistance from a managerial point of view. Bill was concerned about who would pay for the new equipment, but actually it's fantastic for patients. We feel we are leading the way in improving things and it encourages clinicians to come and work with us.

'It also illustrates the need to look at the whole system. The management resistance was, well, who's going to pay for the £200 extra bit of kit that we need in theatre? Over the whole patient journey, we are saving £1,000 because of shorter length of stay. That's a big impediment to innovation and change when people look at their little bit rather than the whole thing. And that's why I got so fed up with my General Manager; talk about dampening the enthusiasm and the innovation of the clinical staff.

'Overall, I've learnt a lot from the experience. Looking back, I can see how right my husband was about me nursing my anger to keep it alive. My righteous indignation might have kept me going in some ways, but sometimes it stopped me seeing the opportunities or reduced my ability to influence others – I made it easier for them to dismiss me by staying in character as the angry clinician.

'I've also reflected on the difficult relationship I had with Bill, my General Manager, and I think in spite of that we've actually achieved quite a bit. Or maybe because of that. If I'd had a people-pleaser

Ch. 2, multiple perspectives of change; pp. 29–31.

as a General Manager, I probably wouldn't have challenged so much. I wouldn't have been so motivated to make it work, and I do believe that in the end it has to be about negotiation and finding a compromise that all sides can live with.

'Involving everyone in my team and telling them the truth along the way was really important to me. I probably did it because it felt ethically the right thing to do, and actually it meant people worked together to look for ways to solve issues and improve our services. If I hadn't told them what was happening, we would've missed out on a lot of great ideas.

'Finally, it was so important to have someone to talk things through with. My husband really helped me gain perspective and enjoy other things in life, even when times were tough.'

Questions for further reflection

- How do you use the various relationships and contacts you have to work back stage to influence organizational politics during change?
- How do you involve the people around you in the reality of what's going on during change and what could you do to encourage more involvement?
- What kind of support do you find helpful when times are tough and whom do you turn to?
- Which groups of people could you connect with that might help you accelerate the change that you're looking for?

Chapter 12

From toxicity to talking: Creating connection through dialogue

Joe's story

An organization was losing money; competitors were taking over some key contracts but no progress was being made on agreeing a strategy to ensure the organization's future. The executives (execs) and non-executives (non-execs) were stuck in fixed positions, both sides highly suspicious of each other. Anything the execs proposed came back from the non-execs with red pen marks in the margins. The execs felt as though they were having their homework marked. Meanwhile, the non-execs felt their questions often didn't receive proper answers, fuelling their fears that the execs didn't know what they were doing or were hiding something. In this case study, we hear how Joe and Damian planned and delivered an offsite away day for the Board, looking at how they engaged people before the session as well as the 'in the moment' choices on the day.

Joe and Damian had worked together in the change team at Devonbridge for three years and knew each other well. They'd been asked to come and meet the HR Director, the Chair and the CEO of one of the sister organizations in the group. They were ushered upstairs to the Board room for the 30-minute meeting. Jane, the HR Director, reiterated the issues she'd mentioned in their briefing on the phone and then asked them to share their ideas for running the day.

Ch. 7, running the session yourself or using a facilitator; see pp. 137–138.

'We'd like to give each board member an opportunity to tell us how they see things before we design the day,' explained Joe. The HR Director nodded in agreement.

Ch. 7, getting input into the design of a session and designing the day; see pp. 138–141.

'Do you really need to ask everyone?' challenged the Chair, Evan. He had a strong Welsh accent. 'Couldn't you just talk to a few to give you a sense of the issues?'

Joe paused. What was the issue here? Time? Money? Did Evan feel they were creating more work than was necessary?

'In our experience, it is important for everyone to be interviewed so they all feel some ownership for the day,' Joe said.

Ch. 4, introducing front and back stage; see pp. 70–73.

Damian added, 'Yes, you don't want to create an "in" group and an "out" group, otherwise some people will feel involved and others will feel sidelined.'

Their points were accepted.

Walking back to the car, Damian said, 'You stood up to that challenge from Evan really well.'

'Thanks. Yes, I felt we needed to stand firm on that. I hope that in calmly explaining our rationale we demonstrated our expertise without provoking him.'

Ch. 6, understanding your own personal drivers; see pp. 110–113.

'Yeah,' laughed Damian, 'And good you didn't let your "Please People" driver kick in.'

Joe laughed. Damian knew him too well.

Ch. 10, seeking out the challenge and support from others; see pp. 204–206.

Ch. 3, introducing 'push' and 'pull'; see pp. 49–56.

Appendix 1, intervention styles questionnaire; see pp. 269–273.

It was a wet day when Joe arrived for his face-to-face conversations. He started with Bob, one of the non-execs who had worked for Railtrack. Bob talked about the differences between the execs and the non-execs. The exec team were all passing through, here for a few years before their careers took off; they weren't local either, not like him and most of the other non-execs. Then he talked about the financial problems besetting the place and the horror and public scandal when the auditors found an £11 million hole after the interim Finance Director left. Joe kept silent, listening carefully to Bob. He could sense the man's feelings of shame and regret. Next Joe met with the new Finance Director, Peter. He had been a Board director elsewhere and said he was shocked at how immature the Board was. 'I find it impossible to know where people are coming from,' he said. 'I'm spending a week per month just preparing for meetings with the Board and, when you present anything, it comes back with red pen like you've had your homework marked.'

Ch. 9, stuckness through stereotyping and over generalizing; pp. 188–191.

Last on Joe's list was Kerry, the CEO, who was in an ebullient mood – getting married in two weeks' time and not returning to work till the day of the offsite away day. Kerry reiterated some of what Joe had heard her say at the initial meeting. Then she suddenly launched into a tirade against Evan: he was never there and when he did come in he was squirreled away in his office, watching the racing on his laptop. Joe just listened. He needed to stay neutral.

When Joe and Damian met up the following week, they started by sharing what they had learned from the inquiry conversations, creating some general themes: lack of trust was a major issue, as was the fact that nobody seemed to know each other – the CEO hadn't even told anyone she was getting married. The offsite session would also be the first meeting attended by the new Business Development Director who was officially joining in the spring.

Joe and Damian felt the day would have to start with a round of introductions – this would take up time, but was vital to ensure everyone would feel welcomed. They discussed different ways of doing this which would also enable people to gain some insight into each other. Joe liked the idea of people standing up and using a technique called 'constellations'. Damian thought that might be a bit too 'edgy' for their first exercise so they decided to do four rounds of speed dating. They probably wouldn't use that phrase on the day but it would be a fast-paced series of paired conversations. The questions they settled on were:

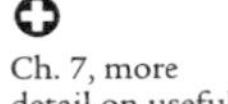
Ch. 7, more detail on useful group exercises; pp. 149–152.

- What made you choose to join Devonbridge?
- What has been your best ever job?
- What hobby do you have outside of work?
- What has been the most disappointing present you've ever received?

They rejected Damian's question about 'first impressions of Devonbridge' – it was probably too long ago for some people to remember. They also rejected Joe's idea of 'Where do you live?' as not being personal enough, so people probably wouldn't learn much new from that question. They considered 'How long have you been at Devonbridge?' but that was a closed question which wouldn't generate enough conversation. With the last question about presents, they began by asking about Christmas, but removed the reference as Rashid, one of the non-execs might have been Muslim and they weren't sure if he would celebrate Christmas. Damian suggested making it your 'most

Ch. 7, beginning: setting the frame for the session; see p. 142.

disappointing present ever' rather than 'worst' as it added more interest and surprise. It took them about ten minutes to get the questions right but they both felt it was worthwhile. This was to be the first part of the day and they wanted it to go well.

In the face to face inquiry conversations, some people had talked of past failures still overshadowing the present; for others there was a fear that history might repeat itself. Yet there was no shared understanding of that history or what it had felt like at the time. How could there be for those who had joined more recently? And why would the old timers have shared their experiences of a time that had been difficult and painful? Thus, the purpose of the second exercise would be to create a mutual understanding of the organization's own story.

Ch. 7, Figure 7.1. example, session, design; see p. 141.

They decided to split the participants into groups of four so that there would be more air time for each person. However, when Joe later briefed Jane, the HR Director, she suggested having just two groups.

Joe and Damien then started thinking about how to feed back the themes from the inquiry conversations. Share the themes too early and there was a risk normal battle lines would be drawn with no listening or inquiry as a result. Giving the feedback after looking at the history felt like the right place in the agenda. Damian and Joe outlined the key themes on a sheet of A4, paying careful attention to the wording of each phrase so that there would be no hint of judgement seeping through. They wanted the comments to present an unvarnished picture of what they had heard, but not to offend anyone or provoke anxiety or anger.

The next question was how to share it? Both Joe and Damian felt uncomfortable turning the feedback into a PowerPoint presentation or even talking it through with the group. It was pretty self-explanatory and unambiguous. The feelings and reactions it might evoke, however – that was a different matter.

'If we present the interview feedback,' Joe reflected, 'there's a risk that, rather than listening, people will just be scanning down to the bullet point they find most interesting or controversial.'

Damian nodded. 'And if we talk it through, it will sound more as though we are judging them. That wouldn't feel right ... How about we just let them each have a copy of the feedback sheet and let them read it on their own?'

'Oh yes,' said Joe, catching on immediately, 'That way they can read at their own pace and experience their own reactions.'

'And after a few moments, we can encourage them to have a conversation about their responses with whoever is sitting next to them.'

'Yes. That would work,' agreed Damian. 'It'll be important that they do talk about this stuff, but doing so as a pair will feel safer and less exposing than having a whole group conversation. And I like your idea of just asking them to turn to the person next to them. This isn't the time for people to get up and find a partner. That would disrupt the reflection we want to encourage.' And then it would be time for lunch. The shape of the day was coming along well.

Ch. 3, creating dialogue or allowing debate; pp. 56–62.

After lunch, they might move onto strategy. Jane, the HR Director, was keen that the Board explored how different stakeholders saw the organization. They could agree the key stakeholders and then work in groups of three or four. Each group could take several of the stakeholders, writing up on flip charts what those stakeholders valued about Devonbridge, as well as what they would like to be different. This exercise would have the virtue of the group working together, creating a different dynamic to their normal pattern of the non-execs marking what the exec had written. They would also be up and doing which would vary the pace. The day could finish with a review and next steps.

Ch. 4, who you need to influence and how: stakeholder mapping; see pp. 75–79.

Ch. 9, in praise of small gestures; see pp. 196–198.

The offsite session was held in a local hotel. Joe and Damian had asked for a room without a table. It was pleasant enough, with golden flock wallpaper and candelabra-style lamps projecting from the walls and windows down one side, looking out onto a small garden. There was a set of upright chairs, upholstered in blue velvet ranged against the back wall. Along another wall, also pushed back, was a set of slightly more comfortable-looking armchairs in orange and red tartan upholstery.

The room was slightly small for fifteen people, but good enough, they thought. The chairs, however, were not looking right at all: rigid, formal and unwelcoming, like a waiting room or, as Damian joked, 'Pushed back for country dancing.' Certainly not creating the conditions to encourage dialogue and conversation. Joe and Damian

Ch. 7, where to hold it; see pp. 136–137.

interspersed the blue chairs with tartan ones so there was no division repeated in the seating arrangements and then arranged them in an oval, careful to make sure everyone could see everyone else easily. Next they quickly revisited the design.

How much of the agenda should they put up on the flip chart? In the end, they decided to put times for the first exercise, lunch and the close, which would allow them to be flexible depending how things were going.

Fifteen minutes before the session was due to begin, people started arriving. Some individuals came up and introduced themselves, while two people carried on a conversation from the two-hour Board meeting they had had first thing. Others were preoccupied with where to sit, put their coats or just with getting a cup of coffee. Damian was very good at making contact with each person, shaking them by the hand, welcoming them to the session – Joe had noticed and learnt from him when they'd worked together before. One slight hiccup was there was one too few chairs. They had counted down the inquiry conversation sheet and forgotten to add the new Business Development Director, Ben. A quick trip up the corridor and that was rectified.

10.30. Joe glanced at his watch and then at Damian. He stood up, aware of his raised heart beat – anticipation rather than anxiety. He welcomed them and in his introduction added, 'We were commissioned by Evan, Kelly and Jane but we very much see you collectively as our clients.' He wanted them to know that he and Damian were not in the pocket of either side.

Joe continued, 'You might like to know what you have let yourselves in for ...' (slight nervous laughter from the group). He stood up and turned the flip chart over. Damian noticed that Joe was careful to include everyone in his gaze as he ran through the agenda.

'Now I know that you normally sit round a table when you meet and that sitting in a circle may feel a bit odd. However, trust us. This is deliberate. We want the rest of the day to feel, and to be, different from how you normally experience each other. We want to give you the opportunity for some different kinds of conversations.

'We also know you're used to having precise timings for agenda items when you meet as a Board. Today we're only committing to the start time, time for lunch and the close at four p.m. This is because we want to have the flexibility to let the conversation go where you as a group have energy, rather than us trying to prejudge this. So again, a request for you to go with the flow. Any questions?'

Damian ran the first exercise. He stood up and got them all to stand, too. There was quite a bit of shuffling and stretching as they got out of their seats and a few jocular remarks. Damian waited, smiling until they fell quiet.

'What was apparent from our inquiry conversations with you is that you don't know each other very well as people. Some of you have only joined recently. Others have only met in formal settings. We want to give you the opportunity to do some connecting. Indeed, a writer on top teams said: "Only connected people do connected work".'

There was an air of of expectancy in the room. Damian told them to find a partner and talk for five minutes on 'Why you chose to work at Devonbridge'. There was a moment of quiet before people began to move. Some turned to the person next to them; others made a beeline for someone. One of the non-execs who was quite an introvert looked a bit uncomfortable, but someone came over and started talking to him. Damian and Joe checked that everyone was paired up and talking and then checked in with each other. There was a good buzz in the room. So far so good. They let people keep talking beyond the five minutes because everyone seemed to be chatting away. Joe did the next round, apologizing for having to break into their conversations.

'So next, find someone else to talk to on the subject of "My best job ever".'

He could hear some intakes of breath, some murmuring, a comment of 'interesting question' and someone saying 'well my best job ever is my current one'. The final two rounds similarly seemed to go well. There wasn't really a need for any collective debrief, but Damian just asked in a jokey fashion if anyone had learned anything they were so surprised by that they wanted to share. A few people did.

The next agenda item was group conversations about the organization's history. Damian's group stayed in the main room while Joe took

Ch. 7, if only it were that neat ...; see p. 148.

his upstairs where the formal Board meeting had taken place earlier. It felt good to give each group space to talk without overhearing the other. However, when he opened the door he saw a long table, so they formed a circle of chairs in the corner near the window.

As they helped get the chairs in place the Company Secretary unprompted, said: 'I'm amazed at how different it's felt sitting without a table. I mean, we've had conversations. We just all seem more relaxed.'

'Perhaps we could run some of our meetings a bit more like this,' agreed one of the non-execs.

Joe was thrilled that, with no comment from them, people were already noticing the difference the physical setting made. This conversation was starting to gather a bit of momentum though, so he interrupted gently but firmly.

'Yes, I absolutely agree with you. How we sit makes a difference to the nature of the conversations we have. I'm also noticing that we could easily spend the next thirty minutes talking about this. However, I think it is even more important to explore Devonbridge's history.' A bit of laughter, a few more comments and they started the exercise.

Joe gave everyone a pad of post-it notes to write down key events that were mentioned during the conversation. He then asked the group how far back they could go into the company's history. Nina, the longest standing exec member, talked about the photo of the founder in the exec corridor when the new site was built, and how it had been the pride of the town. Others started asking questions: Had there really been three different sites? So when was the Fisher building erected? The conversation flowed easily as there was real curiosity, interest and surprise.

One of the newer execs asked when the financial problems started. Bob took the floor, looking at the ceiling rather than his colleagues as if he was seeing himself back then. Joe sensed this was a story he had gone over himself many times before, but rarely with others. It was more detailed than when Joe had interviewed him. He talked about the local media reaction, how isolated the non-execs had all felt, unsure what to do next; the terrible feeling they had let the organization down. The unfairness of it was still raw. The more recent joiners asked more questions about the timing and sequence of events.

There was a knock at the door, and Damian poked his head round. 'We've finished. I suggest you grab a coffee from outside here when you come back as there's not much left downstairs.' Joe looked at his watch. Gosh yes. They were ten minutes over time. He let the person who had been speaking finish and then suggested they stop there.

Joe and Damian had a quick debrief as people got coffees and checked phones. Both groups had had really good conversations. Time now for some group sensemaking. There was flip chart paper along the back wall with dates written in marker pen along the top. Damian asked people to put their post-it notes on it to create a timeline with key events. Some people were more keen than others to put up their notes; others were chatting. Once there was a good smattering of yellow and orange notes, Damian asked everyone to gather round and read what was there. He then facilitated a discussion about key moments in Devonbridge's history, allowing people to ask questions, prompting with some questions of his own. In particular, he asked questions about the impact of different events on morale and on the culture.

People stood up, moved around, listened with interest. Kelly, the CEO, asked many helpful open questions that encouraged others to share more. When there were points of difference about specific dates or details, Damian carefully but lightly said, 'I guess what we know from studying history is that the facts and our interpretation get mixed.' Someone else had been watching a programme on the First World War, and agreed. Joe added that the exercise was about sharing different perspectives rather than uncovering 'the truth'. It had been a good conversation – informative and respectful – and people had learned things about the place.

It was 12.15 – time for one more item before lunch. Joe asked everyone to find a seat so that they reformed into one circle. He waited till calm descended on the group. It was time to share the feedback from the inquiry conversations. Joe noticed that he was breathing slightly more quickly than normal, but then brought his focus back onto the people in the room. There was an expectant hush. He had a momentary thought: should he sit or stand? He decided to stay sitting as he if he had stood up, it might have unconsciously shifted the power dynamic as if he was judging them or was the 'teacher' handing out school

Ch. 5, shifting and moderating power through small gestures; pp. 94–96.

reports. He kept his voice neutral and matter of fact, reminding them that the themes had emerged from the inquiry conversations.

The sheets of A4 were passing around the room. They started reading. Someone muttered 'Crikey' and there was a sotto voce 'OMG' from over near Damian. Joe and Damian stayed silent, waiting, not rushing. Joe caught Damian's eye. 'Move them on now?' Damian slightly shook his head. OK. Perhaps another minute or so on their own. What they were reading was a stark appraisal of the current dysfunctionality of the Board, something they all played a part in perpetuating. Looking round at the group, Joe just hoped today would help them understand how they had got to this place and from this, learn to behave differently together. And he knew that psychologically something shifts when whatever you have personally felt or experienced is voiced aloud and confirmed by others. It has a different weight and impact. In change terms, this one-page A4 document was Kotter's burning platform, or at least that is what he and Damian hoped it would be. Joe brought his attention back to the group. Several people were now looking up from the paper.

Ch. 2, Kotter in introducing directive and facilitative approaches to change; see pp. 35–36.

'OK everyone,' he said. 'I'm imagining that there are things on that paper which resonate with your own views. There may also be some things that you find surprising or even shocking. So, what we would like you to do now is to turn to the person sitting next to you and have a conversation together about what you have just read. We encourage you to use it as an opportunity to ask questions of each other, to learn how others experience the way you function together.'

Like the flick of a switch, there was immediately a low buzz of quiet but intense conversation. They had been talking for about ten minutes when there was a knock at the door. 'Oh no,' thought Joe, 'not lunch coming in'. This was indeed the time they had said but right now lunch was an unwelcome interruption.

'I am going to see if they can put lunch in the room upstairs,' Joe whispered to Damian urgently. It was better to move to a different room for lunch. The waitress was doubtful at first but with a bit of sweet talking she agreed to take the food upstairs to the formal Board room where it was cooler and more spacious.

In the afternoon, Damian and Joe had planned to move on to strategy, looking at the organization through the eyes of different stakeholders. However, over lunch several people said they would like to talk as a whole group about the feedback. Now that everyone had had some time to process the material individually and then in pairs, it felt psychologically safe enough to open the subject to a group conversation. Joe had enjoyed preparing the stakeholder exercise and created some really good posters, so he recognized he had a twinge of regret they wouldn't be using them, but also recognized talking about working as a team was much more important right now than talking about strategy.

After lunch, they went back downstairs to the room they'd been using earlier. Damian contracted with the group about changing the agenda, in response to their desire to understand some of the feedback comments better.

Bob, one of the long serving non-execs, had clearly been itching to say his piece. 'I was quite surprised, well shocked, to read that you execs feel that we sort of mark your work.'

The Finance Director, Peter, responded with some examples which he described briefly and relatively neutrally. He then said quietly, "Bob you need to remember I'm not the interim FD who hid the 11 million quid hole, yet I kind of feel as though you are angry with me, even though I'm new.' There was a pause.

Ch. 8, from difficult to honest conversations; see pp. 168–169.

Bob said, 'Ok, but I'm not angry with you, Peter, I just get worried.' There was no need for Joe or Damian to intervene. Members of the Board were now having the conversation they needed to have.

Ch. 3, 'releasing' in introducing push and pull; pp. 54–55.

After a bit Kelly, the CEO, asked a great question: 'So tell me, Bob, and you, too, Derek, what did it feel like when the financial hole was discovered? I'm just trying to imagine.'

Ch. 6, change curve; see pp. 113–116.

The two didn't need further prompting. What had happened when the news broke, the emotional soundtrack – the shock, the denial, the shame, the sense of failure that they hadn't done their job. Joe and Damian could tell from comments that others were suddenly understanding why these two behaved the way they did. Joe gave a little bit of theory about Transactional Analysis, explaining that if someone is acting like a Parent or Teacher, it evokes the rebellious or compliant

Ch. 3, 'informing' in introducing push and pull; p. 52. Ch. 8, Transactional Analysis; see pp. 161–165.

Child in us, rather than the Adult. He kept his comments quite low key. It didn't feel as though more was required.

Others raised different comments from the feedback. Kelly was particularly good throughout, asking questions in a thoughtful and genuine way. They explored the Board and committee structures and the ridiculous amount of reading required for Board meetings. Others brought up the issue of lack of trust. Evan, being an introvert, hadn't said that much but then offered quietly, 'I trust Kelly 100 per cent so when I ask questions it's for my own understanding, not because of lack of trust.' Gosh – Joe hoped Kelly had heard that comment, given what she had said about Evan during her interview.

It was three o'clock now so they agreed to break for five minutes for a cup of tea. Joe and Damian had a quick chat with each other. They were amazed at how Adult to Adult and respectful the discussion had been. People had listened to some difficult feedback and been able to explore and empathize with each other's positions. But they couldn't linger on that now as they needed to work out what to do next. Joe had an idea which Damian liked.

They brought everyone back together quickly, knowing that the end of a session can creep up on you and they wanted to stick to the four o'clock finish. Joe asked them to get into groups of four round a flip chart, and identify things that would help them work differently together. He gave them just fifteen minutes on this so it would be action orientated and pacey, varying the rhythm. Also they didn't have much time. For speed he split them into groups, numbering everyone one, two three or four, round the room. People were asked to group together according to the number Joe had given them. There were some more furniture removals and then the buzz of talk as they filled the flip charts. Time was ticking but they were OK. Damian gave out three sticky dots for them to identify which suggestions would make the most impact. Joe knew he had a bit of a 'Hurry Up' driver so he was keen to move them on and make the ideas really concrete. He started asking who could take forward the suggestions that had the most votes.

Ch. 7, decision-making exercises; p. 152.

Ch. 6, understanding your own personal drivers; see pp. 110–113.

'Let's not give ourselves lists of actions that we don't then achieve and then feel bad about. Let's discuss this item in April when we have the new IT system live and we've finished the dashboard exercise,' said Peter, the Finance Director. It was a good point. Joe realized he had suddenly slipped into delivery-and-action mode himself and this wasn't needed.

Ch. 10, Connecting with your own experience: the role of reflection; pp. 201–203.

3.50. Time for one last thing. Joe and Damian wanted a simple process to end the session properly which would allow people to reflect on what they had been experiencing and encourage them to make a public commitment to doing something (in a light touch sort of way). While the group had been doing the flip chart exercise, Joe and Damian had experimented with different ways of expressing the closing questions. It had taken a few goes till they were satisfied.

Damian made everyone stand up in a circle. 'No tree hugging or group singing,' he said, causing some laughter. He invited people to step into the circle and say something they had learned from today which was new or surprising, then, as they stepped back out to share one thing they were going to try and do differently or pay more attention to.

It worked well. Ben, the new Director, was first into the circle. He paused and looked round at the faces, 'I'd just like to say that today has absolutely confirmed my decision to come to Devonbridge.' It was a warm affirmation that seemed to radiate a little glow round the room. Bob went next, 'It's been an eye opener hearing how I've unintentionally made some of the exec feel. I'm going to pay more attention to explaining what my concerns are rather than firing out questions.' Derek, the other long serving non-exec said something broadly similar. Comments were thoughtful with the odd joke here and there. At four o'clock, it was over and they were off, picking up coats and bags, with a wave and a hand shake from some.

Joe and Damian sat down amongst the discarded chairs, the bits of screwed up flip chart paper and cups of half-drunk coffee. It had felt good. Who would have believed that Evan would have publicly supported Kelly like that? Or that they would have talked as a group so maturely and authentically? The two of them reflected what had gone well, anything they might have done differently, and then time for a high five, the taking down of the flip charts, checking that there were no feedback sheets left hanging around, and then home.

Joe typed up the flip charts and emailed them to Evan, Kelly and Jane. No reply. No thank you. Busy people don't necessarily spare the time for acknowledgements. Still, they both knew they had really managed to engage a group in real dialogue in a way they would never have thought possible, and they had enjoyed working together. That was actually more than good enough.

A month later over lunch in the staff canteen, Joe and Damian reflected on what they had learnt from the work with the Devonbridge Board. 'Those inquiry conversations at the start were vital and using that information to design the day was invaluable. It meant we could really help them have the conversations that mattered to them. I'm glad we challenged Evan at the start and spoke to everyone,' Joe reflected.

'And it gave us such powerful information to share with people on the day. I've used that technique again. By sharing the feedback themes that emerged from our inquiry conversations, it felt as if we gave people a chance to see things in the round, rather than jumping to defending their own positions,' said Damian. 'Working together was good, too. It would have been hard on my own to spot what was going on in the group and redesign the session there and then. Plus the stakes were quite high with this.'

'Putting the time into the design for the day also made it much easier to chop and change in the moment.' said Joe. 'We really managed to go with the energy of the group, and to keep them focused on talking about what mattered. I still need to watch out for my own need for action though.'

'Well yes,' said Damian, 'but don't get too obsessed about it – it's also what enables you to help people stay focused and full of energy. It kind of all came together; they were ready for the conversation they had, and we helped create a safe enough space for them to have it.'

Questions for further reflection

- With the change you are working on, how could you actively seek out the perspectives of different people involved or impacted?
- How might you create the opportunity to work on a day's session with a colleague?
- How much design time do you allow yourself? Reflecting on this

story, do you think you are doing too much design or not quite enough? What might you want to experiment with?

- When people are coming together for the first time for a meeting or session, what different ways have you tried to make sure people feel welcomed and able to start well?
- What different physical settings might you experiment with when wanting to encourage honest conversation?
- When you have taken part in, or facilitated, a group discussion, what did you do that went well? What skills would you like to develop further?

Chapter 13

Involving people across the system

Emma's story

An American heritage organization undertook a system-wide change project to improve how objects and artworks were acquired and catalogued across their five different institutions. Emma, the Chief Conservator, instigated and led the project. She was convinced that involving people in understanding and designing the acquisitions process would lead to sustainable change. She recruited a project team to lead the work with her, enlisting Terry who became her sounding board and sanity during the inevitable ups and downs along the way.

Terry was a world expert on Roman and Greek artefacts and was normally laid back, with a long pony tail and a preference for wearing jeans and tee shirts, although at fund-raising gala events he would wear a velvet jacket and looked more like an eighteenth-century beau. Today he was absolutely furious, storming into Emma's office. 'Well the hell! Can you believe it? What was he ******* thinking of? How can he just order people to complete forms, talking like we're in kindergarten. ******** outrageous. And after all our good work.'

Ch. 8, Transactional Analysis; see pp. 161–165.

Emma and Terry had been working together for over nine months on a sizeable change project to standardize and professionalize the way art works were purchased and catalogued for a group of three museums, an art gallery and an old Plantation House, with a unique collection of paintings and antiques. Located in the American South, all five organizations had been given to the state by a successful nineteenth-century entrepreneur. Emma's job title was Chief Conservator, which meant she was responsible for all the care aspects of the collections and was based at the rather imposing State Museum in the middle of the city where all the corporate staff worked.

Ch. 9, stuckness at the system level; see pp. 185–188.

What had happened to make Terry so agitated? Emma told him to go and grab them both a coffee while she read the email the Director had just sent. It wasn't good. True, the Director's anger and frustration at what he perceived as lack of progress was evident but it wasn't nearly as bad as she had feared, given Terry's reaction. The email had only gone to senior staff. She knew from a friend that the Director's life wasn't all roses at the moment – his marriage was on the rocks and he was probably expecting a rough ride from the Trustees in a couple of weeks' time following the humiliation of a purchase that had turned out to be a forgery. She suspected this was the source of much of his angst, but it so annoying that he hadn't come to talk to her first before shooting from the hip. She was annoyed with herself, too, that she hadn't made more effort to keep him reassured and in the loop.

Ch. 4, introducing front and back stage; see pp. 70–73.

Ch. 8, the core skills of listening, presence, and suspending; pp. 157–160.

Terry was back with the coffees.

'Tell me what in particular made you so upset?' she inquired.

As he talked and she listened, he became calmer. 'What about you? What do you make of it?' he asked eventually.

She told him how touched she was to see how much he cared about the project and how glad she was that he had come to talk to her. 'At least the email shows everyone how important the change project is', she added.

Ch. 9 reframing resistance; pp. 191–196.

Ch. 6, Appreciative Inquiry; see pp. 128–131.

'Gosh you really are good at seeing the positives in shitty situations', Terry laughed.

Now they had both shared how they felt and vented, they could get on with planning what to do next – an email to the project team and Emma would go talk to the Director today. One of his direct reports happened to walk past where they were sitting. Terry knew him well so grabbed the opportunity to informally update him on the project. Without explicitly referring to the email rant, one of the key players now knew another side to the story.

Ch. 4, understanding your own and others' political style; see pp. 79–83.

Six months later, they were sitting in Emma's office again, reflecting on the whole project. Emma and Terry agreed that the email had been the worst moment for both of them. 'But, hey,' said Terry 'like all good stories, perhaps you should start at the beginning. How did the whole thing start? I don't think I ever knew ...'.

Ch. 10, connecting with your own experience; the role of reflection; pp. 201–203.

Emma smiled. 'When I joined the organization I was kinda surprised at how ad hoc we were in acquiring new works of art and antiques. I guess the process had developed organically over time but there was no way of seeing the objects across all the museums as an overall collection. Nothing was written down. No one used the central data base properly, so we didn't have a complete record of what we owned which was a real challenge for insurance purposes. Also, people didn't always involve the conservation staff at the beginning of the acquisition process, so the costs of renovating or repairing were often significantly more than the cursory estimates people had made without involving the experts. So, lots of reasons for change.'

Emma continued. 'I realized though that if my central team asked for a review of the process, we wouldn't get much support. It would be seen as our problem. So I asked our auditors to review the process. I knew that this would get me the buy-in of the Senior Management team to tackle the acquisitions process. Sure enough, I was right – the auditors came back and reported there was much room for improvement.

Ch. 4, who you need to influence and how: stakeholder mapping; pp. 75–79.

'When I'd worked for the Fitzgerald Museum in New York, I'd seen that involving people across the whole organization to understand what currently happens and to design a new way of doing things was likely to be much more successful than me sitting in a darkened room and rewriting a policy on my own. I also knew that I couldn't just take what we'd done there, because our context and culture is different. It's much more hierarchical here. But having seen something similar elsewhere gave me some ideas about how to approach the change here that helped my confidence.'

Ch. 5, understanding culture in more detail; see pp. 98–103.

Following the auditor's report, the exec team asked Emma to lead a review of the acquisitions process. Some Directors wanted to nominate their people for a project team, but Emma was clear she didn't want that. 'I chose people partly because of their roles, but also those who I thought would be able to work together. Change projects can be hard work and I needed people who I thought would be fun to work with and who would give it a lot of energy.

Ch. 3, introducing 'push' and 'pull'; pp. 49–56.

'There was one really awkward character that one of the Directors wanted on my team, but I knew she would be trouble. She's mistress of the subtle put down. I knew I'd end up spending all my time and

Ch. 6, understanding your own personal driveres; see pp. 110–113.

Ch. 8, from difficult to honest conversations; see pp. 168–173.

energy on her. I kept quiet for a bit and then decided to be brave and just share my concerns with my own Director. That was tough because I don't like asking for help and I even got a bit emotional when talking to him about how I felt. He hates emotion and so, lord bless him, he just said leave it with me and I never heard how he sorted that out but sort it out he did.'

'So why d'you choose me?' Terry asked.

'Well,' she laughed, 'I didn't know you that well but knew you were well liked and respected. You have a reputation for being a bit left field in your thinking and I thought you had been around long enough to know the history of previous attempts to crack this problem. As you were also the Chief Curator at the Grantworth museum, I thought you'd be able to help make sure their particular needs were taken into account.'

'That's interesting,' said Terry. 'Maybe it would have been helpful to know this at the start. Also I was comfortable looking at the problem from beyond the remit of my role but I'm not sure everyone was. You'd told me that your secretary, Cassie, was in the group, not just to be our administrative support, but because she has really creative good ideas. Some in the group didn't realize this. Maybe setting out your intentions and expectations at the start might have been helpful.'

Emma looked surprised. 'Yeah, good call – I never thought about that. Although the organization is hierarchical, as far as I was concerned, it was a level playing field in the team. I expected people to pitch in, but they didn't at the beginning. If I'd done what you are suggesting that might have helped. It was almost as though our first bit of cultural change was in the project group.'

Ch. 9, stuckness through stereotyping and generalizing; see pp. 188–191.

Ch. 7, reimagining meetings; see pp. 133–153.

Emma continued. 'Of course, we knew we needed the curators on board early as they are a really influential group. If we're reflecting on surprises during the project, working with them was a surprise. When we ran that two-hour session for them I discovered that they weren't a cohesive group at all. In fact, some of them didn't even know each other while I had assumed they did. They really enjoyed getting to know each other, even though that wasn't the prime purpose of the session, so that was a bit of a win.'

'Yeah and talk about unexpected consequences ... Did you know they are now meeting as a group every six months?' added Terry.

'Really? That's great. And, tell me, why do you think the five engagement workshops were a success?'

Terry took a glug of coffee. 'The sessions were half a day with refreshments, decent food from our café caterers, not polystyrene cups of instant coffee. There's a certain amount of currency, isn't there, in activities that have good catering. So word spread we were providing the good stuff! Running a session at each of the museums was also important, so that people didn't have to travel, and symbolically we signalled each institution was important.

'I also think the fact you encouraged conversation made a big difference Emma. People here are so used to being lectured and told, it was kinda liberating for them to find there was an interest in their views. Lots of working in pairs and trios also meant opportunities for everyone to speak. I remember some more junior people like the administrators weren't sure if it was their place to come along so needed a bit of extra encouragement. But when we got them there, they really contributed.'

'Yeah, and we didn't want the museum directors to come to the workshops. That sure was the right call. It would've crippled everyone else's involvement. It meant I had to keep them in the loop with a monthly report but that was okay.'

Ch. 5, embedded power; see pp. 96–97.

Terry nodded. 'So much of it is about being smart about how you deal with different people, isn't it? That's something I learned from this. I noticed that when people had very strong views, you encouraged them to say what was on their minds, getting it out in the open so it could be discussed, rather than festering away.'

Ch. 6, dealing with others' emotional pain; see p. 128.

It was Emma's turn to nod. 'But do you remember that particularly irritating guy who'd worked in LA, who kept accusing us of not consulting people enough, even though he'd been to all of the workshops? I remember phoning him. I was dreading the call so Cassie told me to do the call standing up – makes your voice sound more confident, she told me. I tried to find out what his real issue was and then negotiated a compromise: we'd get back to him when we were looking at the database and he would park this for now. Having to do

Ch. 8, responses to conflict; see pp. 165–168.

Ch. 9, reframing resistance; see pp. 191–196.

Ch. 10, connecting with others; see pp. 204–212.

that sort of thing takes time and effort and did get me down a bit at times. I was glad I'd talked to Cassie about him.'

After the five engagement sessions, the project team built a picture of the current process. Terry took up the story: 'We then had those couple of really important sessions as a project team, going through all the information we'd gathered, and used this to redesign the process. It became obvious where departments needed to work together better. People having seen this in the engagement sessions meant something had already begun to shift as people could see what wasn't working.'

The improved acquisitions process was presented as both a written narrative and a visual process map. The project team wanted to test it out with people, to increase engagement and refine it further.

'I loved the way we were able to display the improved process as a big chart all along the wall at the back of the staff canteen in our main museum,' Emma said. 'The way we laid it out meant people could come and almost physically be the object moving through the process. An unexpected win was being able to upgrade the collections management database, COOKIE, properly. Instead of people arguing about whether a probable acquisition should go into the database, people were taking about *when* to put it into COOKIE – we didn't get any arguments about it needing to happen!'

The proposed improved process was presented to the Exec Team and approved. Before it went live, the project team put together training so people understood the new process and accompanying paperwork. Terry chuckled. 'I can't remember how we came up with that idea of writing scenarios and inviting people to come and work through the imaginary acquisition of a piece, culminating in putting in a proposal to the Directors for agreement – role play without calling it that.'

'It was Bernadette's idea – one of the younger members of the project team,' Emma said. 'She got really excited didn't she and chose all kinds of preposterous objects from ebay as potential acquisitions. We had things like a two-foot china rabbit cookie jar and a rainbow-striped teddy bear.

'Doing scenarios and actually getting people to live through the new process worked because it changed the pace. Everyone started embellishing the cases studies, so it became quite raucous! Word got out that these sessions were fun, and people came pre-primed with ridiculous scenarios. There was such a good atmosphere, we were also able to have some heated discussion which threw up some things that we hadn't thought about, such as tackling the database upgrade.'

Several months later, Terry and Emma were finalizing the evaluation report for the exec. 'Remember the team meeting just after that dreadful email from the Director?' said Terry: 'Someone called it "Black Friday."'

Emma did remember. She also remembered how helpful Terry had been. 'Everyone was so upset by that email from further up the hierarchy but when you spoke first, Terry, sharing your initial anger and the way the two of us talking about it helped you get over the emotions and see beyond that, it was really helpful. As you are one of the more senior people in the project team, you sharing your reactions meant others shared theirs too. I had given 15 minutes on the agenda for this and when the time was up, I remember gently moving people on as I didn't want us to wallow.'

Ch. 6, practical actions to mitigate the risks of ignoring emotions; pp. 117–123.

Terry continued, 'And then you spoke about your own feelings and how, as a team, we had some choices. We could feel upset and do nothing, acting as victims, or we could vent all our anger about the Director, or indeed on those who hadn't followed the new process properly. You said you'd had moments that week when all those options seemed really appealing, but that your sensible self knew that none of those would be productive, even if they might temporarily make us feel better.'

'You were so good in that moment, Emma. The team really listened to you. You didn't gloss over what had happened and how you felt. You drew that Victim–Persecutor–Rescuer triangle on the flip chart so people could understand why they were feeling as they did, but at the same time you then helped us see the need to not get stuck in that pattern.'

Ch. 8, the drama triangle; see pp. 179–180.

'Well thank you for saying so, Terry. It was strange as I hadn't known I was going to say all of that. I knew beforehand that it was going to be important to let people share how they felt about the Director's bomb

Ch. 10, seeking out support and challenge from others; see pp. 204–206.

shell. But then I just trusted my own feelings, and because you and I had talked about this before, I think it unconsciously gave me the confidence to just go for it and say what I wanted to say. I also knew I had your support.'

Ch. 6, Appreciative Inquiry, see pp. 128–131.

Terry took up the story. 'Yes it was then that, after a bit of talking, Cassie suggested we go and talk to all ten of the initial users and ask some open questions to understand their experience. The Appreciative Inquiry worked earlier in the programme when talking to users of the old system; why not do so again? People on the team eventually came round to this, although some would have preferred to try and just sell the benefits, reminding the users of what they should have done with the new system.'

Emma added, 'And then the usually quiet Mike said, "If we do 'tell and sell', it would be just as bad as shouting louder when someone doesn't understand English. It won't help at all. It's making the assumption that we're right and they are wrong. How about we create a bit of a script for ourselves and then do this interviewing in pairs. Knowing how to start the conversation in the right way and doing it with someone else would make me feel much more up for it".'

Ch. 5, shifting and moderating power through small gestures; see pp. 94–96.

Terry laughed as he recalled what happened next. 'So I went with Cassie to speak with the Curator at The Plantation House; she's been there for ever; one of those rather prickly people who always knows better than you and has a story to trump yours. We chose to do this conversation face to face as we didn't think it would work well over the phone. We asked her if she would like us to go down to the house or if she would like to meet us when she was coming up to the city. We got a bit of a snappy response about of course she was too busy to come and see us, so anyway, we went down there. Turned out she had her dog curled up in the office. It was on some antibiotics which she had to administer every two hours. Cassie spontaneously just connected with the dog and so we spent the first ten minutes on Cocker versus King Charles spaniels.

Ch. 9, in praise of small gestures; see pp. 196–198.

'It was a real surprise to me how connecting differently at the beginning meant we then had a completely different conversation about the work. I think she expected us to come out all guns blazing, coming down hard on her like the Director did in the email, so finding we were genuinely interested in making things better came as such a surprise to her, and she really thawed.'

'And even then the approach didn't work with everyone. Two out of the ten don't want to be involved in any new process, but we were able to address the concerns of the majority and streamline the documents so they were easier, and IT improved the database access, so we could show that we had listened to people, learnt from them and made adaptions.'

'So, how do you think things are now?' asked Terry.

'Well, six months on, we still have a few issues with people not completing the paperwork properly, although it is much better than it was. It feels as if the Directors now really need to "out" any individuals who don't complete it. There are not really enough penalties in place for not completing it. This is something they know they need to tackle.'

Ch. 2, introducing directive and facilitative approaches to change; see pp. 31–39.

'Overall though,' said Terry, 'my sense is people are using the improved process; it's a simpler clearer process, duplication is avoided and we're able to find objects on COOKIE.'

'True,' Emma agreed, 'and the Directors have the information they need to make acquisition decisions. Anyone new to the organization is now easily able to understand and follow the process.'

Terry shared what he felt good about. 'Also, I'm also really pleased with how the project team engaged people in the change. Do you remember when we did our evaluation survey, we asked people to tick which statement reflected their experience of the redesign of the process? They could choose from:

We created the process

They created the process

The auditors made us do it

The majority of people chose "We created the process". I was really pleased about that!'

'Me, too,' rejoined Emma. 'So, what do you think you've learned from the project?' she asked Terry.

'A number of things ... I definitely think more about how to get the best out of people; I can encourage people because I can make them laugh. I also do a lot of work behind the scenes, helping people understand each other's perspectives. I think this really worked. Giving the project the time it needed made a big difference. Thirdly, it's okay if there is some movement of team membership. As new people joined, their fresh new perspectives helped the project along, and when Bernadette came back from maternity leave, she was able to see how much progress the team had made which was really motivating for us all. And finally, I've seen how people have developed their confidence through being part of the project team. One time, Emma, you were ill but three of the group felt confident to run the session without you – something some people would previously never have done.'

He paused and smiled. 'And what about you Emma? What have you learned? You can't leave until you've answered the question you posed me.'

She grinned, pushing her glasses back into her hair.

'Mmm. So many things. Well, firstly, it's a reminder of the time and effort it takes when you are changing something across a whole system. Second, I certainly tried to be politically astute and to create an authorizing environment so we could do the project. I'm also glad that I listened to my instincts about people and created a project team who worked well together and cared about the work.'

'I'm also pleased that I went against the organizational culture to involve people across the hierarchy and that we created sessions that people wanted to come to. It's been really good working with you, Terry. I'm also glad we took the time to reflect on the story. I've learned a lot just remembering what we did and having your perspective on what happened. Drinks are on me next time.'

Questions for further reflection

- What do you need to legitimize your change in the eyes of senior stakeholders?
- Are you working with the people you want to be in your change team? If not, what might you do about that?

- Who are you involving in supporting you to lead the change? How do their skills and temperament compliment yours?
- What has worked well for you in terms of engaging others from across a system?
- What opportunities do you create for people to recognize and work with their emotions?
- How are you sustaining yourself throughout the process?

In Summary: What does a leader of relational change do in practice?

As a leader of relational change, your role is to create conditions for those around you to make sense of what is happening and what happens next. You no longer feel the need to be a hero, trying to fix everything and feeling you ought to be in control. You are in charge, you might have plans and you recognize that plans are helpful to hold other people's uncertainties and anxieties, as well as your own. However, you hold these plans lightly, acknowledging that there is no guarantee that they describe what will necessarily happen, although they guide and signal intention and direction of travel. So do the stories you tell in conversation with others which allow others to see connections between the past and what may be emerging in the future. You're on the lookout for opportunities to adapt and change direction as the future emerges and you pay good attention to what is going on below the waterline.

You are working in complex circumstances so you recognize that you need to stay connected to yourself. You are reflexive and have insight into your own behaviour and actions so that you can be choiceful in your gestures, in the moment. When you make gestures, you acknowledge that they may not always have the impact you intend, as you cannot control the meaning others take from them. However, as a leader, living in a glass lift, much of what you say and do is seen by others, so your gestures as a leader often carry significant weight. What you choose to notice and amplify, what you say, what you do counts, even though you cannot predict the outcome with absolute certainty.

You are connected to those around you, relating to people through planned, front-stage meetings, as well as taking advantage of emergent opportunities and back-stage conversations. You aim to be an owl while watching out for foxes. You recognize the importance of acknowledging your own emotions, as well as the emotions of those around you. You know you can make gestures to support others' work through their emotions so that they are better able to transition but you are not, and cannot be, responsible for their emotions.

You privilege a facilitative approach, seeking to inquire into others' experiences and gaining their insights and ideas before sharing your own. You create ways for groups of people to be in dialogue, rather than debate and pay attention to creating areas of safe uncertainty. You reimagine meetings so that people can have different conversations.

You encourage experimentation, conversation and reflection around what is working to help unstick stuck patterns, and by working with others, rather than doing to them, you create energy, ideas, enthusiasm and action for change.

You see change as a relational activity that is an art rather than a science.

References

Chapter 1

1. Deming, W. E. (2004) quoted in M. Pedler, J. Burgoyne and C. Brook (2005), 'What Has Action Learning Learned To Become?', *Action Learning* 2 (1): 49–68.
2. Argyris, C. and D. A. Schon (1995) *Organizational Learning II: Theory, Method and Practice*. Reading, MA: Addison-Wesley.
3. Oxford Dictionary. Available online: http://www.oxforddictionaries.com (accessed 10 March 2016).
4. F. W. Taylor (1912) in *Organization Theory: Selected Readings*, edited by D. S. Pugh (1990), 3rd edn. Middlesex: Penguin.
5. Zohar, D. (2008) *Rewiring The Corporate Brain: Using The New Science To Rethink How We Structure And Lead Organizations.* San Francisco: Berrett-Koehler.
6. Gronn, P. (2000) quoted in P. Myers, S. Hulks and L. Wiggins (2012), *Organizational Change: Perspectives On Theory And Practice.* Oxford: Oxford University Press, 244.
7. *Fortune Magazine*, 2002.
8. Grey, C. (2002) quoted in P. Myers, S. Hulks and L. Wiggins, *Organizational Change: Perspectives on Theory and Practice*. Oxford: Oxford University Press, 18.
9. Burke, W. (2009) *Organizational Change: Theory and Practice*, 2nd edn. Thousand Oaks, CA: Sage.
10. Maslow, A. (1954) *Motivation and Personality*. New York: Harper.
11. Likert, R. (1961) *New Patterns of Management*. New York: McGraw Hill.
12. Hershey, P and K. Blanchard (1997), *Management of Organizational Behavior*. Englewood Cliffs, NJ: Prentice Hall.
13. Heifetz, R. (2002) *Leadership on the Line: Staying Alive through the Dangers of Leading*. Boston, MA: Harvard Business School Press.
14. Stacey, R. D., D. Griffen, D, and P. Shaw (2002) *Complexity and Management: Fad or Radical Challenge to Systems Thinking?* London: Routledge.
15. Stacey, R. D. (2011) *Strategic Management and Organisational Dynamics: The Challenge of Complexity to Ways of Thinking about Organisations*, 5th edn. Harlow: Prentice Hall, 18.
16. Shaw, P. (2002) *Changing Conversations in Organizations: A Complexity Approach to Change*. London: Routledge, 120.
17. Weick, K. (1995) *Sensemaking in Organizations*. London: Sage.
18. Stacey, R. D. (2011) *Strategic Management and Organisational Dynamics: The Challenge of Complexity to Ways of Thinking about Organisations*, 5th edn. Harlow: FT Prentice Hall, 192.

19. Mintzberg, H. and B. Ahlstrand (2009) *Strategy Safari: The Complete Guide through the Wilds of Strategic Management*, 2nd edn. Harlow: FT Prentice Hall.
20. Merton, Robert, K. (1948) 'The Self-fulfilling Prophecy', *Antioch Review* 8 (2) (Summer): 195.
21. Gladwell, M. (2000) *Tipping Point: How Little Things Can Make a Big Difference.* Boston, MA: Little, Brown and Company.
22. Stacey, R. D. (2011) *Strategic Management and Organisational Dynamics: The Challenge of Complexity to Ways of Thinking about Organisations*, 5th edn. Harlow: FT Prentice Hall, 292.
23. Stacey, R. (2012) *Tools and Techniques of Leadership and Management: Meeting the Challenge of Complexity*. London: Routledge, 291.
24. Zohar, D. (1997) *Rewiring the Corporate Brain: Using the New Science to Rethink How We Structure and Lead Organizations.* San Francisco: Berrett-Koelher Publishers Inc., 59.
25. Zohar, D. (1997) *Rewiring the Corporate Brain: Using the New Science to Rethink How We Structure and Lead Organizations.* San Francisco: Berrett-Koelher Publishers Inc., 30.
26. Janis, I. L. (1972) *Victims of Groupthink*, Thousand Oaks, CA: Sage.
27. Stacey, R. (2012) *Tools and Techniques of Leadership and Management: Meeting the Challenge of Complexity*. London: Routledge.
28. Weick, K. (1995) *Sensemaking in Organizations*. London: Sage, 61.
29. Baker, A. C. (2000) in P Myers, S. Hulks L. and Wiggins (2012) *Organizational Change: Perspectives on Theory and Practice.* Oxford: Oxford University Press, 297.
30. Binney, G., G. Wilke and C. Williams (2009), *Living Leadership: A Practical Guide for Ordinary Heroes*, 2nd edn. Harlow: FT Prentice Hall, 10.
31. Stacey, R. (2012) *Tools and Techniques of Leadership and Management: Meeting the Challenge of Complexity*. London: Routledge.
32. Morgan, G. (2006) *Images of Organzation*. Thousand Oaks, CA: Sage.
33. Bennett, N. and J. Lemoine (2014) 'What VUCA Really Means for You', *Harvard Business Review* 92 (1/2).
34. Binney, G., G. Wilke and C. Williams (2009) *Living Leadership: A Practical Guide for Ordinary Heroes*, 2nd edn. Harlow: FT Prentice Hall.
35. Gioia, D.A. and E. Pitre (1990), 'Multiparadigm Perspectives on Theory Building', *Academy of Management Review* 15: 584–602, 587.
36. Wiggins, L., B. Marshall and J. Smallwood (2016) 'Pluralism: The Art and Science of Making (Practical) Choices about Change and Improvement Methods'. Paper submitted to the 10th International Behaviour in Healthcare Conference: Attaining, Sustaining and Reading Improvement: Art or Science?

Chapter 2

1. Personal communication: Emma Adams.

2. Lewin, K. (1947) 'Frontiers in Group Dynamics: Concept, Method and Reality in Social Science, Social Equilibria and Social Change.' *Human Relations* 1 (36).
3. Personal communication: Reg Bull, Chief People Officer, LGi.
4. Clayton, T. (2014) *Waterloo, Four Days that Changed Europe's Destiny*. London: Hatchette, 310.
5. Kotter, J. and D. Cohen (2002) *The Heart of Change*. Boston, MA: Harvard Business School Press.
6. Myers, P., S. Hulks and L. Wiggins (2012) *Organizational Change: Perspectives on Theory and Practice.* Oxford: Oxford University Press, 48–9.
7. Stacey, R. (2012) *Tools and Techniques of Leadership and Management: Meeting the Challenge of Complexity*. London: Routledge.
8. Johnson, B. (1996) *Polarity Management: Identifying and Managing Unsolvable Problems*. Amhurst, MA: HRD Press.
9. Sorge, A. and A. van Witteloostuijn (2004) 'The (Non)Sense of Organizational Change: An Essai about Universal Management Hypes, Sick Consultancy Metaphors, and Healthy Organization Theories', *Organization Studies* 25 (7): 1205–31, 1223.
10. Barnes, J. (2015) *Keeping an Eye Open: Essays on Art*. London: Jonathan Cape, 7.

Chapter 3

1. Heron, J. (2009) *Helping the Client: A Creative Practical Guide*, 5th edn. London: Sage.
2. Stacey, R. D. and D. Griffen (eds) (2006) *A Complexity Perspective on Researching Organisations*. London: Routledge.
3. Stacey, R. D. and D. Griffen (eds) (2006) *A Complexity Perspective on Researching Organisations*. London: Routledge.
4. Isaacs, W. (1999) *Dialogue and the Art of Thinking Together.* New York: Doubleday.
5. Argyris, C. and D. A. Schon (1995) *Organizational Learning II: Theory, Method and Practice.* Reading, MA: Addison-Wesley.
6. Isaacs, W. (1999) *Dialogue and the Art of Thinking Together.* New York: Doubleday.
7. Isaacs, W. (1999) *Dialogue and the Art of Thinking Together.* New York: Doubleday, 10.
8. Isaacs, W. (1999) *Dialogue and the Art of Thinking Together.* New York: Doubleday, xvii.
9. Kantor, D. (2012) *Reading the Room*. San Francisco, CA: Jossey-Bass.
10. Isaacs, W. (1999) *Dialogue and the Art of Thinking Together.* New York: Doubleday, xviii–xix.
11. Stacey, R. D. and D. Griffen (eds) (2006) *A Complexity Perspective on Researching Organisations*. London: Routledge.
12. Mason, B. (1993) 'Towards Positions of Safe Uncertainty', *Human Systems: The Journal of Systemic Consultation and Management* 4: 189–200.

13. Chapman, S. (2014) *Can Scorpions Smoke: Creative Adventures in the Corporate World.* London: Can Scorpions Smoke Change and Creativity Ltd, via Lulu.com, 90.
14. Adapted from Stacey by Vanstone, Critchley and Ashridge colleagues.
15. Heron, J. (2009) *Helping the Client: A Creative Practical Guide,* 5th edn. London: Sage.
16. Burnes, B. (2004) 'Kurt Lewin and the Planned Approach to Change: A Re-appraisal', *Journal of Management Studies* 41 (6): 997–1002.
17. Personal communication: David Julien.

Chapter 4

1. Morgan, G. (1986) *Images of Organization.* Newbury Park, CA: Sage, 115.
2. Dutton, J. E., S. J. Ashford, R. M. O'Neil and K. A. Lawrence (2001) 'Moves that Matter: Issue Selling and Organizational Change'. *Academy of Management Journal* 44 (4): 716–36.
3. Buchanan, D. and R. Badham (2008) *Power, Politics and Organizational Change. Winning the Turf War,* 2nd edn. London: Sage.
4. Buchanan, D. and D. Boddy (1992) *The Expertise of the Change Agent: Public Performance and Backstage Activity.* London: Prentice Hall.
5. Lapworth, P. and C. Sills (2011) *An Introduction to Transactional Analysis,* 5th edn. London: Sage, 83.
6. Campbell, A., J. Whitehead and S. Finkelstein (2009) 'Why Good Leaders Make Bad Decisions', *Harvard Business Review* 87 (2): 60–6.
7. Heron, J. (2001) *Helping the Client: A Creative Practical Guide*. London: Sage.
8. Scholes, K. (1998) 'Stakeholder Mapping: A Practical Tool for Managers'. In V. Ambrosini, G. Johnson and K. Scholes (eds), *Exploring Techniques of Analysis and Evaluation in Strategic Management* . Harlow: Prentice Hall Europe, 152–68.
9. Baddeley, S. and K. James (1987) 'Owl, Fox, Donkey, Sheep: Political Skills for Managers', *Management Education and Development* 18 (1): 3–19.

Chapter 5

1. A well-known phrase of Bill Critchley.
2. De Haan, E. and Y. Burger (2005) *Coaching with Colleagues.* Basingstoke: Palgrave.
3. French, J. R. P. and B. Raven (1959) 'The Bases of Social Power'. In D. Cartwright and A. Zander (eds) *Group Dynamics,* 3rd edn. New York: Harper and Row, 259–69.
4. Baddeley, S. and K. James (1987) 'Owl, Fox, Donkey, Sheep: Political Skills for Managers', *Management Education and Development* 18 (1): 3–19.

5. Stacey, R. (2012) *Tools and Techniques of Leadership and Management: Meeting the Challenge of Complexity*. London: Routledge.
6. Shaw, P. (2002) *Changing Conversations in Organizations: A Complexity Approach to Change.* London: Routledge.
7. Coleman, G., L. Wiggins and K. Lavelle (2016) 'Giving Voice to Humanity: Early Findings from Using Action Research and Appreciative Inquiry in Qatar's Ambulance Service'. Organisation Behaviour in Healthcare Conference, Cardiff, April 2016.
8. Schein, E. H. (2010) *Organizational Culture and Leadership*, 4th edn. San Francisco, CA: Jossey-Bass.
9. Vanstone, C. (2010) *An Introduction to Appreciative Inquiry: Change, Performance and Engagement.* Ashridge: Ashridge Consulting.
10. Kotter, J. P. (1995) 'Leading Change: Why Transformation Efforts Fail', *Harvard Business Review* 73 (2): 59–67.
11. Shaw, P. (2002) *Changing Conversations in Organizations: A Complexity Approach to Change.* London: Routledge, 92.
12. Amabile, T. M. and S. J. Kramer (2011) *The Progress Principle*. Boston: Harvard Business Review Press.
13. Kotter, J. P. (1995) 'Leading Change: Why Transformation Efforts Fail', *Harvard Business Review* 73 (2): 59–67.
14. Brown, M. (1998) 'The Invisible Advantage', *The Ashridge Journal* (November): 20.
15. Gladwell, M. (2000) *Tipping Point: How Little Things Can Make a Big Difference.* Boston: Little, Brown and Company.

Chapter 6

1. Kübler-Ross, E. (2003) *On Death and Dying*. New York: Scribner.
2. Kahneman, D (2012) *Thinking, Fast and Slow*. Penguin, London.
3. Campbell, A., J. Whitehead and S. Finkelstein (2009) 'Why Good Leaders Make Bad Decisions', *Harvard Business Review* 87 (2): 60–6.
4. O'Neill, M. B. (2000) *Executive Coaching with Backbone and Heart.* San Francisco, CA: Jossey-Bass.
5. Kahler, T. and H. Capers (1974) 'The Miniscript'. *Transactional Analysis Journal* 4 (1): 26–42.
6. Kübler-Ross, E. (2003) *On Death and Dying.* New York: Scribner.
7. Sugarman, L. (2001) *Life-span Development: Frameworks, Accounts and Strategies*, 2nd edn. Hove: Psychology Press.
8. Kübler-Ross, E. (2003) *On Death and Dying.* New York: Scribner, 35.
9. Stuart, R. (1995) 'Experiencing Organizational Change: Triggers, Processes and Outcomes of Change Journeys', *Personnel Review* 24 (2): 3–87, 30.

10. Frost, P. J. and S. Robinson (1999) 'The Toxic Handler: Organizational Hero – and Casualty', *Harvard Business Review* 77 (4): 96–106.
11. Eriksson, C. B. (2004) 'The Effects of Change Programs on Employees' Emotions', *Personnel Review* 33 (1): 110–26.
12. Brockner, J., S. Grover, T. Reed, R. DeWitt and M. O'Malley (1987) 'Survivors' Reactions to Layoffs: We Get By with a Little Help for Our Friends', *Administrative Science Quarterly* 32 (4): 526–41.
13. Wiggins, L. (2008) 'Managing the Ups and Downs of Change Communication'. *Strategic Communication Management* 13 (1): 20–3.
14. Frost, P. J. and S. Robinson (1999) 'The Toxic Handler: Organizational Hero – and Casualty', *Harvard Business Review* 77 (4): 96–106.
15. Fairhurst, G. T. and R. A. Sarr (1996) *The Art of Framing: Managing the Language of Leadership*. San Francisco, CA: Jossey-Bass
16. 'The Power of Words'. Available online: https://www.youtube.com/watch?v=Hzgzim5m7oU (accessed 7 November 2015).
17. Bridges, W. (2009) *Managing Transitions: Making the Most of Change*, 3rd edn. London: Nicholas Brealey.
18. Day, A. (2011) 'Changing the Social Fabric of Organisations: The Importance of Participation', *The Ashridge Journal* (Summer).
19. Janssen, C. Available online: http://www.fourroomsofchange.com.au/claes-janssen-h.php (accessed 14 November 2015).
20. Clair, J. A. and R. L. Dufresne (2004) 'Playing the Grim Reaper: How Employees Experience Carrying out a Downsizing', *Human Relations* 57 (12): 1597–625.
21. Wright, B. and J. Barling (1998) 'The Executioners' Song: Listening to Downsizers Reflect on their Experiences', *Canadian Journal of Administrative Sciences* 15 (4): 339–54.
22. Clair, Judith A. and R. L. Dufresne (2004) 'Playing the Grim Reaper: How Employees Experience Carrying out a Downsizing', *Human Relations* 57 (12): 1597–625, 1608.
23. Vanstone, C. (2010) *An Introduction to Appreciative Inquiry: Change, Performance and Engagement*. Ashridge: Ashridge Consulting.
24. Barrett, F. J., R. E. Fry and H. F. M. Wittock (2005) *Appreciative Inquiry: A Positive Approach to Building Cooperative Capacity*. Chagrin Falls, OH: Taos Institute Publications, 37.
25. Barrett, F. J., R. E. Fry and H. F. M. Wittock (2008) *Appreciative Inquiry: A Positive Approach to Building Cooperative Capacity*. Chagrin Falls, OH: Taos Institute Publications, 36.

Chapter 7

1. Shaw, P. (2002) *Changing Conversations in Organizations: A Complexity Approach to Change*. London: Routledge, 10.
2. Isaacs, W. (1999) *Dialogue and the Art of Thinking Together*. New York: Doubleday.
3. Thank you to Debbie Bunyan.
4. Kantor, D. (2012) *Reading the Room*. San Francisco, CA: Jossey-Bass.
5. Thank you to Janet Smallwood.
6. Thank you to Cathy Sharpe.
7. Barrett, F. J., R. E. Fry and H. F. M. Wittock (2008) *Appreciative Inquiry: A Positive Approach to Building Cooperative Capacity*. Chagrin Falls, OH: Taos Institute Publications, 11.

Chapter 8

1. 'You and I' by Roger McGough (© Roger McGough, 2016) is printed by permission of United Agents (www.unitedagents.co.uk) on behalf of Roger McGough
2. Clive Wiggins: personal communication.
3. Senge, P. M., C. O. Scharmer, J. Jaworski and B. S. Flowers (2005) *Presence: An Exploration of Profound Change in People, Organizations, and Society*. London: Brealey Publishing, 42.
4. Isaacs, W. (1999) *Dialogue and the Art of Thinking Together*. New York: Doubleday, 134–5.
5. Stacey, R. (2012) *Tools and Techniques of Leadership and Management: Meeting the Challenge of Complexity*. London: Routledge.
6. Runcorn, E. (2015) *Dust and Glory*. Oxford: The Bible Reading Fellowship, 43.
7. Lapworth, P. and C. Sills (2011) *An Introduction to Transactional Analysis*, 5th edn. London: Sage, 1.
8. Berne, E. (1968) *Games People Play: The Psychology of Human Relationships*. Harmondsworth: Penguin, 11.
9. Original research by K. W. Thomas and R. Kilmann. Available online: http://www.kilmanndiagnostics.com/overview-thomas-kilmann-conflict-mode-instrument-tki (accessed 8 February 2016).
10. Stone, D., B. Patton and S. Heen (2000) *Difficult Conversations*. London: Penguin.
11. Argyris, C. (1990) *Overcoming Organizational Defenses*. Harlow: Prentice Hall, 88–9.
12. Stone, D., B. Patton and S. Heen (2000) *Difficult Conversations*. London: Penguin.

13. Karpman, S. B. (2011) 'Fairy Tales and Script Drama Analysis', *Group Facilitation* (11): 49.
14. Casey, D., P. Roberts and G. Salaman (1992) 'Facilitating Learning in Groups', *Leadership and Organization Development Journal* 13 (4): 8–13.
15. Lapworth, P. and C. Sills (2011) *An Introduction to Transactional Analysis*, 5th edn. London: Sage.
16. Casey, D., P. Roberts and G. Salaman (1992) 'Facilitating Learning in Groups', *Leadership and Organization Development Journal.*
17. Griffin, D. and R. Stacey (eds) (2005) *Complexity and the Experience of Leading Organisations*. New York Routledge, 2.
18. Rogers, J. (2010) *Facilitating Groups.* Glasgow: OUP McGraw-Hill Education.
19. Rogers, J. (2010) *Facilitating Groups.* Glasgow: OUP McGraw-Hill Education.
20. Bion, W. R. (1961) *Experiences in Groups.* London: Tavistock.
21. Karpman, S. B. (2011) 'Fairy Tales and Script Drama Analysis'. *Group Facilitation* (11): 49.
22. Bird, J. and S. Gornall (2016) *The Art of Coaching: A Handbook of Tips and Tools.* Abingdon: Routledge.
23. For more on this and how to get out of the cycle see J. Bird and S. Gornall (2016) *The Art of Coaching: A Handbook of Tips and Tools.* Abingdon: Routledge.

Chapter 9

1. Watzlawick, P., J. H. Weakland and R. Fisch (1974) *Change: Principles of Problem Formation and Problem Resolution.* New York: W. W. Norton.
2. Zohar, D. (2008) *Rewiring the Corporate Brain: Using the New Science to Rethink How We Structure and Lead Organizations.* San Francisco, CA: Berrett-Koehler.
3. Grint, K. (2008) 'Wicked Problems and Clumsy Solutions: The Role of Leadership', *Clinical Leader* I (II), BAMM Publications.
4. Grid by Vanstone, Critchley and Ashridge colleagues, adapted from original ideas by Ralph Stacey.
5. Oshry, B. (2007) *Seeing Systems: Unlocking the Mysteries of Organizational life*, 2nd edn. San Francisco, CA: Berrett-Koehler.
6. Oshry, B. (2007) *Seeing Systems: Unlocking the Mysteries of Organizational Life*, 2nd edn. San Francisco, CA: Berrett-Koehler, xiii, xiv.
7. Oshry, B. (2007) *Seeing Systems: Unlocking the Mysteries of Organizational Life*, 2nd edn. San Francisco, CA: Berrett-Koehler, xvi.
8. Sims, D. (2003) 'Between the Millstones: A Narrative Account of the Vulnerability of Middle Managers' Storying', *Human Relations* 56 (10): 1195–211.
9. Nickerson, R. S. (1998) 'Confirmation Bias: A Ubiquitous Phenomenon in many Guises', *Review of General Psychology* 2 (2) (June): 175–220.

10. Stern, D. N. (1985) *The Interpersonal World of the Human Infant.* London: Karnac Books.
11. Gladwell, M. (2002) *The Tipping Point: How Little Things Can Make a Big Difference.* Boston: Little, Brown and Company.
12. Knights, D. and T. Vurdubakis (1994) 'Foucault, Power, Resistance and All That'. In J. M. Jarmier, D. Knights and W. R. Nord (eds), *Resistance and Power in Organizations.* London: Routledge, 191.
13. Piderit, S. K., (2000) 'Rethinking Resistance and Recognizing Ambivalence: A Multidimensional View of Attitudes toward an Organizational Change', *Academy of Management Review* 25 (4): 783–94.
14. Bridges, W. (2009) *Managing Transitions: Making the Most of Change*, 3rd edn. London: Nicholas Brealey.
15. Rousseau, D. M. (1995) *Psychological Contracts in Organizations: Understanding Written and Unwritten Agreements.* Thousand Oaks, CA: Sage.
16. Landsberger, H. A. (1957) *Hawthorne Revisited: A Plea for an Open City.* Ithaca: Cornell University Press.
17. Clark, R. E. and B. M. Sugrue (1991) '30. Research on Instructional media, 1978–1988'. In G. J. Anglin, *Instructional Technology: Past, Present, and Future.* Englewood, CO: Libraries Unlimited, 327–43.
18. Midgley, G. (2008) 'Systems Thinking, Complexity and the Philosophy of Science', *Emergence: Complexity and Organization* 10 (4): 55.
19. Stacey, R. D. (2011) *Strategic Management and Organisational Dynamics: The Challenge of Complexity to Ways of Thinking about Organisations*, 5th edn. Harlow: FT Prentice Hall, 291.
20. Kotter, J. P. and D. S. Cohen (2002) *The Heart of Change.* Boston, MA: Harvard Business School Press.
21. Stacey, R. D., D. Griffen and P. Shaw (2002) *Complexity and Management: Fad or Radical Challenge to Systems Thinking?* London: Routledge.
22. Amabile, T. M. and S. J. Kramer (2007) 'Inner Work Life: Understanding the Subtext of Business Performance', *Harvard Business Review* 85 (5): 72–83.
23. Martyn Brown (1988) 'The Invisible Advantage', *The Ashridge Journal* (November).
24. Chapman, S. (2014) *Can Scorpions Smoke: Creative Adventures in the Corporate World.* London: Can Scorpions Smoke Change and Creativity Ltd, via Lulu.com, 92.

Chapter 10

1. Griffin, D. and R. D. Stacey (2005) *Complexity and the Experience of Leading Organizations.* London and New York: Taylor & Francis.
2. Binney, G., G. Wilke and C. Williams (2009) *Living Leadership: A Practical Guide for Ordinary Heroes*, 2nd edn. Harlow: FT Prentice Hall.

3. Clance, P. R. and S. A. Imes (1978) 'The Imposter Phenomenon in High Achieving Women: Dynamics and Therapeutic Interventions', *Psychotherapy: Theory, Research and Practice* 15 (3): 241–7.
4. Sandberg, S. (2013) *Lean In: Women, Work and the Will to Lead.* London: W. H. Allen.
5. Steve Chapman. Available online: https://canscorpionssmoke.wordpress.com (accessed 20 March 2016).
6. Stacey, R. (2012) *Tools and Techniques of Leadership and Management: Meeting the Challenge of Complexity.* London: Routledge, 110.
7. Gilmer, B. and R. Markus (2003) 'Personal Professional Development in Clinical Psychology Training: Surveying Reflective Practice', *Clinical Psychology* 27: 20–3.
8. Stacey, R. (2012) *Tools and Techniques of Leadership and Management: Meeting the Challenge of Complexity.* London: Routledge, 110.
9. Schön, D. A. (2013) *The Reflective Practitioner: How Professional Think in Action.* Farnham: Ashgate.
10. Rowling, J. K. (2014) *Harry Potter and The Goblet of Fire.* London: Bloomsbury.
11. Argyris, C. and D. A. Schon (1995) *Organizational Learning II: Theory, Method and Practice.* Reading, MA: Addison-Wesley.
12. Heron, J. (2009) *Helping the Client: A Creative Practical Guide,* 5th edn. London: Sage.
13. Haan, E. de (2012) *Supervision in Action: A Relational Approach to Coaching and Consulting Supervision.* Berkshire: Open University Press, 2.
14. Cathy Reilly and David Birch: personal communication.
15. Weick, K. (1995) *Sensemaking in Organizations*. London: Sage
16. Myers, P., S. Hulks and L. Wiggins (2012) *Organizational Change: Perspectives on Theory and Practice.* Oxford: Oxford University Press, 143.
17. Coleman, G. (2015) 'Core Issues for Modern Epistemology in Action Research: Dancing between Knower and Known'. In H. Bradbury, *Handbook of Action Research*, 3rd edn. London and Thousand Oaks, CA: Sage.
18. Argyris, C. and D. A. Schön (1995) *Organizational Learning II: Theory, Method and Practice*. Reading, MA: Addison-Wesley.
19. Coleman, G., L. Wiggins and K. Lavelle (2016) 'Giving Voice to Humanity: Early Findings from Using Action Research and Appreciative Inquiry in Qatar's Ambulance Service'. Organization Behaviour in Healthcare Conference, Cardiff, April 2016.
20. Mead, G. (2014) *Telling the Story: The Heart and Soul of Successful Leadership*. San Francisco, CA: Jossey-Bass.
21. Okri, B. (2011) 'Novelist as Dream Weaver'. *The National* (1 September).

Appendix 1

Intervention styles questionnaire

In Chapter 3, we examine the impact on others of different ways of asking questions and commenting in one-on-one conversations. Drawing on the work of John Heron, we explore two broad ways of intervening in conversations – push and pull. 'Push' interventions are quite directive, while 'pull' interventions are more facilitative. Within each of these categories, Heron characterizes a further three styles, making six in total. As a relational leader of change, it is helpful to be aware of your own style preferences so that you can then practice those that you use less often and perhaps reduce your reliance on other styles. This questionnaire is based on one developed by Richard Phillips and further refined by Erik de Haan at Ashridge and will give you a guide as to your preferred intervention styles.

It has been designed to help you assess your interventions as a leader. It lists a number of different ways in which you might act towards people and asks you to think about how often you act in each of these ways. For each item, please indicate your perception of how often you react in that way in the right-hand box. None of these behaviours are good or bad in themselves – there are no 'right' or 'wrong' answers. You will get the most value from this exercise by being completely honest with yourself. Don't spent too long considering your replies: your spontaneous answer is most likely to be the most appropriate one.

If you find it difficult to give just one answer to a question (perhaps because you consider that you act differently towards different people), we suggest that you try to give an answer based on your average behaviour in such circumstances.

Questionnaire

'When working with others as a leader, I tend to do the following ...'

0 – Not at all (or not applicable)

1 – Rarely

2 – Sometimes, but not often

3 – Moderately often

4 – Often

5 – Very often

		Score (0–5)
1	Advise them of the appropriate action to take	
2	Explain the purpose of a task	
3	Raise their awareness of their own learning needs	
4	Ask them to tell me about a negative incident which they have experienced	
5	Encourage them to set their own learning goals	
6	Show my respect for them as individuals	
7	Give them feedback about the impact of their behaviour	
8	Invite them to talk about a difficult personal experience of theirs	
9	Help them to reflect on their experiences	
10	Express my concern to help them	
11	Suggest that they choose a particular solution	
12	Inform them about a learning opportunity	
13	Ask them what they have learnt from a particular incident	
14	Acknowledge the value of their ideas, beliefs, opinions	
15	Persuade them to take a particular approach	
16	Interpret their experiences or behaviour	
17	Ask questions to uncover what they are hiding or avoiding	
18	Encourage them to express their emotions	
19	Apologize for anything I do which is unfair, forgetful, hurtful	

20	Ask them how they can apply what they have learnt	
21	Help them to recognize their own emotions	
22	Challenge their denials or defensiveness	
23	Make them aware of the choices open to them	
24	Ask that they change their behaviour	
25	Ask them how they feel about a success which they achieved	
26	Make them aware of their mistakes	
27	Offer them an explanation of what has happened	
28	Inform them about the criteria for measuring success in performing a task	
29	Ask open questions to promote discovery	
30	Praise them for a job well done	
31	Encourage them to find their own solutions and answers	
32	Ask them why they are upset or angry	
33	Offer them emotional support in difficult times	
34	Present facts which contradict their opinions	
35	Demonstrate skills or actions that I want them to copy	
36	Give them information which they need to achieve a task	
37	Draw their attention to facts which they have missed	
38	Reflect their feelings by describing what I see in their behaviour	
39	Make them feel welcome when they visit me	
40	Recommend the best way to do something	
41	Challenge their assumptions	
42	Ask them to evaluate their own performance	
43	Give them feedback about their results	
44	Propose the best course of action for them to take	
45	Ask them to express feelings which are blocking their progress	
46	Show them the consequences of their actions	
47	Ask them to set their own work objectives and targets	
48	Make myself accessible to them when needed	
49	Help them 'with my hands in my pockets': i.e. without interfering	
50	Ask them how they feel about a current difficulty	

51	Encourage them to feel good about themselves	
52	Tell them where to go to find information and help	
53	Show them how to correct their mistakes	
54	Confront issues of poor performance	
55	Tell them how to get started on a new task	
56	Reveal information about my own experiences	
57	Affirm positive qualities or actions of theirs which they are denying	
58	Help them to express their insights after an emotional experience	
59	Help them to map out their present understanding	
60	Share information about my own failures and weaknesses	

Table Appendix 1.1 from Haan, E. de and Y. Burger (2005), *Coaching with Colleagues: An Action Guide for One-to-One Learning*, Basingstoke: Palgrave Macmillan.

Score sheet

For each question, please transfer your score to the appropriate box below, making sure you are putting the right score against the right question number. Then please add up the totals for each column.

Q No.	Your score	Q No.	Your score	Q No.	Your score	Q No.	Your score	Q. No.	Your score	Q. No.	Your score
1		2		3		4		5		6	
11		12		7		8		9		10	
15		16		17		18		13		14	
24		23		22		21		20		19	
28		27		26		25		29		30	
35		36		34		32		31		33	
40		37		41		38		42		39	
44		43		46		45		47		48	
53		52		54		50		49		51	
55		56		57		58		59		60	
TOTALS FOR EACH COLUMN*:											
PR:		**IN:**		**CH:**		**RE:**		**DI:**		**SU:**	

Table Appendix 1.2 from Haan, E. de and Y. Burger.

*** Preferred intervention styles:**

Push styles:

PR: Prescribing

IN: Informing

CH: Challenging**

Pull styles:

RE: Releasing**

DI: Discovering**

SU: Supporting

The styles with the highest scores are those that you use most frequently. If you have low scores for some styles, this suggests that these are currently not a significant part of your behavioural repertoire. For many leaders the behaviours that go with the push styles are often more familiar. However, as a relational leader of change, it is important to develop the pull styles. For a full explanation of each of these styles, and examples of their use in change situations, please turn to pages 51–56 in Chapter 3.

** Heron in his original nomenclature used the terms 'confronting', 'cathartic' and 'catalytic' for what we refer to above as 'challenging', 'releasing' and 'discovering'.

Appendix 2

In Chapter 6, we examine recognizing and working well with the emotions that inevitably are evoked when engaged in change situations. As a relational leader of change, it can be very helpful to understand your own personal drivers as these will affect how you respond personally to change. This questionnaire enables you to make that assessment. With increased personal awareness, you can then have more choice about how you respond to the emotions and behaviours of others, rather than relying on your default mode.

Personal drivers questionnaire

We do not know the origin of this questionnaire. It is based upon behavioural drivers that were first proposed by Taibi Kahler in 1975 and is included in E. de Haan and A. Kasozi's *The Leadership Shadow: How to Recognize, and Avoid Derailment, Hubris and Overdrive*, London: Kogan Page, 2014.

A full explanation of drivers is given on page 110, but as a brief reminder, drivers are:

- unconscious internal pressure that makes us do things certain ways, e.g. with speed, perfection, little emotion, etc.;
- often (although not always) inappropriate or unhelpful in obtaining results. They tend to satisfy inner needs rather than actual events;
- a warning sign that strong internal processes may be at play.

Completing the questionnaire

Study every section in the table below, carefully, reading through the five (a–e) statements listed under each of the twelve sections.

For each section, from a–e, pick out the statement that is *most true* for you and give it a score of 7, 8, 9 or 10, depending how true you feel the statement is for you.

Next, find the statement that is *least true* for you and give it a score of 0, 1, 2 or 3, depending how untrue the statement is for you.

Finally, arrange the other three statements in an order that reflects how much you agree with them, giving each a mark which ranks them between your lowest and highest (4–6). Please ensure that one statement is given a mark of 5.

Scoring the first section may take a little while. Once you get going, the others will not take as long though. The whole questionnaire should take between 20 and 30 minutes to complete.

Table Appendix 1.1

0–3 Low

4–6 Medium

7–10 High

Section		**Statement**	**Score (0–10)**
1	a	Endurance is a valuable asset.	
	b	I like to see people doing their best to get things right.	
	c	Considering all the effort I put into things I should get more done.	
	d	I find myself doing too many things at the last minute.	
	e	On balance, I adapt more to other people's wishes than they do to mine.	
2	a	Casualness and carelessness bother me.	
	b	It's keeping on doing things that interest me more than finishing with them.	
	c	When people are slow about saying something I want to interrupt or finish their sentence.	
	d	I have a fair amount of imagination when it comes to guessing what people need.	
	e	When someone gets emotional my reaction is often to make a joke of it or else be critical	

3	a	I don't mind things being hard. I can always find the energy.	
	b	I prefer to use just the minimum necessary time to get to a place.	
	c	If someone doesn't like me I either try hard to get them to like me or I walk away.	
	d	It is rare for me to feel hurt.	
	e	If it's a question of doing something properly I'd rather do it myself.	
4	a	I get impatient with slow people	
	b	Normally I prefer to take people's wishes into account before deciding something.	
	c	I show a calm face even when my feelings are running high.	
	d	I don't make excuses for poor work.	
	e	There's something about coming to the end of a job that I don't like.	
5	a	I put a lot of effort into things.	
	b	Sometimes it is better to just do something and leave the discussion until later	
	c	I'm cautious about asking favours.	
	d	I don't let people look after me much.	
	e	I sometimes find it hard to stop myself correcting people.	
6	a	Sometimes I talk too quickly.	
	b	I'm uncomfortable when people are upset or displeased with me.	
	c	I dislike people making a fuss about things.	
	d	Things can always be improved on.	
	e	I don't believe in the 'easy' way.	

7	a	I think I do a lot to be considerate towards others.	
	b	I usually manage to cope even when I feel I've had more than enough.	
	c	I prefer doing things really well even if it takes longer.	
	d	I tend to start things and then gradually lose energy or interest.	
	e	I want to get a whole lot of things finished, then I run out of time.	
8	a	I'm not what you would call soft.	
	b	I prefer to do things right first time, rather than have to re-do them.	
	c	I sometimes repeat myself because I'm not sure I've been understood.	
	d	My energy is often at its highest when I have a lot of things to do.	
	e	It's quite hard to say no when someone really wants something.	
9	a	I like to use words correctly.	
	b	I like exploring a variety of alternatives before getting started.	
	c	It's quite like me to be already thinking of the next thing before I have finished the first.	
	d	When I'm sure someone likes me I am more at ease.	
	e	I can put up with a great deal without anyone realizing it.	
10	a	People who just want to finish something tend to irritate me.	
	b	I prefer to just plunge into something rather than have to plan.	
	c	If a person doesn't know what I want, I'd rather not have to ask directly.	

	d	Other people start whining and complaining before I do.	
	e	I prefer to correct myself rather than have other people correct me.	
11	a	If I had 20% more time I could relax more.	
	b	I often smile and nod when people talk to me.	
	c	When people get excited I can stay very cool and rational.	
	d	I can do something well and still be critical of myself.	
	e	There are so many things to take into account it can be hard to get to the end of something.	
12	a	I have a good intuitive sense if someone likes me or not.	
	b	I think duty and reason pay off better than emotion in the long run.	
	c	I tend to see quickly how something could be improved on.	
	d	Some people have a habit of over simplifying things.	
	e	Sometimes the more there is to do, the more I get done.	

Adapted from de Haan and Kasozi.

When you have finished scoring all the sections, transfer the marks onto the scoring sheet following (Appendix Table 1.2), listing each number you have awarded it against the appropriate letter (a, b, etc.) and add them up to give you a total for each of the five drivers.

Being aware of your own personal drivers helps you understand and make sense of your own emotional reactions to particular situations during change. For a full explanation of each driver, please turn to pages 110–113.

Question number	Item number	Your score	Item number	Your score	Item number	Your score	Item number	Your score	Item number	Your score
1	a		b		C		d		e	
2	e		a		B		c		d	
3	d		e		A		b		c	
4	c		d		E		a		b	
5	d		e		A		b		c	
6	c		d		E		a		b	
7	b		c		D		e		a	
8	a		b		C		d		e	
9	e		a		B		c		d	
10	d		e		A		b		c	
11	c		d		E		a		b	
12	b		c		D		e		a	
Total	**Be strong**		**Be perfect**		**Try harder**		**Hurry up**		**Please people**	

Table Appendix 2.2 Personal Drivers' questionnaire scoring chart

Adapted from de Haan and Kasozi.

Further reading suggestions

Barrett, F. J., R. E. Fry and H. F. M. Wittock (2008), *Appreciative Inquiry: A Positive Approach to Building Cooperative Capacity,* Chagrin Falls, OH: Taos Institute Publications.

Binney, G., G. Wilke and C. Williams (2009), *Living Leadership: A Practical Guide for Ordinary Heroes,* 2nd edn, Harlow: FT Prentice Hall.

Bird, J. and S. Gornall (2016), *The Art of Coaching: A Handbook of Tips and Tools*, Abingdon: Routledge.

Bridges, W. (2009), *Managing Transitions: Making the Most of Change,* 2nd edn, London: Nicholas Brealey Publishing Ltd.

Buchanan, D. and R. Badham (2008), *Power, Politics and Organizational Change: Winning the Turf War,* 2nd edn, London: Sage.

Caulat, G. (2012), *Virtual Leadership: Learning to Lead Differently*, Oxford: Libri Publishing.

Chapman, S. (2014), *Can Scorpions Smoke? Creative Adventures in the Corporate World*, London: Can Scorpions Smoke Change and Creativity Ltd, via Lulu.com.

Kantor, D. (2012), *Reading the Room,* San Francisco: Jossey-Bass.

Lapworth, P. and C. Sills (2011), *An Introduction to Transactional Analysis,* 5th edn, London: Sage.

Morgan, G. (2006), *Images of Organization*, Thousand Oaks, CA: Sage.

Myers, P., S. Hulks and L. Wiggins (2012), *Organization Change: Perspectives on Theory and Practice,* Oxford: Oxford University Press.

Oshry, B. (2007), *Seeing Systems: Unlocking the Mysteries of Organizational Life,* San Francisco, CA: Berrett-Koehler.

Rogers, J. (2010), *Facilitating Groups*, Glasgow: OUP McGraw-Hill Education.

Shaw, P. (2004), *Changing Conversations in Organizations: A Complexity Approach to Change,* London: Routledge.

Stacey, R. (2012), *Tools and Techniques of Leadership and Management: Meeting the Challenge of Complexity,* London: Routledge.

Index

The letter *f* after an entry indicates a page that includes a figure.
The letter *t* after an entry indicates a page that includes a table.